hotels · lodges · spas

southafricachic

hotels · lodges · spas

southafricachic

To obtain preferential rates and amenities at the hotels
featured in *South Africa Chic*, please register online at:
www.theworldsbesthotels.com
info@theworldsbesthotels.com

hotels • lodges • spas

southafricachic

text sally roper • bridget hilton-barber • elaine meyers • jacqueline tan

Abercrombie & Kent Travel

acknowledgements

In creating *South Africa Chic*, a small number of people were responsible for giving the book its initial momentum. While thanking all the wonderful properties that have participated, there are a few individuals to whom I am particularly in debt.

In February 2004 I met Gavin Varejes, a proud and patriotic South African who shares my passion for rugby. Gavin organised my first trip to Johannesburg and Cape Town. There he introduced me to Richard Weilers of Southern Sun and his very professional team, including Lindiwe Sangweni-Siddo, who in turn introduced me to the new CEO of South Africa Tourism, Moeketsi Mosola. My thanks to Liz McGrath who was totally supportive from our very first meeting at her wonderful property The Cellars-Hohenort in Cape Town; Chris Weir of Inspirational Places for his encouragement and endorsement; and South Africa Tourism for their introductions and access to photography. My thanks to our sponsors, Cellfind and Abercrombie & Kent Travel. Later in the book you will find three itineraries suggested by A & K that will help you plan your trip.

Last but not least, to the team who created this book: Sally Roper for writing, suggesting and networking, and to editors Melisa Teo and Ng Wei Chian who sourced the photography, edited the copy, dealt with all the properties and got the job done.

It has been a privilege for me to discover South Africa at such a wonderful time for the country. I hope that readers of *South Africa Chic* will feel the same.

Nigel Bolding
editor-in-chief

managing editor
melisa teo

assistant editor
ng wei chian

contributing editors
christopher khoo • elaine meyers

designers
chan hui yee • norreha sayuti

production manager
sin kam cheong

first published in 2005 by
bolding books
nigel.bolding@theworldsbesthotels.com
www.theworldsbesthotels.com

designed and produced by
editions didier millet pte ltd
121 telok ayer street, #03-01
singapore 068590
edm@edmbooks.com.sg
www.edmbooks.com

©2005 bolding books
design and layout © editions didier millet pte ltd

first published in great britain 2005 by
kuperard
59 hutton grove, london n12 8ds
telephone : +44 (0) 20 8446 2440
facsimile   : +44 (0) 20 8446 2441
sales@kuperard.co.uk
www.kuperard.co.uk

Kuperard is an imprint of Bravo Ltd

Printed in Singapore

isbn: 1-85733-405-1

COVER CAPTIONS:
1–2 AND 19–22: Singita lodges.
3: Pool at The Outpost.
4: The Mweni Valley in the Drakensberg.
5: Rock art by the San, also regarded as 'the first South Africans'.
6: Baobab tree abstract.
7: Magnificent rural landscape of yellow sunflowers.
8: Bridge swinging from the Gouritz Bridge on the Garden Route.
9: Soweto residential areas.
10: Ndebele wall detail.
11: Kosi Bay in KwaZulu-Natal.
12: A rural Ndebele homestead.
13–14 AND 17–18: South Africa's signature wildlife.
15: A spectacular sunset viewed in solitude at Royal Malewane.
16: Guests at Makanyane Safari Lodge can get close to nature.
PAGE 2: This solitary elephant is one of the splendid beasts that make up the famed Big Five.
OPPOSITE: Postcard views from the stylish rooms of Singita Lebombo.
THIS PAGE: Noble leopards roam the wilds of South Africa.
PAGES 8–9: Fields of rapeseed and canola bloom under stormy skies in the Western Cape region.

contents

southafrica**by**provinces

Namibia

Atlantic Ocean

southafrica**by**chapters

Limpopo

Mpumalanga

Gauteng + Free State

KwaZulu-Natal

Northern Cape + Northwest Province

Eastern Cape

Atlantic Ocean

Eastern Cape

Western Cape

Indian Ocean

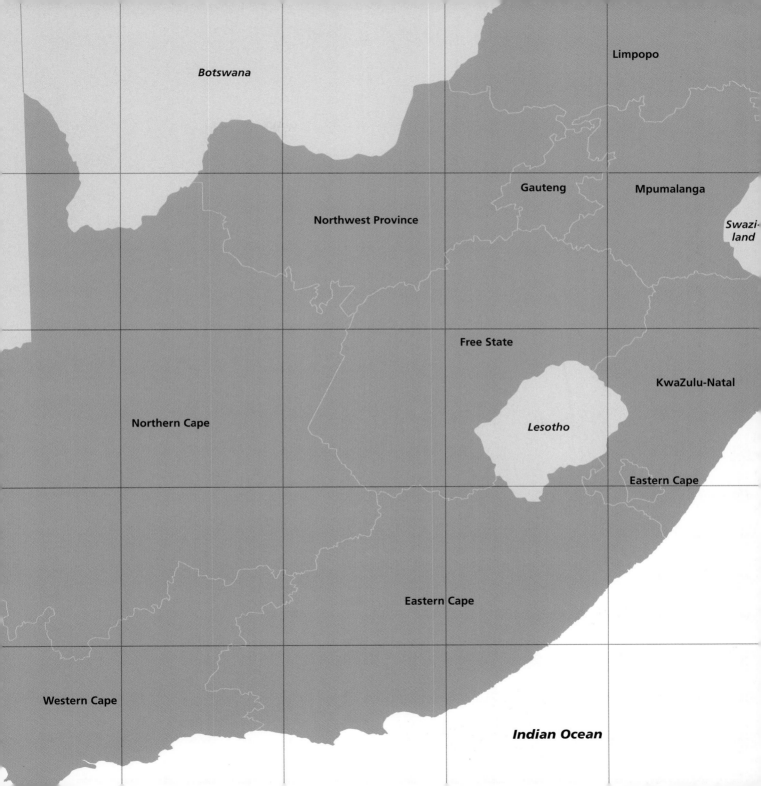

introduction

the rainbow nation of hope

In a world riven with strife and conflict, South Africa's emergence like a butterfly from the chrysalis of its solitude and isolation is a great story of the triumph of the human spirit. In Africa, there is an indigenous philosophy, known as ubuntu, which describes the paramount importance of human relationships. Simply translated, ubuntu means 'I am a person because of other people', a remarkable statement that sums up in a single phrase the impetus behind the country's magnificent act of reconciliation and the creation of its much admired new democracy.

One of the major personalities of the anti-apartheid struggle, Bishop Emeritus Desmond Tutu, coined the truly evocative name 'the rainbow nation' for this 'new South Africa', the place emerging from many decades on the world's front pages as a country of sorrow and conflict. Many nations have a rich kaleidoscope of cultures, but this rainbow nation is rare, for those remarkable political solutions have been actively crafted by, and for, South Africans themselves, with thought and provision for every citizen, wherever on the social, cultural or religious spectrum they might be. After only one short decade, South Africa has burst upon the world stage in an explosion of exuberance in virtually every field of creative endeavour. There is no more rewarding experience in travel today than to see, touch, feel and taste this firsthand, and to plunge right into the heart of the ongoing celebration.

a spectacular backdrop

Aside from the riveting human drama of the past 15 years, South Africa has always been a place of fascination for the environmentalist and nature lover. This huge country, with a land area which exceeds that of Italy, France and Germany combined, has a relatively small population of some 48 million people. Falling between its two spectacular ocean boundaries, the warm Indian Ocean to the east and the icy waters of the Atlantic to the west, is a staggering variety of landscapes and climates. In sultry KwaZulu-Natal one finds dense tropical coastal dune forests, while a short three-hour

THIS PAGE (FROM TOP): The post-1994 South African flag is a powerful symbol of the values of freedom and democracy; South Africa's children have a strong sense of community as a result of their history.

OPPOSITE: This was the first extraordinary glimpse the world had of Nelson Mandela in February 1990 after over 27 years' incarceration. After making the symbolic gesture of walking through the prison gates, Mandela was driven to central Cape Town, where he made his first momentous speech from the balcony of the City Hall.

THIS PAGE: *The high-adrenalin extreme sport of bridge swinging—seen here from the Gouritz Bridge on the Garden Route—has become a huge drawcard for young, adventurous travellers.*

OPPOSITE (FROM TOP): *A typical roadside stall selling local produce—a quintessential sight throughout South Africa; South Africa's 350-year-old tradition of viticulture produces some of the world's most sought-after wines today. Here, winemakers from the Cape's successful new black empowerment wine entreprise, New Beginnings, inspect the grapevines.*

drive inland brings one straight to the province's imposing mountain range, the Drakensberg. To the northwest of the country stretch the timeless desert wastes of the legendary Kalahari, and in the centre of the country, in the wondrous Eastern Cape province, lies one of the world's most ancient pieces of primordial land, the Karoo. Here, in an area of immense semi-desert biodiversity, can be found traces of the earliest creatures to have walked the earth, primitive beings which pre-dated the dinosaurs by millennia. To the south lie the fertile and verdant valleys of the Cape, which is blessed with a Mediterranean-like climate comparable to that of the south of France, while to the north are huge tracts of classic African bushveld, which is home to the famous Big Five. The term Big Five is used to denote the animals which were most sought after as trophies by big game hunters of the 19th century, namely lion, elephant, leopard, rhinoceros and buffalo.

adrenalin heaven

For well over 100 years, South Africa's seductive safari experiences have been a magnet for the adventurous. But since the advent of democracy in 1994, the field of extreme sports has grown in popularity and South Africa is riding on the trend, with kloofing (known as canyoning to some), surfing and abseiling being just a few of the many options you have. But those looking for something milder will also find an abundance of healthy outdoor activities for all fitness levels which take full advantage of the country's balmy climate and plentiful sunshine. Scenic hikes ranging from just a few hours to over a week or even longer can be made in any of the 9 provinces.

The ocean and air have yet more to offer. There are bungee jumps, including the highest in the world, bridge swings and high forest canopy rapels in the Tsitsikamma region of the Eastern Cape. South Africa also has some of the world's top hot-air ballooning spots, notably in the Magaliesberg in Gauteng and the Free State. There are also clubs in virtually every province offering skydiving or gliding. In the ocean one can dive in search of wrecks, reefs and sharks, sail the rough seas off Cape Town or seek out gentler swells further north along the Indian Ocean coast where sailing routes head out eastwards towards the tropical archipelagoes of the Indian Ocean.

a new world of food and wondrous wines to match

Because of its political isolation, the new culinary fusion trends of the 1980s and 1990s that swept the world largely passed South Africa by, but in the 1990s younger members of South Africa's culinary circles travelled out of the country, apprenticing themselves to established chefs around the world, fielding the lowliest tasks in as many famous kitchens as possible while learning their craft.

Today, many of these talented people have returned home, bringing great skill and flair to the new South African cuisine. There are also restaurants in most big centres which serve wonderful traditional South African food, which is a mix of Dutch stews, breads and desserts which has remained unchanged since the 18th century. This cuisine includes strong, fiery influences from Southeast Asia, with some dishes originating from Malaysia and Indonesia, which were the home countries of the slaves who came with their masters from the Dutch East India Company territories. One can add to this the piquant tastes of the Indian subcontinent, especially in KwaZulu-Natal.

Under apartheid, the excellent potential of the Cape vineyards, which date from the 1600s, could not be realised as the international boycott of South African products meant that there was a severely limited export market. After 1994, however, it was as if the Cape wine industry had awakened from a long slumber. Talented young South Africans finally had an incentive to pursue careers in the industry, and a number of important winemakers emerged, fronting boutique wineries that also happened to make superb products. The world began to sit up and take note, and South African wines now feature on the best wine lists around the world, and the annual Nederberg Wine Auction has become a major international event.

join the celebration

South Africa offers a feast for the fan of the performing arts, especially music, dance and theatre. Current Hollywood heavyweight Charlize Theron, a Johannesburg native, brought home the Oscar for Best Actress in 2004 for *Monster*. The country has also produced an illustrious line of rock legends, from Trevor Rabin of 1970s prog-rock group Yes, Shania Twain's husband and globally respected producer Robert John 'Mutt' Lange, reggae mega-star Lucky Dube from Durban, to jazz legends Miriam Makeba, Hugh Masekela and the peerless Cape-born jazz pianist Abdullah Ibrahim. Kwaito, a distinctly South African mélange of R & B, hip-hop and house with chanted lyrics that speak to the country's black youth, was born in the post-apartheid years, and boasts its own mega-star in Soweto native Mandoza.

Classical ballet, traditional African, modern, jazz, tap and avant-garde dance all thrive here and can be seen in a variety of explosive dance shows which have been so successful they regularly tour internationally. Visitors should definitely try to catch the fabulous *African Footprint*, a spectacular dance musical showcasing these indigenous styles which has become a recurring fixture in most major South African cities. The energy of the new South Africa is truly palpable, and a visit to the country is the very best way to experience its vibrant pulse.

THIS PAGE: Jo'burg-born trumpet virtuoso Hugh Masekela is a revered father of the African jazz sound. A talented songwriter who still performs, he spent many years in exile during the height of apartheid.

OPPOSITE: Ballet sensation Noliyanda Mqutwana dances in front of her family home in Kayelitsha township, Cape Town. A dynamic programme of dance outreach run by the Cape Town City Ballet has resulted in a flood of new talent coming to the fore.

The energy of the new South Africa is truly palpable...

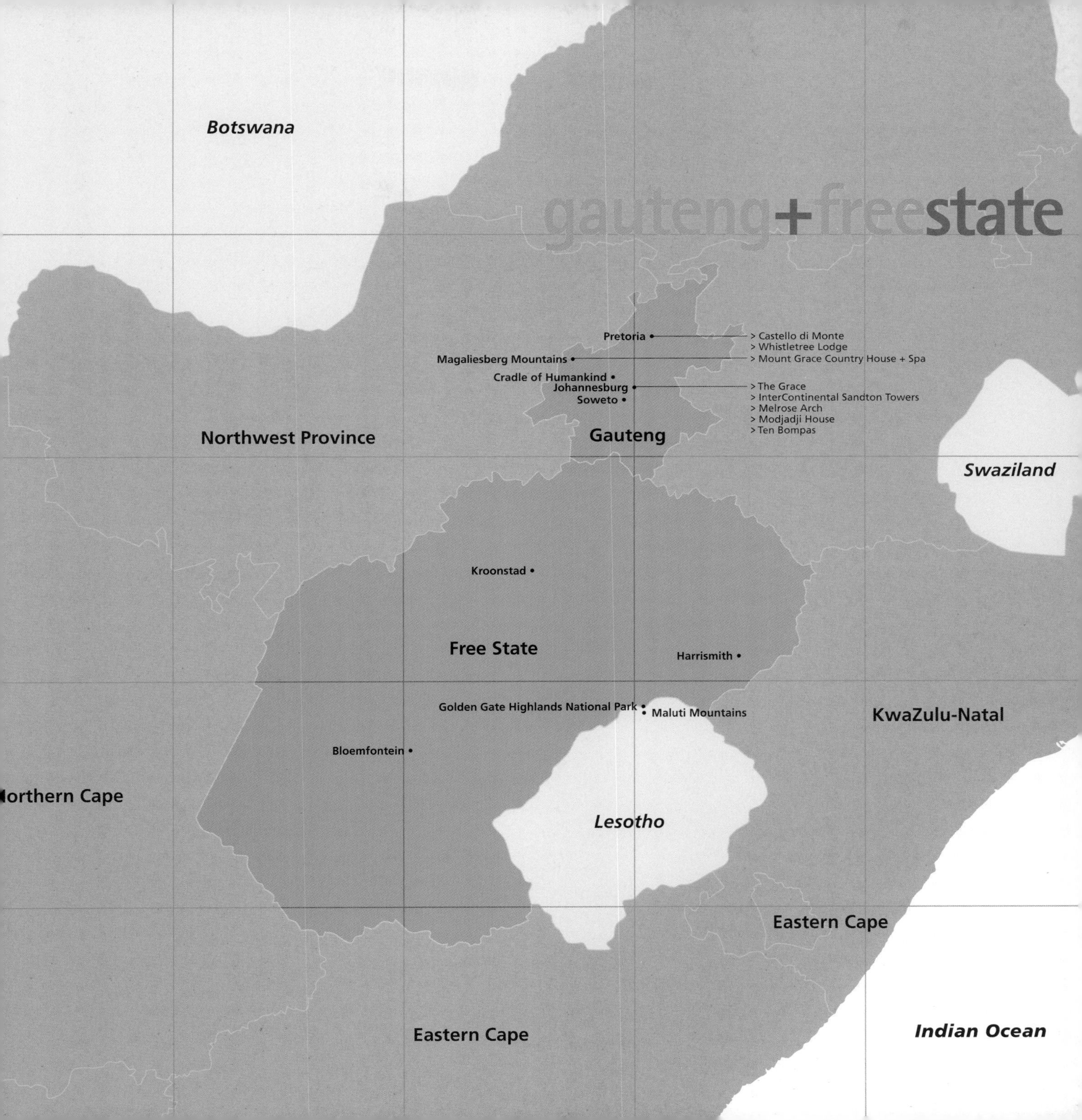
gauteng+freestate
Botswana
Pretoria
> Castello di Monte
> Whistletree Lodge
Magaliesberg Mountains
> Mount Grace Country House + Spa
Cradle of Humankind
Johannesburg
Soweto
> The Grace
> InterContinental Sandton Towers
> Melrose Arch
> Modjadji House
> Ten Bompas
Northwest Province
Gauteng
Swaziland
Kroonstad
Free State
Harrismith
Golden Gate Highlands National Park
Maluti Mountains
KwaZulu-Natal
Bloemfontein
orthern Cape
Lesotho
Eastern Cape
Eastern Cape
Indian Ocean

the heart of an ancient land

The regions of Gauteng and the Free State together form the literal and metaphorical heart of the diverse land that is South Africa. The two provinces, though very different in some ways (the Free State is intensely rural, a land of huge spaces and infinite horizons, whilst Gauteng is the dynamic, urban, go-getting industrial engine of the entire region), have a great deal in common. Together, before the great gold discovery of 1886, these regions comprised a continuous, flattish plain, formed through the gradual erosion of huge pre-historic mountain ranges.

Underneath the seemingly dull surface, however, lie unimaginable quantities of gold which still remain today, even after over 100 years of deep-level gold mining. The remarkable Witwatersrand goldfields are the remains of a primordial inland sea into which ancient rivers carrying the gold particles emptied, as if into a collecting bowl. The goldfields span both provinces, and though the largest concentration of mines occurs within Gauteng, the Free State has some of the most modern and largest operations. The precious gold ore is sent to the Rand Refinery, the world's largest gold refinery, near bustling Johannesburg for processing. The great megalopolis of Johannesburg, encompassing a host of industrial satellite towns, is the economic dynamo of the country, whilst the Free State retains its 'olde worlde' feel, a place of reflection sought after by artists and which offers great beauty and solitude. The two provinces, so similar in origin yet so different in experience, offer an intriguing and convenient travel combination.

gauteng: the cradle of humankind

One of the fascinating elements of this small province is its huge contrasts. Some of the world's most influential political philosophies, as devised through the political genius of Nelson Mandela in the 1940s and 1950s, were developed here. Here too is one of the world's major industrial regions, a great sprawl of human activity and energy, making everything from ball bearings to TV commercials. But Gauteng is so much more than the political and economic powerhouse of the region. It has many other unique

PAGE 18: The multitude of ochre and yellow hues which dominate this Free State scene, adjacent to the Golden Gate Highlands National Park, perfectly epitomises the grandeur and beauty of this sparsely populated, magical landscape.

THIS PAGE: Johannesburg, fabled 'city of gold'. The city's unique history, which includes the world's greatest gold discovery and its primary role in South Africa's booming economy, make it an utterly absorbing destination for those who want to reflect upon its rich heritage.

OPPOSITE: The rich, red earth of Free State wheatfields.

attributes, including the delightful mountain playground of the Magaliesberg, that it shares with its neighbour the Northwest Province, and a cluster of mysterious caves known as the Cradle of Humankind, in which have been found the world's largest concentration of very early (some 3 million years old) hominid, or early human, fossil remains.

the pump engine of commerce

In terms of scenery, Gauteng pales in comparison with the natural splendour of many other parts of South Africa, but it possesses assets that the rest of the country cannot begin to rival, in terms of the sweep of human drama that has played out on its stage. It is here in the 1950s that the extraordinary strategies of Mandela and his compatriots in the ANC (African National Congress) were developed, based upon the ideal of a free, multi-party democracy that would welcome diversity.

But not only was Gauteng the crucible of conflict and exceptional political strategising, it was also the theatre of several previous political and military upheavals, each in their own way as dramatic as the last days of apartheid. And in many ways, all the many dramas of this flat, dry plateau stem from one thing: gold.

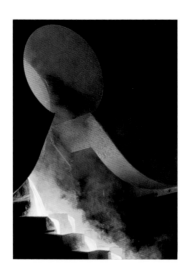

Gauteng is a word from the African language Sotho meaning 'gold'—a truly appropriate name for the region which can justifiably be called a mineral wonderland. No other gold deposit has been found anywhere which can rival the mammoth Witwatersrand goldfields, which stretch in an arc from the Johannesburg area southwestwards into the Free State. A measure of the primary importance of Gauteng's mines and secondary industries can be seen from the fact that some sixty percent of GDP is generated from a minuscule five percent of the country's land area.

Johannesburg (or Jo'burg as it is affectionately known) is where this is at—frenetic, creative, a true 'new world', an ultra-modern city with indigenous values edged with a sharp global consciousness teeming with creative individuals. This is partly because Jo'burg has been a city of immigrants from the day the first news of the great gold strike was published, drawing people from Europe, America, India and all corners of Africa, each bringing their language and customs with them. The influx has continued and increased ever since, with the past 10 years seeing a new wave of foreign businesses seeking opportunity in the politically stable post-apartheid environment.

early history

The precolonial history of this region is effectively that of a crossroads—which it still is even today—making it a superb gateway both to South Africa and the wildlife and adventure playgrounds of the region, including neighbouring states such as Mozambique, Botswana and Namibia. But in days gone by, indigenous groups of varying origins would have moved through the region periodically, seeking wetter grazing grounds such as the lush Apies Valley, around which the modern city of Pretoria is situated.

THIS PAGE: Jo'burg's 'Manhattan on the Highveld' night skyline.

OPPOSITE (FROM TOP): Johannesburg's great gold reserves have drawn workers from every corner of Africa for over a century, giving rise to a unique urban culture focused on the mines; the fascinating sight of a gold pour, the process whereby the molten precious metal is poured into moulds to make gold ingots.

There was a myth—perpetuated by the early European pioneers of Dutch origin who had decided to leave the confines of the southern Cape Colony in the 1830s because of conflict with its new colonial British overlords—that the interior was 'empty' of people. To them it may well have seemed so, but humans have lived in this region for many thousands of years; in fact even well before the advent of *Homo sapiens*, his early hominid ancestors evolved and thrived here some three million years ago. This most ancient thread of history, only fairly recently receiving both wider scholarship and publicity, has become a topic of major importance and increasing fascination not only for visitors but also for the wider South African public.

The Voortrekkers (early pioneers of Dutch origin who were also known as Boers, a word meaning 'farmer' in their Dutch-derived language, Afrikaans) moved slowly into the interior with only their thin wagon hoods, ornate Bibles lettered in High Dutch and their primitive firearms to protect them from a land rife with danger. The sheer doggedness, determination and tenacity of these intrepid groups who struck out beyond the borders of the early colony at the Cape remains a remarkable feat and a triumph of human endurance, even up till today.

the arrival of the voortrekkers

The Boer Voortrekkers underwent great travails on their wanderings in search of a region they could call their own, and where they could set up an independent state that adhered to a republican style of government which they dreamt of basing on the United States model. Relatively few in number, however, the Boer Voortrekkers had many difficulties to overcome before finally succeeding in setting up two Boer Republics deep within the African interior.

THIS PAGE: *Artist's depiction of the Voortrekker migration of the 1830s, when they headed north from the Cape Colony.*

OPPOSITE (FROM TOP): *The dramatic Free State sandstone formation The Sentinel, floodlit at night; beautiful gold jewellery, a quintessential South African product.*

One of these was known as the Orange Free State (named in memory of their Dutch origins, for the Dutch monarch was known as the Prince of Orange), and the other the Zuid Afrikaansche Republiek, or ZAR (South African Republic). The Orange Free State was located in the vicinity of the post-1994 province known today as the Free State, and the ZAR corresponded largely with present-day Gauteng.

By the time these republics had emerged, their citizens were determined to forge a distinct, independent identity at all costs. These were the people who conquered the Highveld region, where Gauteng and the Free State lie today, when their worst fears were realised with the discovery of gold on the Witwatersrand.

the irony of the great gold discovery

The discovery of gold irrevocably changed the fate of the Boer Republics, and indeed the entire African sub-continent. It led, inevitably, to rising tension between the Boer Republics and Britain, represented in the region by her two colonies of the Cape and Natal, over control of the goldfields and the political independence of the Republics. The deterioration of relations culminated in the outbreak of one of the modern world's most significant, though often neglected, conflicts, the Anglo-Boer War of 1899–1902.

The war saw the Boer economies smashed and the first large-scale military use of concentration camps for Boer civilians, and was to be the germination ground for an extreme form of Afrikaner nationalism. Some 26,000 Boer women and children died in the camps (as well as an estimated 14,000 black internees) as the British generals strove to subdue the Boers and attain political and military control of the region. After the trauma of the war, and within a few short years after the British victory, South Africa was awarded self-rule, and the government's policies were dictated by Afrikaner nationalism, from which sprang the phenomenon of apartheid. An extreme form of racial segregation which privileged the Afrikaner minority over the black majority and other coloured groups, it effectively lasted for almost 100 years, and can perhaps best be understood as a reaction to the Afrikaner experience of the Anglo-Boer War.

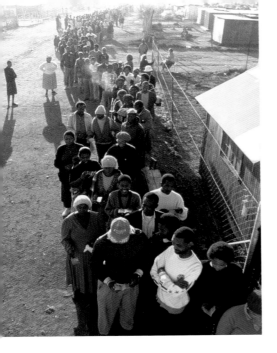

political betrayal

After the Treaty of Vereeniging had been signed by a Boer nation on its knees on 31 May 1902, a period of reconstruction overseen by the British followed. But by 1910, Britain had decided to relinquish the notion of colonies governed by indirect rule. Britain effectively handed over sovereignty in 1910 to the officials of the pre-war Boer Republics. The former British colonies of the Cape and Natal, along with traditional African territories, were to be unified to form the huge new modern state which was simply to be called South Africa.

But what of the African communities throughout the country at this time? Significant black communities had begun to develop in the (ironically) more politically liberal British colonies of the Cape and Natal, where there was universal male suffrage based on wealth instead of race. Black intellectuals were dismayed at the terms of the Union of South Africa, for the negotiations between the Boers and British had not made mention of African rights at all—indeed not even preserving the limited rights black people had possessed in the British colonies. This signalled the beginning of a long battle for political equality by the black majority, which culminated on that unforgettable day in 1994 when all South Africans went to the polls on free and equal terms.

the growth of dissent and the fall of apartheid

As early as the 1960s there was a discernible groundswell of internal dissent which encompassed all groups, including prominent Afrikaners and English-speaking South Africans. However, apartheid had become a colossal structure, which was to take decades to undermine. As the 21st century drew nearer, the insane and costly system of running multiple bureaucracies based on race and the tragic entrenching of millions of black South Africans in under-resourced ghettos masquerading as 'separate cities', along with the escalation of gross human rights abuses in the name of defending the system, began to take its toll. South Africa went on to achieve what many thought could never happen: an internally negotiated just dispensation worked out by South

Africans for South Africans. During this process, pro-democracy activists painstakingly ensured that South Africa's new constitution enshrined respect for all the issues of the modern world, such as environmental responsibility and the rights of minorities.

Almost every visitor who transits through Gauteng's Johannesburg International Airport and has a day to spare in the province visits Soweto, one of the world's truly unique cities, and certainly an essential part of any South African travel itinerary. But Soweto is only one of three major cities in Gauteng. The others are Pretoria, which was established in the 1850s, and Johannesburg, which dates from 1886, the fateful year the world's largest goldfield was struck.

stately pretoria rules

The oldest of these cities is Pretoria. Founded in the mid-1800s as the capital of the ZAR Boer Republic, the city has always been a beacon of identity for Afrikaners. Even in its early years, Pretoria had a grand, tree-lined collegiate townscape, with public buildings reminiscent of those in Vienna, Rome or Amsterdam. They are a particularly intriguing and incongruous sight, located as they are in the heart of Africa.

The Puritan city fathers had in mind a city modelled upon a typical European town. The first constructions, therefore, were built around a market square, and one of the earliest buildings was a church. The church is no more, but the square remains the spiritual heart of Pretoria, set about as it is with a quadrangle of splendid buildings dating from various eras. The oldest buildings were designed by German and Italian architects, and today house the city government. Other buildings date from the short period of British rule in the early 1900s, with others representing some truly magnificent offerings from South Africa's prolific Art Deco period.

As the administrative capital of the country, Pretoria was associated with the enforcement of the apartheid system. Today it is a place with much happier memories, notably the ceremony of the president's inauguration after each democratic election, the first of which marked the inauguration of Nelson Mandela in May 1994.

BELOW: Pretoria's exquisite Union Buildings date from the early 20th century. They house key government offices, and are where the inauguration of South Africa's post-1994 presidents takes place in grand style.

ABOVE AND OPPOSITE TOP: The historic day when all South Africans went to the polls as equals.

OPPOSITE BELOW: Mandela and FW de Klerk going head-to-head during the hustings.

but jo'burg jumps!

If Pretoria is the decorous, responsible older sibling, Jo'burg is the younger wild child, which was, as historian Charles van Onselen put it, 'fathered by gold and mothered by money'. The city sprang to life with a torrent of energy that is still characteristic of its brash, forward-looking inhabitants. Everyone came here to make a quick buck when news of the gold strike broke. This was, and still is, a city quite literally paved with gold, for roads have often been made with tailings from the gold mines, which still contain tiny particles of gold dust.

The Witwatersrand gold reserves are an estimated 30 times larger than any other known gold deposit, and the activity of deep-level gold mining which began in the 1880s has spawned a vast heavy industrial base which supports an array of secondary industries ranging from soft drink manufacture to clothing. More recently, the modern industries of IT development, telecommunications, advertising and PR, to say nothing of the large banking industry, have all burgeoned in the new and heady air of the post-apartheid period. Jo'burg's modern services and superb infrastructure make it an ideal place to do business. While Johannesburg has a bad reputation for crime, it is in fact no different to any other large city in that it is really a question of understanding its ways, knowing which areas should be avoided, and how best to navigate the city.

and soweto buzzes!

From the dark day of the student uprising on 16 June 1976, through the turbulent 1980s and early 1990s, Soweto grew to become one of the best-known but least understood cities in the world. Constantly in the news, this remarkable urban sprawl has become a watchword for large-scale conflict resolution and the beginnings of peace in South Africa, as it had been the place where ordinary citizens made their protests against apartheid heard. Despite its past as a segregated city, it is now filled with a lively pulse that continually draws ex-Sowetans back even after they have moved to Johannesburg.

The earliest settlement in the region dates from around 1904, when Indian and African artisans were evicted from the fast-growing Johannesburg railhead district and relegated to the banks of the Klip River. A community began to grow here, living in tiny houses meant as transient dwellings for a population viewed solely by the government as 'temporary migrant workers'. The authorities deliberately neglected to build facilities such as municipal swimming baths, food markets, shops or cinemas, for the workers were supposed to leave when their contracts were over.

Many people, however, lost contact with their traditional homelands and settled into the urban, fast-paced life in Soweto. Despite the immense poverty, people adapted to the city and created an extraordinary urban culture they could call their own. This is evident not only in the areas of popular culture such as music and dance, but also in the field of political innovation. New waves of grassroots resistance rose and swelled, inspired by the tactics of mass-based passive resistance used by Mandela with great success in the 1950s, which were actually pioneered and first practised in South Africa by Mohandas Gandhi some 35 years earlier.

the free state, south africa's prairie land

The Free State, whose name harks back to that of the Orange Free State, one of the 19th-century Boer Republics, is a place of huge skies that either blaze a relentless azure or rumble with great purple-bruised cumulus clouds and spectacular lightning storms. Relatively few people live here, leaving the magnificent landscapes devoid of cities, many covered in great swathes of corn and yellow sunflowers, which are framed by towering sandstone cliffs.

This is the breadbasket of the region, where European-style farming and animal husbandry have seen the cycles of the agricultural year go round for almost some 150 years. Traditional Afrikaner life here has changed little since the days when the ox wagons first appeared over the horizon and this prairie province hides a beauty that reveals itself slowly but surely to the patient traveller.

THIS PAGE: Soweto miscellany: the neglect of African residential areas under apartheid meant that many people have no choice but to live in shacks. However, major housing programmes are being implemented to make up for present conditions.
OPPOSITE (FROM TOP): The sights and sounds of Johannesburg: shooting the breeze in typical township style; browsing in a flea market; urban bustle at night.

images of power and magic

Among one of the sights not to be missed in the Free State are the San rock paintings, such as those at sites near Ladybrand, close to the Lesotho border. South Africa's rock art is said to range from 250 to 5,000 years in age, and was painted by a group of people known as the San. Sometimes called 'the first South Africans', this ancient people, who now generally only exist in tiny communities on the outskirts of remote rural towns, had a hunter-gatherer culture dating back at least 5,000 years, and their art and culture is only coming to light in the post-apartheid era. As other indigenous groups moved southwards some 2,000 years ago and European settlers moved north from the Cape after 1652, the San suffered encroachment upon their territories and endured a virtual genocide, brought about by over 350 years of colonisation and urbanisation. Studies of San art have revealed that many of the works served a spiritual purpose, and it represents the movement of man's consciousness, symbolised by an animal, between Earth and the spirit world beyond the veil of the rock surface.

the maluti mountains, rock stars and middle earth

For the hiker, the Free State is irresistible. The Golden Gate Highlands National Park, a small gem, can be found adjacent to the Maluti Mountains. In this wide open country, it is also perhaps not surprising that one of South Africa's most exciting open-air rock festivals takes place here every Easter. Known as Rustlers' Valley, the Easter festival attracts absolutely everyone from Jo'burg yuppies needing a break to hippies, New Age travellers and the merely curious—who all come to listen to the cream of the country's rock acts. Rustlers' Valley also hosts a now-legendary New Year's Eve party.

Despite all the stories linked to the Free State, few associate it with JRR Tolkien, who was born in Bloemfontein in 1892 to an English father who had been sent out to run a bank in the expanding frontier region of South Africa. Tolkien left South Africa as a child, but *The Lord of the Rings* fans can still be found poring over his trilogy, seeking clues as to which South African landscape might have inspired Middle Earth and its hobbits.

THIS PAGE (FROM TOP): Sunflowers blaze against an azure sky; South Africa's magnificent rock art heritage allows a glimpse into the cultures of the ancient peoples who created these outdoor 'galleries'.

OPPOSITE: The rural lives of these animal herders echo powerfully in Tolkien's characters on their epic quest in his magnificent work The Lord of the Rings.

The regions...form the literal and metaphorical heart of the diverse land that is South Africa.

Castello di Monte

Situated on a hillside, Castello di Monte is a private property where the dream and vision of a builder combined with the owners' passion to create a beautiful, luxurious property located in Waterkloof Ridge, Pretoria. Its high walls and massive rustic copper gates open to reveal a unique property reminiscent of a 16th-century Italian villa. In this little slice of Tuscany, lavender bushes and olive trees grow in a lush garden out front while lemon trees pepper the garden around the swimming pool. Inside, a granite spiral staircase with a copper rail leads the eye upwards to the lofty ceiling.

There are nine sumptuously-appointed and individually-decorated rooms, leaving one spoilt for choice. Choose between the presidential suite with a fireplace and four-poster bed or the honeymoon suite with a spa bath and handpainted bathroom murals, or a terrace room. In addition to the luxuries just mentioned, the spacious 150-sq m (1,600-sq ft) presidential suite also comes complete with a walk-in dressing room, DVD player, a balcony and a bathroom with a separate shower.

The formal lounge with its high fireplace, dark wooden bookcase and

BELOW: A bird's-eye view of Castello di Monte reveals the sweep and grandeur of the architecture of the guest house.

OPPOSITE (FROM TOP): An ornate four-poster bed is the centrepiece of the honeymoon suite; murals in the bathroom bring one back in time to the Roman baths of antiquity.

works of art is a welcoming place. In the main dining room, a painted ceiling that echoes the Sistine Chapel presides over cuisine that is lovingly prepared by the guest house's resident chef. For a unique experience, dine on the panoramic deck on the top floor of the villa as you soak up 360-degree views of Pretoria. At least half a dozen other dining areas are scattered throughout the villa.

A veritable warren, the guest house is full of surprising nooks and crannies waiting to be discovered, and each space is filled with its

own charm and inimitable character, thanks to the careful attention paid to décor details.

If you need to burn off some extra calories, a Roman-style swimming pool is ideal for laps, while the nearby Virgin Active gym is open to all residents. Those who want to practise their golf swing will find two golf courses within a short 3-km (1.8-mile) radius. Return to a refreshing sauna and steam shower, or relax in an

outdoor jacuzzi that sits cosily by a fireplace. Stroll around the rustic garden and have fun with an oversized chess set. A tranquil rock pond beckons, and the soothing sound of running water creates an atmosphere of calm.

By the front door of the villa is a wishing well that is neatly hidden. Cast your wish as you enter, and watch it magically materialise before your very eyes.

FACTS		
ROOMS	4 classic rooms • 3 terrace rooms • 1 presidential suite • 1 honeymoon suite	
FOOD	dining room: international • salad bar • Italian Courtyard: Italian • Barbeque Terrace: South African braai • 8 intimate dining areas	
DRINK	wine cellar • bar	
FEATURES	pool • outdoor jacuzzi • sauna • steam shower • landscaped garden	
BUSINESS	Internet access	
NEARBY	Pretoria city centre • Johannesburg • Virgin Active gym (with complimentary return transfers) • golf courses	
CONTACT	402 Aries Street, Waterkloof Ridge, Pretoria 0181 • telephone: +27.12 346 6984 • facsimile: +27.12 460 6739 • email: info@castello.co.za • website: www.castello.co.za	

PHOTOGRAPHS COURTESY OF CASTELLO DI MONTE.

Whistletree Lodge

Tucked away in the northeastern quarter of Gauteng Province's lush 'garden city' of Pretoria, the exquisite Whistletree Lodge is a well-kept secret and magnificent surprise, whether one is a world-weary executive or an intrepid African explorer.

The lodge comprises an exclusive set of superbly decorated luxury suites in a magical park-like setting on the northern slopes of Pretoria's distinctive landscape of low parallel east-west ridges. Within this sheltered and tranquil valley, a curious microclimate keeps the temperature balmy and the air moist, a welcome relief from the stark dryness found elsewhere in Gauteng.

Whistletree is the spectacular result of the vision of owner Kobus Farrell, who founded the boutique hotel in the mid-1990s as a creative outlet for his love of collecting fine art and furniture. Thus, Whistletree does not have a rigid, generic style, but is more of a character-filled home bursting with stories and decorated with remarkable museum-quality furniture from many eras.

In the main public area is a stunning black Art Deco bar. There, one glimpses fine French armoires, an oil portrait of a chatelaine, and a warm animal skin thrown across the beautiful floor. Every suite has luxurious features such as a balcony overlooking the tropical garden, a refreshment station and other thoughtful elements.

...the exquisite Whistletree Lodge is a well-kept secret and magnificent surprise...

The combination of Whistletree's features attracts a sophisticated clientele, including the many academics who visit the city's prestigious research institutes and business travellers, along with the stream of guests who grace Pretoria's impressive diplomatic offices and residences. Over 100 foreign embassies and consular missions occupy premises in the tree-lined diplomatic quarter of the city's Arcadia district nearby. These illustrious visitors to Pretoria choose Whistletree not only for its great location, superb food and wonderful interiors, but also because of its beguiling options for relaxation. The lodge has the air of an exclusive private health club, with a heated pool, sauna and immaculate tennis court.

Whistletree is also utterly irresistible to the nature-lover. Nearby is a tranquil nature reserve and a running track where one can stroll or jog the day's cares away, or perhaps partake of some spectacular bird-watching. Romantics will derive pleasure from knowing that Whistletree was the setting for a tumultuous and tragic love affair dating back to the Anglo-Boer War of 1899, which is now depicted on the hotel's walls. Whistletree offers a brand of true South African hospitality that pampers the body, and delights the heart and soul.

THIS PAGE: Rooms at Whistletree Lodge are decorated with a blend of old world charm and contemporary African style.

OPPOSITE: The jazzy lounge and bar that overlook the pool are excellent for evening drinks.

FACTS

ROOMS	12 luxury rooms
FOOD	dining room: South African fusion
DRINK	wine cellar • cocktail bar
FEATURES	heated pool • sauna • tennis court • cigar room
BUSINESS	boardroom • conference services
NEARBY	golf course and driving range • shopping centres • Pretoria city centre • cinemas • restaurants • nature reserve
CONTACT	1267 Whistletree Drive, Queenswood, Pretoria 0186 • telephone: +27.12 333 9915 • facsimile: +27.12 333 9917 • email: wtree@icon.co.za • website: www.whistletreelodge.com

PHOTOGRAPHS COURTESY OF WHISTLETREE LODGE.

Mount Grace Country House + Spa

Set in acres of exquisite gardens in the Magaliesberg Mountains, Mount Grace Country House & Spa exemplifies South African country living at its best. The property is divided into four villages, each with its own style and ambience.

At Thatchstone Village, English-style country gardens complete with daffodils and other spring flowers hug the rooms, each of which possesses a distinctive character. Quaintly thatched, the rooms exude a quiet charm, and are located at a convenient but discreet distance to the main hotel and its facilities.

Over at Grace Village, the units are endowed with either a verandah or balcony which overlooks manicured gardens and the swimming pool. At Treetops Village, spacious rooms are adorned with life's little luxuries, such as underfloor heating, air-conditioning and a dressing room. Rooms

THIS PAGE (FROM TOP): The cosy ambience of the verandah at The Spa; pools such as this one abound in the grounds of The Spa, which emphasises hydrotherapy treatments.

OPPOSITE: The stone façade of The Spa with a waterfall in front, which is part of the hydrotherapy spa garden.

with a generous balcony or verandah enjoy a magnificent, uninterrupted view of the deep ravine, dotted with trees and inhabited by abundant bird life.

Golf carts are available to transport guests around the property, especially to and from Upper Mountain Village rooms, and those who make the trip are rewarded with a breathtaking view of the Magaliesberg Mountains from their private verandah. Situated on an elevated plateau, each suite has private access. Guests can enjoy a languid dip in their suite's private plunge pool, then curl up inside with a cup of hot tea and a movie on a DVD player. The distance between the Upper Mountain Village and the main hotel ensures exclusivity. Instead of checking in at the front desk, guests register directly at the spa's reception, close to the village. Breakfast is served at the Spa Café instead of The Copperfield Grill with the rest of the guests. Come late afternoon, sundowners are delivered to each room at the Upper Mountain Village, while in-room massages can be ordered from the spa.

Home-cooked country-style buffets are served at The Copperfield Grill, which is where most guests come to fill up on breakfast and dinner. Do not be fooled by the casual air of this eatery. Its hearty rustic cooking, including dishes such as beef

THIS PAGE: *Float your worries away at The Spa's brine flotation pool. The salinity of the water allows you to be naturally bouyant, which is a very calming experience.*

OPPOSITE: *The outdoor jacuzzi is set amongst the lush vegetation of the Magaliesberg Mountains.*

carpaccio dressed in thyme vinaigrette, duck and cherry pie, and chicken liver pâté with melba toast, has earned it a firm place in rankings of South Africa's top 100 restaurants.

To make the most of the African sunshine, Mount Grace conducts its lunch and afternoon tea service on the verandah or in the fresh, verdant garden. Intimate meals can be taken at The Stoep, the hotel's elegant à la carte restaurant, which seats 35 guests. The food is 'country with French flair'. This translates to dishes like coq au vin, mushroom râgout and fancy confit of pork belly, and Brie wanton parcels served in a

sweet onion soup. Light breakfasts and lunches are served at the Spa Café. Guests who prefer a healthy regime may opt for a detox menu tailored to suit their diets.

The Spa complex is a destination in itself. It has, after all, been the recipient of glowing accolades from the beauty and spa industry. The complex is built from organic materials like stone, clay and thatch, which blend in soothingly with the surrounding landscape. Like a secret playground for adults, the outdoor hydrotherapy spa garden instantly relaxes work-weary muscles and stressed-out minds. Who can resist the lure of

heated al fresco rock pools and cool gushing waterfalls? For the ultimate in relaxation, guests are encouraged to try out the brine flotation pool enhanced with soothing underwater music, which induces a state of ultimate repose and calm—rather like the effect of warm camomile tea on a rainy evening. Hydrotherapy is a recurring theme in the spa's treatment menu, which has recently grown to include the signature Thaba ('mountain' in Sotho) massage, where two therapists skilfully wield the knopkierie, a knob-headed rod traditionally used by the Zulu as a weapon, to relieve tension. A range of body wraps and skin care treatments are also offered at the six treatment rooms and three outdoor safari-style spa treatment tents.

There is no lack of activities here. History buffs will be gratified to discover the historical sites of the Old English Block House, Battle of Nooitgedacht and the Cradle of Humankind. Cheese connoisseurs should make a pit stop at the Van Gaalen Kaasmaker, a cheese factory that still makes cheese the traditional Dutch way. Sports enthusiasts can get their adrenalin flowing with tennis, mountain biking or swimming, while nature-lovers have a wealth of options including bird-watching, fly-fishing and nature walks, while thrill-seekers have hang-gliding and hot-air balloon safaris, and guests will also appreciate the hotel's monthly classical music concerts. Mount Grace is the perfect place to rejuvenate a weary soul.

FACTS		
ROOMS	80 rooms	
FOOD	Copperfield Grill: buffet • The Stoep: French country • Spa Café: light healthy meals	
DRINK	Hartley's Bar and Billiard Room	
FEATURES	3 swimming pools • gift shop • library • spa and hydrotherapy garden • snooker and pool tables • croquet lawns • bowling green • tennis courts • picnic grounds	
BUSINESS	conference facilities • facsimile • Internet facilities • secretarial services	
NEARBY	Pecanwood Golf Estate • Battle of Nooitgedacht site • Old English Block House • Cradle of Humankind • Van Gaalen Kaasmaker • microlighting • balloon safaris	
CONTACT	Private Bag 5004, Magaliesburg 1791 • telephone: +27.14 577 1350 • facsimile: +27.14 577 1202 • email: mountgrace@grace.co.za • website: www.grace.co.za	

The Grace

Grace Hotels are a small group of award-winning boutique hotels in South Africa. The Grace is a sophisticated urban hotel set in the heart of the exclusive Johannesburg suburb of Rosebank. Here, residents and visitors enjoy tree-lined streets, upscale shops and department stores, and a host of fine restaurants and bars.

The Grace was opened in 1997 and is currently owned by African Sun Hotels, which runs and manages hotels throughout Africa, with the jewel in their crown being the Victoria Falls Hotel in Victoria Falls, Zimbabwe. The success of The Grace is evident in the accolades that have been heaped upon it by critics and trendsetters in the travel and leisure industry. In 2004 alone, it was voted 'Best Business Hotel in Africa and the Middle East' and 'Top Hotel in Johannesburg' by *Travel + Leisure*, and ranked among the top three hotels in Africa by *Condé Nast* readers.

At The Grace, guests have the option of staying in either luxurious twin or double rooms, suites or one-bedroom penthouses. To maintain a personal level of service and hospitality, the total number of rooms is kept deliberately low for an urban hotel. Suites come with a separate lounge which is ideal for private business meetings or dinner parties for up to six people. A guest bathroom ensures that the privacy of the master bedroom need not be intruded upon when guests need to use the facilities. Penthouses are located on the 10th floor and boast stunning views of the town. Elegant French doors open out onto

balconies that overlook downtown Rosebank. Like the suites, the penthouses also have a separate lounge with a guest bathroom. Children are well catered for here. Young ones are welcome to stay in their parents' room, while older children are provided with a complimentary room so that mum and dad can sleep in peace.

Dining at The Grace is a sumptuous affair. Its fine dining restaurant is called The Dining Room, and the simplicity of this name echoes the restaurant's elegant yet down-to-earth ambience and single-minded mission to dish out great food. Executive Chef Raymond Rundle is a master of creativity and skill. Using only the freshest ingredients, he conjures up African-inspired dishes that have delighted guests from all over the world. Try his oak-smoked springbok served on hot multigrain with white balsamic vinegar and cranberry sauce, or his Key lime soufflé made with Swazi limes. Many well known businessmen and celebrities will testify to the excellence of The Dining Room, and its monthly food and wine evenings have become a popular attraction.

THIS PAGE: The Grace's stunning lap pool and manicured lawns make the perfect retreat after a hectic day in the city.

OPPOSITE: The hotel's rooftop is a veritable English country garden where al fresco breakfasts, lunches and evening cocktails are served in summer.

On the fifth floor of the hotel is the fitness centre. Your room key will admit you to this fully-equipped gym which is open round the clock. When you are done working out, slip into the spa next door and let experienced therapists pamper you with a range of soothing treatments. Luxuriate in a seaweed wrap, Hawaiian massage or hot stone treatment, either in a treatment room or, if you prefer, the privacy of your suite.

Business travellers will find everything they need here. A 12-seater boardroom and a 30-seater conference room provide ample facilities for large meetings, while a business centre with full secretarial services has all the office support you require while on the road. All rooms and suites have facsimile and Internet connections.

THIS PAGE (FROM TOP): The elegant lounge is well stocked with international newspapers and a wide selection of books; the crafts at Rosebank's African curio market are authentic and of superb quality.

OPPOSITE: A cosy fireplace in The Dining Room, the hotel's fine dining establishment, provides warmth on cool winter nights. If that does not warm you up, the hearty, mouth-watering food here will.

Alternative dining options at The Grace include The Dining Room's garden terrace. Set by a croquet lawn and a lap pool, and lined with manicured rose bushes, the terrace is excellent for an al fresco meal. The hotel's rooftop garden is also open-air. During the summer it hosts leisurely breakfasts, lunches and evening cocktails. Small groups might prefer The Vinoteque, the hotel's vintage wine cellar, which also has dining facilities for parties of up to 20 people.

Leisure visitors and business people taking a break from work have plenty at their disposal. A covered, elevated walkway links The Grace to designer shops at The Mall at Rosebank for convenient access. On the rooftop of The Mall is a weekend craft market, arguably one of South Africa's best. Within walking distance of the hotel are more exclusive shops, an eclectic mix of over 200 restaurants, art galleries, movie theatres, including an art-house cinema, and a reputable permanent African curio market.

Nearby is Johannesburg's city centre with its multitude of sights and attractions, including many notable museums. Further afield but still within easy reach is the mountain retreat of Mount Grace, the first hotel in the Grace collection. This is the ideal place for your next stop or a weekend away from the city. At The Grace you enjoy the best of all worlds—an idyllic suburb, the bustling, cosmopolitan city and rugged countryside are just a stone's throw away.

FACTS

ROOMS	60 twin or double bedrooms • 10 suites • 3 penthouses
FOOD	The Dining Room: South African and international • The Vinoteque: private parties
DRINK	wine cellar • bar • lounge
FEATURES	pool • fitness centre • spa • library • croquet lawn • English garden
BUSINESS	boardroom • conference centre • business centre • facsimile • Internet facilities
NEARBY	The Mall at Rosebank • art galleries • cinemas • craft markets • Johannesburg city centre • Sterkfontein limestone caves • Mount Grace Country House & Spa
CONTACT	54 Bath Avenue, Rosebank, Johannesburg 2196 • telephone: +27.11 280 7200 • facsimile: +27.11 280 7474 • email: graceres@thegrace.co.za • website: www.thegrace.co.za

InterContinental Sandton Towers

The gleaming, modern towers of Sandton are home to South Africa's most sophisticated shopping malls, its largest corporations and the most comprehensive conference facilities. It is little wonder then that this vibrant suburban metropolis attracts large numbers of local and international travellers for both business and leisure. The InterContinental Sandton Towers has earned a reputation among discerning visitors for being ranked among one of the finest hotels in the Southern hemisphere.

Sandton Towers is one of the most striking architectural features of the suburb's skyline, and its graceful external lines are mirrored in the breathtaking reception area. The atrium boasts Grecian friezes and soaring vaulted ceilings, and its honey-gold granite and marble finishes are beautifully offset by the natural warmth of maplewood.

This magnificent welcome is found throughout the hotel. Friendly staff are on hand to anticipate one's needs. Rooms are tastefully decorated and equipped with every possible convenience. All rooms have satellite television and pay-per-view channels, air-conditioning, a mini-bar and 24-hour room service. The lavishly-appointed penthouse in Sandton Towers is the last word in luxury, with a splendid bedroom, lounge, dining area, kitchenette and guest bathroom, allowing one to entertain in privacy.

As befits its cosmopolitan setting, the InterContinental Sandton Towers offers cuisine that reflects cultures and tastes from around the world. Traditional African dishes, Afro-fusion fare, Portuguese meals, delectable seafood and authentic Japanese delights are all served. The sophisticated Upper West Side Café Bar serves light meals and snacks, accompanied by live entertainment.

Whether for exercise or recreation, guests have access to superb sports facilities. A fully-equipped gymnasium has trainers who offer personal instruction. Transport can also be arranged to any of the

THIS PAGE: All rooms and suites at InterContinental Sandton Towers come with satellite TV, a mini-bar, a tea- and coffee-maker, bathrobes and video check-out facilities.

OPPOSITE: A glorious sunset as seen from one of the hotel's two outdoor pools and decks. There is no better place to refresh yourself after a day of shopping, sightseeing or meeting with business associates.

numerous golf courses, tennis courts and other facilities nearby. Alternatively, two beautiful pool decks provide the perfect excuse to bask in the African sunshine while being served exotic drinks and nibbles.

For guests who prefer shopping or light entertainment, South Africa's premier shopping complex, Sandton City, is literally a few steps away, and the glamorous boutiques, gift shops, restaurants and cinemas are likely to prove irresistible.

Sandton Towers offers exceptional business and convention facilities, with venues accommodating up to 850 guests. Excellent communication and presentation facilities can be found at the business centre. To cater to the hotel's stream of international guests, kosher, halal, Greek and Japanese functions can be arranged.

For visitors to Sandton or Johannesburg, a stay at InterContinental Sandton Towers is guaranteed to enhance the pleasure and success of the trip.

PHOTOGRAPHS COURTESY OF INTERCONTINENTAL SANDTON TOWERS.

FACTS		
ROOMS	564 rooms • 35 suites • 3 presidential suites • 1 penthouse	
DINING	Ferns: African seafood • Daruma: Japanese • Vilamoura: Portuguese seafood • Upper West Side: snacks and coffee • Atrium: international	
BARS	Atrium • Upper West Side	
FEATURES	2 pools • gym • sauna • beauty salon • car rental desk	
BUSINESS	conference facilities • international business centre • Club floor	
NEARBY	Sandton City Shopping Centre • Sandton Convention Centre • Montecasino	
CONTACT	Corner of Fifth and Alice Streets, Sandton 2146 • telephone: +27.11 780 5000 • facsimile: +27.11 780 5022 • email: icsandtonsunandtowers@southernsun.com • website: www.southernsun.com	

Melrose Arch Hotel

THIS PAGE: Melrose Arch Hotel pushes the boundaries of conventional design. By the swimming pool, ficus trees grow out of giant buckets, while tables and chairs are immersed in a wading pool.

OPPOSITE: A 22-seater long table forms an arresting centrepiece in the hotel with artistic lighting adding to the mood.

Melrose Arch precinct in the suburbs of Johannesburg is a microcosm of all that is new and great in South Africa today. In the midst of this thriving complex of high street shops, modern offices, hip bars and restaurants, and stylish residences, stands Melrose Arch Hotel. A five-star boutique establishment, this cheerfully progressive hotel redefines what suburban hotels should be. Its design is completely innovative, eclectic and even unusual and when you enter this hotel, you could be forgiven for thinking you've just stepped into a wonderland.

Lighting is a fundamental design feature in this aesthetically-conscious hotel. Waves of light greet you on entry at the impressive Zanzibar doors—intricately carved traditional wooden doors originating from Stone Town in Zanzibar. The entrance has under-lit floors that run the length of the room, right up to the reception area. Columns are lit dramatically and oversized lampshades with cable chandeliers dazzle the eye. Even the pool is lit. Underwater lights change from yellow to red to purple in a kaleidoscope of colour.

Swimming in this pool will certainly be an experience hard to repeat elsewhere. Besides being accompanied by rainbow coloured underwater lighting while you do laps, you will also hear the strains of piped music. The surprises do not stop here. Set in a shallow area of the pool are chairs and tables. Leave your footwear by the side of the pool and wade to a table where waiters will be happy to serve you lunch. As if this were not enough, larger-than-life 1.8-m- (6-ft-) tall steel buckets planted with ficus trees line the poolside and garden.

Contemporary art forms a major component of this hotel. In support of the

South African art community, Melrose Arch Hotel commissions domestically and internationally-acclaimed local artists to produce works of art, which are found in the hotel's public spaces, the Sound Room and the five boardrooms. Not merely for display, the art is an integral part of the hotel's design. Works of art are commissioned with specifically-designated spaces in mind, and artists regularly replenish their works, thereby ensuring that what is on view is always current and exclusive.

The Sound Room is the hotel's state-of-the-art audio-visual room. Encased in glass with manoeuvrable shutters, the room comes with a large plasma screen and a high-tech stereo sound system for your viewing pleasure. Replay your safari home videos here or enjoy the latest blockbuster on DVD.

Guests who want to unwind in the hotel will find the library a perfect place. Timber-panelled bookcases stained to the colour of cherry wood creak under the weight of 5,000 books. Workable catwalks provide access to the higher shelves. Adding to the ambience is an antique billiard table lined in black velvet and illuminated by a chandelier.

March, the hotel's restaurant, offers guests fusion food in a relaxed and inviting atmosphere. Like the hotel, the restaurant's menu is experimental and enthralling. While conventional dishes form the backbone of the menu, delightful, unusual combinations of flavours and ingredients are thrown in for good measure. Every season the menu is redesigned to keep it new and exciting. The restaurant's signature features are its classic tandoor and wood-fired ovens.

An exclusive penthouse suite crowns the 117 luxury bedrooms that this hotel offers. Rooms are colourful and full of unexpected design elements. With all these amenities, it is no wonder that Melrose Arch Hotel sees a constant stream of South African and international guests who frequent the area for both business and pleasure.

FACTS

ROOMS	117 rooms • 1 penthouse suite
FOOD	The March Restaurant: international fusion • coffee shop
DRINK	The March Restaurant bar
FEATURES	experimental design • pool • library • The Sound Room • The Veranda
BUSINESS	boardrooms • business centre • full secretarial and business services • ISDN lines • Internet kiosks
NEARBY	shops • bars and restaurants • Johannesburg city centre • Sandton City
CONTACT	1 Melrose Square, Melrose Arch, Johannesburg 2196 • telephone: +27.11 214 6666 • facsimile: +27.11 214 6600 • email: info@melrosearchhotel.com • website: www.africanpridehotels.com

Modjadji House

An ancient African rainforest legend comes alive in a sophisticated modern setting at Modjadji House. At the heart of this stylish boutique hotel in the Johannesburg suburb of Floracliffe is a 0.8-hectare (2-acre) garden with a beautiful collection of prehistoric cycads, reminiscent of those in the Modjadji Rainforest. The Rain Queen, a divine transformer of clouds, is believed to dwell in that rainforest. Her power lies in her feminine nature, fair skin and fertility, and she is widely revered as a goddess of growth as well as destruction.

This legend inspired the property's owners to transform the original house they built in 1960. With the help of architect

THIS PAGE (CLOCKWISE FROM TOP): Suites at Modjadji House are tastefully decorated in contemporary African style; the tranquil pool is nestled amidst a cycad garden; modern fittings sit alongside natural materials in the bathroom of a suite.

OPPOSITE: The hotel's elegant lounge with its small but growing wine selection.

Georg van Gass, the rather austere 1960s structure blossomed into a work of art. Keeping the stone used in the original house, van Gass reinvented the rest of the building, creating open, fluid spaces, sleek modern lines and stylish decorations. The garden is a key feature of this property and was designed to integrate with the house so that the two form one entity. The two-storey house overlooks the garden, which, with its cycads, exudes an almost mystical quality.

Six luxurious suites promise exclusivity and total privacy. Each one is uniquely decorated, and collectively the suites offer outdoor showers, balconies, private gardens and open-plan bathrooms. Suite three is the grandest, with a huge bathroom and its own garden. All suites come with generous king-size beds.

Breakfast is served in the inner courtyard, and evening cocktails on the outdoor terraced deck. Lunch and dinner are provided on request. A pool beckons, and is especially inviting after a day spent exploring Johannesburg. Business people will find Modjadji House an excellent venue for conferences. A fully-equipped meeting room comfortably seats 25 people, and conference packages include refreshments as well as a sumptuous lunch.

Complimentary transfers to the numerous shopping centres nearby are available. Johannesburg city centre also boasts a host of attractions. To discover the history of this city, visit Gold Reef City which is built around the gold mines that drew so many European fortune seekers here in the 1900s. To learn about African cultures, visit Lesedi Cultural Village, where you will find authentic recreations of villages of the major tribes of this continent. To see Johannesburg at her best, take the lift to the 50th floor of Carlton Shopping Centre for a panoramic view. When you are done, retire to Modjadji House with its age-old cycads and be refreshed in the comfort of your suite.

FACTS		
ROOMS	6 suites	
FOOD	courtyard: breakfast • lunch and dinner upon request	
DRINK	terraced deck • lounge	
FEATURES	pool • lounge • cycad garden	
BUSINESS	boardroom • Internet facilities	
NEARBY	Cradle of Humankind • Walter Sisulu Botanical Gardens • shopping centres • restaurants • bars • Johannesburg city centre	
CONTACT	23 Oosthuizen Drive, Floracliffe, Roodepoort, Johannesburg • telephone: +27.11 674 1421 • facsimile: +27.11 672 4570 • email: info@modjadjihouse.co.za • website: www.modjadjihouse.co.za	

PHOTOGRAPHS COURTESY OF MODJADJI HOUSE.

Ten Bompas

In the quiet, exclusive Dunkeld suburb of Johannesburg lies a pleasant surprise. Tucked amongst the comfortable upper middle-class homés here is a top boutique hotel for leisure and business travellers alike. Ten interior designers were asked to decorate one of the hotel's 10 suites in their interpretation of an African theme. The result is 10 unique representations of Africa, unified by their use of art, sculpture and masks.

But where this hotel has really made its mark is with its unparalleled personal service. Directors Christoff van Staden and Peter Aucamp were driven to inject intimacy into typically impersonal business travel. Fuelled by their own disappointing business travel experiences, they created service that instantly makes a traveller feel cherished.

The close-knit staff greet you by name, and personally see you off to work in the

morning when you hand in your keys at reception. Upon your return in the evening, staff are waiting at the end of the driveway with your room keys in hand and a smile on their faces. Dinner is served in the restaurant if you request it—if not, you will be left to the privacy of your suite.

Nothing is overlooked at this incredible home away from home. Staff note which type of wine you prefer and have a bottle waiting. Laundry service is complimentary, and if it is noticed that you are running out of shirts, one will be ironed and delivered to your suite in time for your next meeting. The mini-bar is also complimentary, a gesture unprecedented in the hotel industry. Generously stocked with standard-size bottles, it offers a privilege all guests have respected. With this degree of hospitality, you might well feel that you are staying in your best friend's home.

At Ten Bompas, everybody knows your name.

Suites come with fireplaces, steam showers and fax machines. Each suite also has a lounge with a guest bathroom. This allows business associates who come to your suite for meetings to use the facilities without intruding upon your bedroom. Wardrobes are big enough to comfortably store large suitcases—an important but highly underrated factor.

Ten Bompas' five-star restaurant, Sides, offers excellent food and wine. Going back to basics, it serves classic cuisine and old home-style favourites. Wine comes from the two-storey, 10,000-bottle cellar stocked with a fine selection of Cape Winemakers Guild labels. Order from your personal waiter or browse the cellar yourself. At Ten Bompas, everybody knows your name.

FACTS

ROOMS	10 suites
FOOD	Sides: international
DRINK	wine cellar
FEATURES	complimentary mini-bar • complimentary laundry service • in-suite guest lounge and bathroom • fireplaces
BUSINESS	in-suite facsimile • boardroom facilities and services • transfers to and from meetings
NEARBY	Johannesburg city centre • suburban towns of Illova, Sandton and Hyde Park
CONTACT	10 Bompas Road, Dunkeld West, Johannesburg • telephone: +27.11 325 2442 • facsimile: +27.11 341 0281 • email: tenbompas@mix.co.za • website: www.tenbompas.com

PHOTOGRAPHS COURTESY OF TEN BOMPAS.

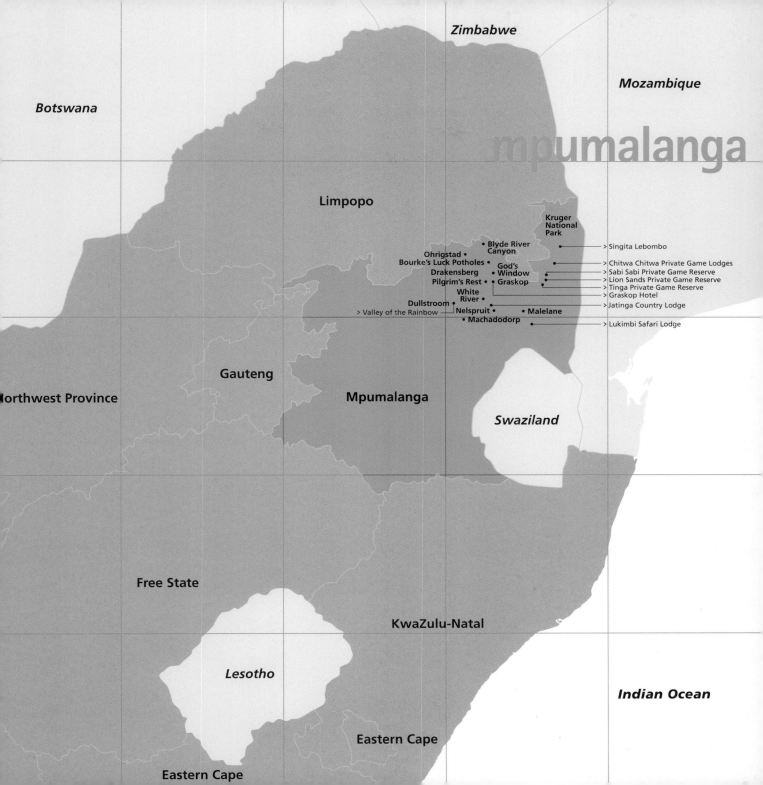

Botswana

Zimbabwe

Mozambique

mpumalanga

Limpopo

Kruger
National
Park

• Blyde River
Canyon

Ohrigstad •
Bourke's Luck Potholes •
God's
• Window
Drakensberg •
Pilgrim's Rest • • Graskop
White
River •
Dullstroom •
> Valley of the Rainbow —— Nelspruit •
• Machadodorp

• Malelane

> Singita Lebombo

> Chitwa Chitwa Private Game Lodges
> Sabi Sabi Private Game Reserve
> Lion Sands Private Game Reserve
> Tinga Private Game Reserve
> Graskop Hotel
> Jatinga Country Lodge

> Lukimbi Safari Lodge

Gauteng

Northwest Province

Mpumalanga

Swaziland

Free State

KwaZulu-Natal

Lesotho

Eastern Cape

Eastern Cape

Indian Ocean

africa's eden

Mpumalanga is truly Africa's Eden. A province whose melodious name means 'the place where the sun rises', it is home to rugged, mountainous cliffs, forested valleys and the slow, sluggish flow of the aptly named Crocodile River. This game and adventure playground is one of Africa's most thrilling, beautiful and alluring regions. Mpumalanga is a large (78,000 sq-km/30,119 sq-mile), lush province, furrowed with several expansive watercourses and stretching across what is known as the Lowveld. One of the country's major drawcards, the mighty Kruger National Park, takes up a large, elongated easterly segment of the region, forming most of South Africa's international border with the neighbouring country of Mozambique. An easy half day's drive from the central province and travel gateway that is Gauteng province, Mpumalanga is most often associated in the imagination with the Kruger, but for a region so strongly linked with wildlife and game, it offers a range of unexpected surprises.

Some two hours out of Johannesburg, for example one comes across the little hamlet of Dullstroom, a trout fishing area of rolling forested hills and fast-flowing streams which reminds one of nothing so much as the Scottish highlands. As one drives further on into the province the altitude drops, the temperature and humidity rise and one enters the regions which struck fear into the hearts of 19th-century wagon train drivers, for this was the start of the fever belt that stretched all the way to the coastal port of Lourenco Marques in Mozambique. Today there is less to fear, though malaria prophylactics are always advised within the Kruger and other tropical areas, but Mpumalanga still offers one of the most seductive safari experiences, where nature can be enjoyed from the comfort of the world's top game lodges.

a cultural + historic patchwork

These eastern parts of the country are rich with fables, sagas, stories of half-remembered wars and the area's remarkable variety of cultures past and present. Mpumalanga is home to a large number of the Ndebele people, whose intricate

PAGE 52: Vultures stand guard over a brilliant sunset.

THIS PAGE: In Big Five territory where the animals roam freely, wandering without an armed game ranger is ill-advised.

OPPOSITE: Mpumalanga is home to a diverse spectrum of wildlife, which makes the most of its rolling landscapes.

geometric designs may be seen in their beadwork and exteriors of their homes. Mpumalanga also borders the independent African kingdom of Swaziland, a territory which was instrumental in assisting many anti-apartheid activists to flee the country.

the charm of the dorp

Other important places in Mpumalanga to note are the little towns of Machadodorp (dorp meaning 'rural village' in Afrikaans), associated with the Anglo-Boer War; Ohrigstad, which is rich with Afrikaner settler history; White River, a small gateway town on the edge of the wildlife region and pretty Sabie, situated in the heart of the huge Lowveld forestry region. The route to all these places takes one through increasingly spectacular terrain, culminating in the majestic Blyde River Canyon. The capital of the province, which has a recently improved airport, is called Nelspruit. Nelspruit was once a sleepy agricultural centre servicing the large citrus, banana and avocado pear plantations here, but in recent years it has become a busy and rewarding tourism and business centre. You are as likely to overhear conversations in Portuguese as in Siswati, Ndebele, Shangaan, Zulu, English or Afrikaans at this cultural crossroads.

There is one historic spot, however, which no visitor to the eastern Lowveld should miss—the little mining town of Pilgrim's Rest. Before the great gold rush of 1886 in the Gauteng region, alluvial gold was discovered in the hills and streams of present-day Mpumalanga. As is always the case with gold discoveries, huge numbers of people flooded Pilgrim's Rest and tiny Barberton nearby, hoping to seek their fortune. One of the earliest stock exchanges in the world was set up in unseemly haste here, with fortunes being made and lost on the hope and a prayer that the gold would last. It did not, and so Pilgrim's Rest and Barberton were abandoned as suddenly as they were founded. The bitter experience that many gold investors had with this very early gold rush put them off losing money again with the great 1886 Witwatersrand strike—something which was soon eclipsed, of course, when people realised that El Dorado really did exist—just a few hundred miles southward. The atmospheric

THIS PAGE (FROM TOP): An excellent example of a rural Ndebele homestead, with its distinctive geometric house decoration. The woman standing in the doorway wears a traditional dress, which displays remarkable beadwork; Victorian gable and window.

OPPOSITE (FROM TOP): A typical rural general store in the historic town of Pilgrim's Rest, once the site of a short-lived 19th-century gold rush; one of the endlessly varied habitats of the sprawling Kruger.

Victorian buildings of Pilgrim's Rest have been preserved, and today the village makes a great pit stop en route to Kruger, one of the star attractions being the saloon of the Royal Hotel, a confection of corrugated iron with a splendid wooden Victorian bar.

the jewel in the crown

The dominant feature by far of this province, however, is the mighty Kruger National Park which, at some 20,000 sq km (7,722 sq miles) is larger than Israel or Massachusetts. The Kruger, which is a household name for those familiar with wildlife, has a fascinating history, for it was one of the world's first formally conserved pieces of wilderness. In 1898, Puritan Boer leader Paul Kruger, four-time president of the South African Republic, proclaimed that a large area in the vicinity of the Crocodile River be protected from farming so that the herds of game could multiply. Kruger—after whom the park is of course named—was a truly extraordinary set of contradictions. He was a man who refused to read any book but the Bible, and believed dancing to be the work of the Devil, but he was far-sighted enough to perceive the immense bounty, physical and spiritual, that the African bushveld had to offer mankind.

the drama of life in the wild

The Kruger is a place which, despite its popularity, always delivers. On one morning you might come face to face with a lioness in mid-hunt. On another morning you might happen upon the comical sight of a pied kingfisher, mohawk ruffled and motionless on a reed by a dank and greasy pool, intent on breakfast, or perhaps a family of elephants ducking one another in a waterhole.

The Kruger succeeds so remarkably because, due to its size, it encompasses a wide range of habitats, which includes forests, plains, damp, lush corners and drier regions, ensuring that the full range of southern Africa's animal denizens may find a niche. And when it comes to game viewing, miniature dramas of the bush can be equally entrancing as those involving the

usual wildlife giants. Watching a baboon comically pick his toes or snatch up a scorpion as a snack, the swagger of a giraffe sashaying down the road before you or hearing the sound of a mother zebra whickering to its young to stay close—these are the sights and sounds that remain with you long after the flight home.

which lodge?

The great vistas and plains of the Kruger are surrounded in turn by a cluster of privately-owned bush concessions, and it is here where many of the country's world-famous bush lodges are located. Names such as Sabi Sands and Malelane, as well as the Timbavati and Manyeleti concessions, which fall further north on the Kruger border in Limpopo province, are now legendary in certain circles. Although these lands are privately owned, they have no fences, meaning that effectively each and every guest at any of the lodges has the entire stretch of one of the world's most magnificent wilderness areas at their personal disposal. No matter who you are, your time in the African bush will profoundly alter the way you see the world.

adrenalin rush

Mpumalanga lies at the northeastern tail end of South Africa's largest and youngest range of mountains, whose soaring peaks are known as the Drakensberg (Dragon Mountain). The most notable scenic feature of the province is the Blyde River Canyon, which ranks third only in size to America's Grand Canyon. The entire length of the Blyde, however, is a locus of outdoor and adventure activities of every kind, so getting a tan whilst exploring the surrounds is de rigueur. Activities on offer include bridge swinging, rock climbing and kloofing (canyoning), white-water rafting (though these rivers are not for novices) and horse trails in Big Five country. And there is always the frisson to be had in doing any outdoor activity in the Blyde, for although it lies outside the borders of the Kruger, the canyon is ideal terrain for the wily leopard whose pug marks are regularly seen in the dust of its elevated trails.

ABOVE AND OPPOSITE: South Africa's luxury game lodges are invariably set in breathtaking locations, allowing you to feel you are immersed in nature.
BELOW: The thrill of white-water rafting is certainly not for the unfit or faint-hearted.

...your time in the African bush will profoundly alter the way you see the world.

Singita Lebombo

Voted 'Top Hotel of the World' in 2004 by the UK's *Tatler* magazine, Singita Lebombo is an exciting and original combination of the contemporary and the traditional, in which conventional boundaries between indoors and outdoors are redefined.

Singita Lebombo is set within South Africa's legendary Kruger National Park, a private world of winding rivers, ancient mountains and vast stretches of ochre bushveld that boasts abundant wildlife. Constructed almost entirely of bleached wood and glass, Lebombo Lodge comprises 15 luxury suites with private wooden decks that look out onto the Nwanetsi River and the Lebombo foothills. A further six exclusive suites which overlook the Sweni River make up Sweni Lodge.

The décor evokes the textures and colours of the wild. While each suite has its own private pool, the lodge's cliffside swimming pool is an experience not to be missed, and close-up views of game while swimming here are not uncommon. The Lebombo area

is famed for its wealth of leopards and other big cats, and the surroundings here are home to a wide variety of other wild animals. Observe prides of lions lazing under trees, gaze at herds of skittish impala, and watch giraffe nibbling the tops of thorny acacia trees.

After a morning game drive, you can look forward to being thoroughly pampered at the Singita Lebombo spa. Masseuses offer treatments ranging from traditional Thai massages and seaweed wraps to African hot stone therapies and head massages. A workout at the fitness centre with its glorious views of the bushveld is equally invigorating.

Fine dining is an essential part of the experience here. The cuisine is flavoursome and original, inspired by Africa and guided by the West. Choose your wines from Singita's silo-style bush cellar, which has some 12,000 bottles of South African and international wines. If there is a special wine you would like to take home, Singita's Premier Wine Direct club can deliver.

The African bush also creates an unparalleled atmosphere of romance. Wedding ceremonies are held at a venue overlooking the Nwanetsi River, and guests will find themselves being serenaded by fish eagles and purple-crested louries as vows are exchanged. As a fitting conclusion, the couple and their party then set out into the bush, where cocktails can be savoured under the African sky.

FACTS		
ROOMS	Lebombo Lodge: 15 suites • Sweni Lodge: 6 suites	
FOOD	dining room: African and Western fusion	
DRINK	Singita Premier Wine Boutique	
FEATURES	cliffside pool • spa • fitness centre • African gallery • wedding package • 4-night honeymoon package	
NEARBY	game-viewing spots • Lebombo Mountains • Nwanetsi and Sweni Rivers	
CONTACT	The Oval, Oakdale House, 1 Oakdale Road, Newlands, Cape Town 7700 • telephone: +27.21 683 3424 • facsimile +27.21 683 3502 • email: singita@singita.co.za • website: www.singita.co.za	

PHOTOGRAPHS COURTESY OF SINGITA LEBOMBO.

Chitwa Chitwa Private Game Lodges

THIS PAGE (CLOCKWISE FROM TOP): *A dramatic monochrome colour scheme dominates Chitwa Chitwa Game Lodges; a luxury suite at Game Lodge, one of two lodges at Chitwa Chitwa.*

OPPOSITE (FROM TOP): *The eclectic and cosy bar at Game Lodge; the tranquil swimming pool and shady sundeck overlook one of Sabi Sand Game Reserve's largest lakes.*

Chitwa Chitwa Private Game Lodges is openly unpretentious, and its homely atmosphere is the first thing that strikes guests. Situated in Sabi Sand Game Reserve and owned by Charl and Italian-born Maria Brink, Chitwa Chitwa began life as a family home. The transformation from family premise to luxury game lodge took eight years, with the addition of a bar, lounge, dining and entertainment area, sundeck and swimming pool. Maria added her personal touch by painting Italian phrases on the screed stone floors. Indeed, her vibrant Italian personality and heritage are gently reflected in the large-than-life paintings and murals on the walls.

To up the chic factor, Lantis Bain Scorgie, an interior decorator with a highly individualistic style, installed a graphic monochromatic theme throughout the lodge. He added to that a dash of European and African influences to create a cocktail of styles that is quirky yet harmonious. In tune with this eclecticism, flea-market treasures are mixed with family silverware, and heirloom antiques with slick, chrome furniture. The result is a comfortable setting where a healthy sense of humour is always appreciated, and where guests are beckoned to chill out.

The accommodations at Chitwa Chitwa are split into two camps: Chitwa Chitwa Safari Lodge and Game Lodge. The Safari Lodge, once a hunting lodge, is a group of five chalets nestled beneath a luxuriant blanket of knobthorn trees. In unwavering

where guests mingle with rangers and staff to catch up on the day's game sightings.

Sabi Sand Game Reserve borders Kruger National Park. With no fences between the two, animals wander around as they please and graze on vast plains. Home to the Big Five, Sabi Sand offers ample opportunities to rub shoulders with these majestic animals during safari drives. Dozens of other species can be observed from the comfort of the lodge. At Chitwa Chitwa, the African wilderness calls.

African tradition, the chalets are thatched and seem to melt seamlessly into the surrounding bushveld. This makes Safari Lodge a prime location for animal- and bird-watching.

Game Lodge, its sophisticated sibling, peeps over a glassy lake—one of the Sabi Sand Game Reserve's largest. Here, guests are rendered practically invisible to the animals which gather on the open plain on balmy evenings. Luxury suites are fitted with glass-walled showers which offer splendid views of the surroundings. Among the other outstanding features of Game Lodge are elevated baths and private sundecks. Honeymooners have the exquisite Boulders Suite all to themselves, which boasts a dip pool that overlooks the savannah, a lounge area and a corner bath by the window.

Like any self-respecting family-run lodge, food is the focal point of the Chitwa Chitwa experience. The cuisine is a hearty mouth-watering fusion of Mediterranean and African fare, often in the form of Maria's speciality dishes. Meals are a social affair

FACTS

ROOMS	Safari Lodge: 5 chalets • Game Lodge: 5 Standard Rooms and 3 Suites
FOOD	dining room and boma: African-Mediterranean • poolside lapa: lunch
DRINK	Game Lodge: wine cellar • Safari Lodge: bar
FEATURES	pool • rangers
NEARBY	Big Five viewing spots • Johannesburg (1.5 hrs by air)
CONTACT	Sabi Sand Game Reserve, Mpumalanga • telephone: +27.11 883 1354 • facsimile: +27.11 783 1858 • email: info@chitwa.co.za • website: www.chitwa.co.za

PHOTOGRAPHS COURTESY OF CHITWA CHITWA PRIVATE GAME LODGES.

Sabi Sabi Private Game Reserve

THIS PAGE (CLOCKWISE FROM TOP):
The magnificent Amber Suite in Sabi Sabi's Earth Lodge. Like the rest of the lodge, this suite was carved out of the earth and boasts organically-designed architecture; a couple's hydrotherapy bath at Bush Lodge's Nature Spa; a secluded plunge pool in a suite at Earth Lodge.

OPPOSITE: The suites at Bush Lodge have played host to princes, presidents and stars from all over the world.

Situated in the heart of the South African bush, Sabi Sabi Private Game Reserve has been enthralling visitors with its natural beauty for decades. It sits in the 65,000-hectare (160,620-acre) Sabi Sand Wildtuin on the southern edge of the famed Kruger National Park. No fences exist between Sabi Sand and Kruger Park, so animals wander around freely. Sabi Sabi offers guests three unique safari experiences: Earth Lodge, Bush Lodge and Selati Camp.

Earth Lodge is a tranquil sanctuary. Its architecture was inspired by the age-old bush building technique of carving out a building from a slope and then covering its roof with earth and plants. Almost perfectly camouflaged, Earth Lodge has been hailed as the most ecologically sensitive lodge in Africa. This haven's respect for the land pervades its interior. The walls of the boma were sculpted from tree roots, and the rooms of the lodge burrow deep into the earth.

Luxury and modern conveniences, however, are not compromised. Earth Lodge comprises 13 suites including the spectacular Amber Suite. Each suite is tended to by a butler and comes with a plunge pool and an open-air shower. In the generously-sized Amber Suite, guests also enjoy their own study, kitchen, steam room and exercise room.

Bush Lodge has been entertaining international guests for 25 years. Hospitality and warmth characterise the staff here. Guests mingle every morning over freshly-brewed coffee before embarking on a game drive with seasoned rangers. In the evenings, guests congregate over an open-air boma dinner to swap bush tales and celebrate newly-forged bonds.

Selati Camp recreates colonial Africa. Perched near the historical Selati Railway, this is an intimate, all-suite camp. Train enthusiasts will delight in 19th-century railway memorabilia that dot the camp. With original steam engine name plates,

shunters' lamps and other collectors' items, this camp is a veritable railway museum. Selati also lies on an ancient animal migration path between the Sabi and Sand Rivers, and wildlife cross what is left of the old railway bed daily as they go about their search for food and water.

A deep sense of peace dwells at Sabi Sabi, and all who stay here are moved by a sense of being at one with Mother Earth.

FACTS		
ROOMS		Earth Lodge: 13 suites • Bush Lodge: 25 suites • Selati Camp: 8 suites
FOOD		bomas: African
DRINK		full bar facilities • wine cellar in Bush Lodge and Earth Lodge
FEATURES		pools at both lodges and camp • private airstrip • Earth Lodge: library and plunge pools at all suites • Bush Lodge: private plunge pool at Mandleve Suite and Bush Nature Spa • Selati Camp: private plunge pool at Ivory Suite
BUSINESS		Bush Lodge and Earth Lodge: conference facilities
NEARBY		wildlife-viewing spots • savannah, bush and scrub habitats
CONTACT		PO Box 52665, Saxonwold 2132 • telephone: +27.11 483 3939 • facsimile: +27.11 483 3799 • email: res@sabisabi.com • website: www.sabisabi.com

PHOTOGRAPHS COURTESY OF SABI SABI PRIVATE GAME RESERVE.

Lion Sands Private Game Reserve

THIS PAGE (FROM TOP): The pool at River Lodge overlooks the river and bush, and is a superb spot for viewing game while doing your laps; outdoor luxury can be enjoyed at the Tree House.

OPPOSITE (FROM TOP): A spacious bedroom in an Ivory Lodge suite looks out over the majestic wilderness; dinners at the River Lodge boma are illuminated by the soft glow of paraffin lamps.

A disproportionately high population of Nile crocodiles made the historical Sabie River one of the most dangerous in the region in years gone by. The Sabie River borders Kruger National Park, and magnificent parades of wild animals stop to quench their thirst at the river's edge, making the area ideal for animal watching.

Lion Sands Private Game Reserve sits in the southern portion of Sabi Sand Reserve, and guests get exclusive access to Sabie River. Lion Sands boasts two lodges, River

and Ivory. Built amongst trees that date back almost 800 years, River Lodge is a family-run property. Decked out in cream and purple, each thatched bedroom has a viewing deck and is linked to all areas of the lodge by raised wooden walkways.

The Game Reserve's chic new sibling, Ivory Lodge, is the last word in elegant living. Each suite has a view magnificent enough for game watching. With a private patio, a plunge pool, a lounge with a fireplace and the services of a host at the mere touch of a button, it is possible to go through an entire day without seeing other guests or staff. Even private bush drives can be arranged. It is little wonder that Lion Sands has seen its fair share of affluent tourists and celebrities.

Those who do wrench themselves away from their lush surroundings can experience the Tree House. Perched atop a century-old jackalberry tree, it has basic amenities and

a bed for guests to spend the twilight hours completely immersed in the wilderness. On full moon nights, guests are accompanied by rangers on unlit walks—a truly magical way to see the savannah. Other equally interesting activities include star-gazing sessions, hippopotamus tours and clay pigeon shooting.

Mealtimes are, more often than not, elaborate outdoor affairs. Breakfast is served in either the river hideout or on an open plain. Delicious barbecue aromas herald dinner at the River Lodge boma. Lit by paraffin lamps, a dry river bed or open plain is transformed into the lodge's makeshift dining room. In typical South African manner, boerewors (meat sausages), sticky ribs and sosaties (marinated spiced meat skewers) are cooked slowly over an open bush fire.

The surge of tourism to the area has not diluted the owners' sense of duty towards the land. Lion Sands is the only reserve in Sabi Sand that employs a full-time ecologist. Enjoy your safari experience with full assurance that the impact of your presence on the natural environment here is well-managed.

FACTS		
ROOMS	River Lodge: 18 rooms • Ivory Lodge: 6 suites	
FOOD	dining room • boma dinners • bush dinners • bush breakfasts • picnic lunches • riverbed dinners	
DRINK	Ivory Lodge: wine cellar • River Lodge: bar	
FEATURES	exclusive access to the Sabie River • indoor and outdoor showers • spa • curio shop • ranger • River Lodge: 2 swimming pools, private hammocks and bird hideout • Ivory Lodge: private lounge with fireplace and private plunge pool	
BUSINESS	meeting facilities • Internet access	
NEARBY	Sabie River • Skukuza Golf Course • game viewing spots • Johannesburg	
CONTACT	PO Box 30, White River 1240 • telephone/facsimile: +27.11 484 9911 • email: res@lionsands.com • website: www.lionsands.com	

Tinga Private Game Lodge

A gentle, primal spirit prevails at Tinga Private Game Lodge. Set within South Africa's world famous Kruger National Park, this lodge overlooks the confluence of the Sabi and Sand Rivers. One of the first private concessions in the park, Tinga offers rewarding game viewing, with an abundance of the Big Five, and more than a dash of luxury in its two private retreats.

In true African tradition, Tinga Legends is set around a giant jackalberry tree, while Tinga Narina is named after a gorgeous and furtive forest bird. Both of these elegant, understated lodges overlook the river, and sport a pared-down colonial look which combines wood, leather and stone.

Romance is definitely high on the list here. Each suite is absolutely private, with

THIS PAGE (CLOCKWISE FROM TOP):
Fine dining at Tinga Private Game Lodge's restaurant; the elegant foyer of the lodge lit up at twilight; in the suites gossamer mosquito nets surround cotton-lined beds.

OPPOSITE: Outdoor dining is a regular affair at the lodge, and is an excellent opportunity for guests to socialise.

wooden decks looking across the river. Dark timber, open thatch, pale ochres, cane and rattan dominate. All suites are air-conditioned, and include a generous lounge, large bedroom and en suite bathroom. Beds are lined with cool cottons in white and stone, and protected by ethereal mosquito nets. Spend mornings lazing on your game-viewing deck, or take a dip in your secluded heated plunge pool, after which you can take a nap, lulled by the soothing sounds of birds and insects. All suites command resplendent views of the Sabi River.

Tinga safari vehicles have access to all of Kruger National Park, so you are practically assured of meeting all the locals—lions, elephants, buffaloes, rhinoceroses, cheetahs, zebras, leopards and an assortment of antelopes. You can choose between dusk or dawn safaris, guided bush walks or bird-watching expeditions. Tinga's expert rangers and trackers will make sure you get the most out of your safari.

Brunches are a languid affair under the shade of a tree, and dinners are hosted at the lodge's traditional boma to the flicker of an open fire and the twinkle of stars. The menu is contemporary with an African twist, and includes rather exotic specialities like line fish, crocodile and kudu fillet. For the perfect companion, select a bottle of wine from Tinga's well-stocked cellar.

You will definitely want to linger a while longer at Tinga, and you may also want to plan for a round of golf at one of Africa's most unique and scenic courses nearby. At this golf course set in the heart of the Kruger National Park, you can expect to share the fairways with an assortment of local wildlife. You can also arrange for a helicopter ride to see some of the attractions along the appropriately named Panorama Route, a dramatic and sculpted escarpment. And before you leave, remember to buy a memento from Tinga's lovely little curio shop. Tinga is without doubt the ultimate safari destination.

PHOTOGRAPHS COURTESY OF TINGA PRIVATE GAME LODGE.

FACTS

ROOMS	Tinga Legends: 9 suites • Tinga Narina: 9 suites
FOOD	restaurant and boma: African and international
DRINK	wine cellar • bar and lounge
FEATURES	library • pool • gym • shop
BUSINESS	Internet facilities • facsimile • satellite television
NEARBY	game-viewing spots • golf course
CONTACT	PO Box 88, Skukuza 1350 • telephone: +27.13 735 8400 • facsimile: +27.13 735 5722 • email: reservations@tinga.co.za • website: www.tinga.co.za

Graskop Hotel

A good balance between civilised comfort and wild landscapes makes up the picturesque town of Graskop. Perched comfortably on the edge of the Klein Drakensberg Escarpment in Mpumalanga, it boasts spectacular views of the Lowveld some 1 km (0.6 miles) below. The village is the gateway to the famous Panorama Route, and lies in close proximity to the major game and Big Five parks in the region.

The quaint village of Graskop was founded to accommodate settlers during the gold rush era of the late 1800s. Till today, it still maintains something of the feel of a Wild West town. Its gold-mining days are long gone though, and a thriving timber industry stands in its place. Row upon row of pine and eucalyptus trees lace its hills and valleys, making the plantations of Graskop some of the largest man-made forests in the world.

Not least because it is within the only malaria-free zone which lies within easy driving range of Kruger National Park, the town of Graskop is a wise choice for accommodations when in the region. The Graskop Hotel, with its delightful artistic spirit, stands out here.

The story goes that the hotel survived a fire which burnt down the original verandah that embraced the entire timber building. A new building in an unassuming 1960s style was built in its place, which was slowly restored to its current splendour. The hotel's active interest in the contemporary South

THIS PAGE (CLOCKWISE FROM TOP):
Contemporary South African art features prominently—this oversized cactus sculpture standing at the entrance is by Strijdom van der Merwe; an avant-garde group of busts decorates a corner of the lounge; a more conventional sculpture graces the garden of the hotel.

OPPOSITE (FROM LEFT): Pastel drawings of African doors by Helena Scholtz adorn this bedroom; an unusual wall sculpture adds interest to a double bedroom.

The hotel's active interest in the contemporary South African art scene is apparent.

African art scene is apparent. Each room is currently being systematically decorated by established young South African artists. The striking result is that each bedroom is characteristically different and unique in style.

The hotel serves a scrumptious breakfast with homemade muffins, croissants and scones, while The Coffee Shop dishes out light à la carte meals. Most guests head out to Harrie's Pancakes at least once for brunch or lunch. Famous for its meal-sized pancakes, this pancake house serves up

mouth-watering savoury and dessert pancakes with a plethora of fillings from the traditional to the imaginative. Bobotie, roasted butternut, chicken liver and trout are favourite fillings for main course pancakes. For dessert, dark chocolate mousse and banana caramel are big hits.

When guests do decide to leave their comfortable lodgings, they have a myriad of choices in which to roam. At the doorstep of Graskop are famous sights like the scenic Pinnacle Rock, the misty God's Window

mountain fissure and the ancient town of Pilgrim's Rest. Graskop is flanked by cascading waterfalls—including Lisbon Falls, Mac Mac Falls and Berlin Falls, trickling streams and hiking trails. Nature buffs can have their fill of Mother Earth at her best by 4x4 drive, motorbike or quad bike. A short drive from Graskop are Bourke's Luck Potholes, Blyde River Canyon and Kruger National Park, the latter a flagship game reserve in South Africa, and indeed the whole of Africa, for the quintessential safari excursion.

FACTS		
	ROOMS	19 bedrooms • 15 garden suites
	FOOD	restaurant: home-style cooking • The Coffee Shop: à la carte
	DRINK	Ladies' bar
	FEATURES	lounge • swimming pool • African Arts & Crafts shop • Contemporary South African Art Gallery
	BUSINESS	Internet access
	NEARBY	Mpumalanga • Kruger National Park • Pilgrim's Rest • Pinnacle Rock • God's Window • Bourke's Luck Potholes • Blyde River Canyon
	CONTACT	3 Main Street, Graskop 1270 • telephone/facsimile: +27.13 767 1244 • email: graskophotel@mweb.co.za • website: www.graskophotel.co.za

Jatinga Country Lodge

English country living can be experienced in the heart of South Africa. Situated right on the outskirts of White River town in Mpumalanga and only a short drive from Kruger National Park is the lovingly restored Jatinga Country Lodge. The original homestead dates back to the 1920s, and today forms the main lodge.

Ten superior rooms and four luxury suites offer guests a variety of elegant country themes. Take your pick between Victorian, Colonial, Provençal, French Country, African Colonial and English Country. Each themed room has unique features—Provençal rooms have enormous bathrooms with half-ton

concrete baths, while Victorian rooms boast outdoor showers, and Colonial and English Country suites have private lounges. All suites and rooms have patios that look out over the lodge's impeccably kept grounds.

Jatinga runs an award-winning restaurant that is frequently voted amongst South Africa's top 100. An extensive à la carte menu is on offer, which will impress even the most discerning gourmet. Begin a meal with a Jatinga salad of fresh asparagus and crispy prosciutto layered between a fusion of salad greens, topped with shavings of Parmesan, followed by tender, partially-deboned duck either à l'orange or with

chocolate and chilli sauce. If you have room, sample the lodge's delectable homemade ice cream for dessert.

Pick any wine from the lodge's superb wine cellar, where intimate meals for up to 12 can also be organised. Wine-tasting sessions are held regularly. At each tasting, only one estate is showcased and the master from that estate attends to share his knowledge with guests. The tasting is accompanied by a meal that is specially crafted to enhance the wines of the evening.

The cosy Lord Milner pub offers a range of drinks with a great old-world ambience, after which you can wander down one of the lodge's garden paths until you reach a beautiful deck overlooking White River. Built around two shady indigenous trees, the deck is a sublime and much favoured spot for sundowners while watching the river flow by. For the epitome of country living, request for a traditional English high tea to be served on the verandah of the main lodge.

Day-trippers heading out to one of the many historic and scenic attractions nearby may want to take with them a specially prepared gourmet picnic hamper.

With its undulating green lawns, superb cuisine and luxurious accommodation, Jatinga is a paradisiacal country retreat.

THIS PAGE: Jatinga Country Lodge's emerald-green lawns flank a garden path that leads to the banks of the White River.

OPPOSITE (FROM TOP): The wine cellar can accommodate dinner parties of up to 12 guests; each of Jatinga's suites is decorated to reflect European country elegance.

FACTS		
ROOMS	10 superior rooms • 4 suites	
FOOD	restaurant: South African and European	
DRINK	wine cellar • Lord Milner pub	
FEATURES	riverside deck • pool • bowling green • croquet lawn • walking paths • billiard table • wedding chapel	
BUSINESS	function room	
NEARBY	Kruger National Park • God's Window mountain fissure • Blyde River Canyon • Bourke's Luck Potholes • Casterbridge Farm • White River Country Club	
CONTACT	Jatinga Road, Plaston, White River, Mpumalanga • telephone: +27.13 751 5059 • facsimile: +27.13 751 5119 • email: info@jatinga.co.za • website: www.jatinga.co.za	

PHOTOGRAPHS COURTESY OF JATINGA COUNTRY LODGE AND PETER FROST, GETAWAY.

Lukimbi Safari Lodge

African myth comes alive at Lukimbi Safari Lodge. The spirit of the Lukimbi—half-giant owl, half-lion—safeguards travellers in the African bush. Lukimbi's comrades, Great Eagle Owl and King Cheetah, lend their presence to the lodge's two executive suites, and throughout the lodge are decorative elements that reflect African myth and art. Guests staying at this lodge also find themselves treated to bush dramas, enacted by the lodge's resident staff, while trackers amaze game viewers with stories of the colourful customs of the local communities.

This safari lodge is located in a private concession on the southern part of Kruger National Park, on 15,000 hectares (37,000 acres) of prime game area. All roads in the concession are private, and you will not see any other vehicles besides Land Rovers from the lodge. One of the roads that cuts through the concession is actually an old trading route that was used by ox-drawn wagons to transport goods from the interior to the coast of Mozambique, and is still clearly visible.

At the lodge, a myriad of interesting activities and luxurious facilities await. The swimming pool comprises a waterfall cascading into a jacuzzi that connects to the main pool, which often doubles as a watering hole for elephants in the evening.

Expect the unexpected during mealtimes. Lukimbi delights in beautiful,

THIS PAGE (FROM TOP): The rustic façade and grounds of Lukimbi Safari Lodge; the lounge is decorated with traditional African art and other objets d'art.

OPPOSITE (CLOCKWISE FROM TOP): Couples on their honeymoon will receive a complimentary bottle of chilled Champagne in their suite; the lodge's traditional African boma; the luxurious bathroom of a suite overlooking a private plunge pool.

unusually presented food which will both surprise you and titillate your taste buds. Breakfast is taken outdoors in the bush, lunch is a lazy affair around the pool and dinner is served either in the open dining area that overlooks the river or in an unusual boma. Accompany your meal with one of the many fine wines from the lodge's wine cellar, or order a cocktail from the bar.

Talks on conservation and the culture of the local community are held regularly, while a library provides endless information on those topics as well as light holiday reading.

Should you find yourself wanting some first hand experience, the lodge organises visits to nearby villages and helicopter rides to places of stunning natural beauty. On game drives and bush walks, the lodge's highly-experienced rangers and trackers regularly impress guests with their rich knowledge of the local bush and unforgettable wildlife sightings. Africa's Big Five and a wide variety of other game are frequently spotted.

All who visit Lukimbi will certainly be enthralled by their experience and the wonders of the African bush.

PHOTOGRAPHS COURTESY OF LUKIMBI SAFARI LODGE.

FACTS		
ROOMS	14 suites • 2 executive suites	
FOOD	boma and dining area: South African and international	
DRINK	bar • wine cellar	
FEATURES	pool with jacuzzi • viewing decks • library • curio shop • gym • children's play area • wedding chapel	
BUSINESS	conference centre • Internet facilities	
NEARBY	wide variety of game • local villages • golf courses	
CONTACT	PO Box 2617, Northcliff, Johannesburg 2115 • telephone: +27.11 888 3713 • facsimile: +27.11 888 2181 • email: info@lukimbi.com • website: www.lukimbi.com	

Valley of the Rainbow

Dullstroom, South Africa's favoured fly-fishing region, has a thriving village and farm environment where nature enthusiasts converge. But while bird-watching and horseback riding rate high on the list of must-dos, a scattering of art galleries and historic sites make for a multi-faceted visit.

Accommodation options abound. One option is The Valley of the Rainbow Country Estate and Nature Reserve. A mere two-hour drive from Johannesburg, the reserve lies in a secluded valley embraced by misty mountains, threaded with shimmering rivers and laced with thick forests.

In this private reserve, nature is in its element. Rather like a home away from home, it exudes charm and personality. Personal butlers are replaced by indigenous animals, infinity pools by glassy rivers, and modern suites by country cottages.

A triumvirate of accommodations peppers the estate and appeals to those in search of the rustic. Country houses and tented chalets blend into the environment. At Witpoort Park Estate on the northern slopes of Witpoort Mountain, 10 furnished country houses, each with five double bedrooms, are sprinkled along the grounds. Each room

THIS PAGE (CLOCKWISE FROM TOP):
A cheerful fireplace awaits in a country lounge at Valley of the Rainbow; indigenous forest lines the grounds of this lakeside property; meals here are fresh, simple and tasty.
OPPOSITE: The old lakeside mill has been lovingly converted into Mill Restaurant.

...the reserve lies in a secluded valley embraced by misty mountains...and laced with thick forests.

leads out to a spacious verandah offering breathtaking views of the valley. The present Country House can accommmodate large parties of up to 10 guests quite comfortably.

Two-bedroom chalets with en suite bathrooms at the Valley of the Rainbow Lake Resort are built either in the midst of the foliage overlooking the lake, or on decks reaching over the water. The perennial Witpoort River which feeds five dams flows through the entire property, and is central to

a handful of activities at the lodge. Chock-full with rainbow and brown trout, guests can go fly-fishing or boating, docking their boats right by their lake chalets.

Exuding old-world charm is Tierkloof Mountain Estate, snuggled in the peaks and troughs of Tierkloof Mountain. Bridges built over streams and old stone weirs down which trickle fresh river water add suitably rustic touches. Tierkloof's entourage of estate houses are interwoven with a plethora of

cultural stops. The old Transvaal Trading Store and the Picture Museum take visitors back in time. Vestiges of the Anglo-Boer War and old Transvaal and Ndebele culture on display at the latter tell of the land's chequered past.

While The Valley's existing Manor House is being remodelled as a luxury boutique hotel, upmarket additions like the Natural Wellness Centre and Equestrian and Polo Centre promise a whole new holiday experience at this property.

FACTS		
ROOMS	Manor House: 5 rooms • Country House: 5 rooms and 5 tented chalets • Valley of the Rainbow Lake Resort: 10 chalets • Witpoort Park Estate: 10 furnished country houses • Tierkloof Mountain Estate: 10 furnished estate houses	
FOOD	The Manor Restaurant and Mill Restaurant: traditional South African	
FEATURES	Valley of the Rainbow Lake Resort: pool, lakeside decks • Witpoort Park Estate: landscaped park • Tierkloof Mountain Estate: stone weirs and bridges, trading store, barn theatre, Picture Museum, arts and crafts centre and hiking trails	
NEARBY	Johannesburg (2 hrs by car)	
CONTACT	PO Box 20366, Noordburg, Potchefstroom 2522 • telephone/facsimile: +27.13 272 7050 • email: rainbowlodge@telehost.co.za • website: www.rainbowvalley.co.za	

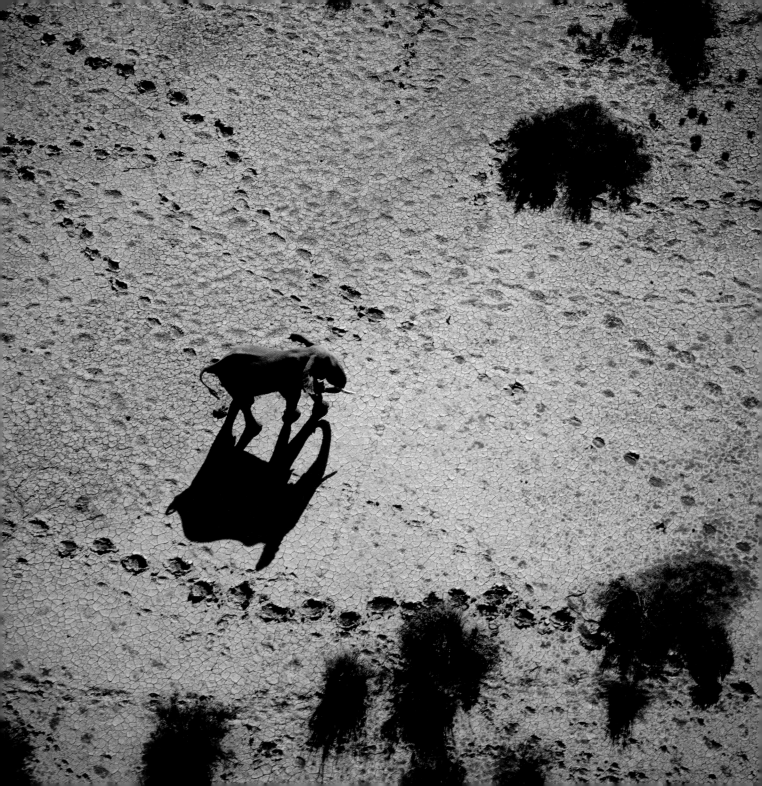

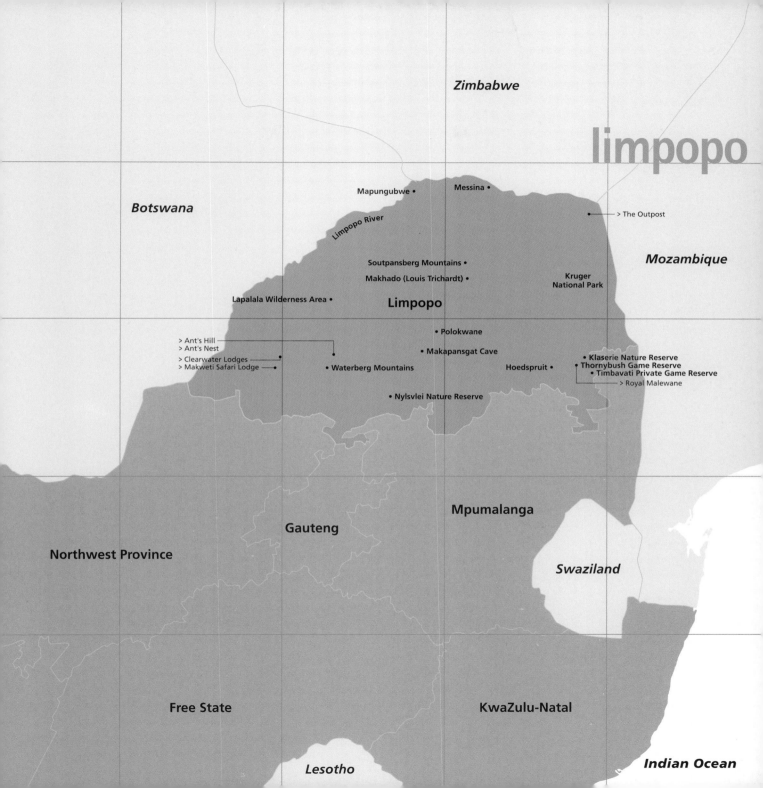

limpopo

Zimbabwe

Botswana

Mapungubwe •   • Messina •

Limpopo River   • > The Outpost

Soutpansberg Mountains •   Mozambique

Makhado (Louis Trichardt) •   Kruger
                                          National Park

Lapalala Wilderness Area •

                    Limpopo

> Ant's Hill   • Polokwane

> Ant's Nest

> Clearwater Lodges   • Makapansgat Cave   • Klaserie Nature Reserve
                                                                    • Thornybush Game Reserve
> Makweti Safari Lodge   • Waterberg Mountains   • Timbavati Private Game Reserve
                                                Hoedspruit •   > Royal Malewane

                    • Nylsvlei Nature Reserve

                                                          Mpumalanga

                    Gauteng

Northwest Province

                                                          Swaziland

Free State   KwaZulu-Natal

        Lesotho   Indian Ocean

'the great north is great in its vastness and beauty'

From the 19th-century big game hunter legends that tell of the biggest elephants ever seen to fables of the Land of Ophir, the wanderings of Christian ruler Prester John and tales about great vanished African states, their city ramparts overgrown and deathly silent. Modern scholarship is building a spellbinding picture of ancient empires here which operated a sophisticated trade in ivory, gold and animal skins with the potentates of Arabia and even remote Southeast Asia.

It is a place worthy of the time taken to explore its great secrets, and to see first-hand a frontier land of magnificent bushveld, characterised by its awe-inspiring baobab trees, the thickets and plains of the northern half of the mighty Kruger National Park and the art of the Venda. The air is filled with the shriek of cicadas and the searing heat conjures up mirages and illusions as you drive northward, straight as an arrow, on the province's principal traffic artery, the aptly named Great North Road, the road leading straight to Africa's interior.

The most exceptional game experiences anywhere in southern Africa can be found here in the internationally-rated conservancies of Timbavati and Klaserie, alongside the fascinating history of the Voortrekkers in the Makhado district, formerly known as Louis Trichardt. There is also a long list of some of eco-tourism's most extraordinary sanctuaries such as the Nylsvlei birding haven, remarkable prehistoric sites and intriguing tales of the Venda peoples, with their mystical art, belief in water sprites, and one of the Lost Tribes of Israel, the Lembe.

Here too are magnificent traditions of wildlife conservation stretching back to the late Victorian period, and a number of the country's best wildlife teaching institutions, specifically the Lapalala Wilderness School in the Waterberg and the Moholoholo Centre at Hoedspruit, home to 'South Africa's Dr Doolittle', Brian Jones, whose work with the public has brought home to thousands of mesmerised listeners from all corners of the globe an understanding of why the natural environment is of such enormous importance to man's own survival.

PAGE 78: *One of the many breathtaking scenes that abound throughout Limpopo's many nature reserves.*
THIS PAGE: *Baobab abstract.*
OPPOSITE: *Loxodonta africana, the African elephant, is the world's largest terrestrial creature, and an endless source of fascination for the nature lover.*

legends of crooks, scoundrels + ivory

Academic research in recent years has confirmed many of the seemingly wildly exaggerated stories of enormous herds of elephant (and indeed other plains game) which once traversed these parts. Historic sources talk of literally hundreds of animals being killed on a single hunting trip. These numbers are also indicated in even earlier sources from precolonial times, when oral traditions spoke of such numbers of game in the time of King Shaka of the Zulu. Today, whilst the spread of human habitation and the consequent reduction in wild bushveld has reduced the numbers of game, Limpopo province is undoubtedly still big game territory. Here wandered the lone hunters of Victorian legend. With their quarries—the great bull tuskers, known individually by name and the unique shape of their ivories to the hunters—these men handed on a rich storehouse of first-hand accounts down to others. Today the Kruger National Park still has displays which tell of the tuskers, their lives and their deaths.

Inevitably, these remote bushveld regions, which abut the two international boundaries of Zimbabwe and Mozambique, also attracted more than their fair share of renegades and buccaneers. The triangle of land where the three borders meet has thus long been humorously known as Crook's Corner. Gun runners, shady ivory hunters, poachers and any numbers of fugitives from the law lived here in the early years of the 20th century in this distant corner of South Africa, where it was but a simple matter to cross a nearby border to escape pursuit.

a place of miracles + wonders

If the frontier renegades of yore worshipped the freedom of the open range, then other inhabitants here had their own intriguing religious rites. Under apartheid, this region was designated as one of the independent rural homelands to which urban Africans were supposed to return when their work contracts in the cities ended. Deprived of even the most fundamental ingredients for successful economic activity such as electricity and elementary education, many of these areas tragically grew to become

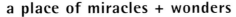

depressed, overpopulated rural slums. However, the other side of the coin was that in some places, indigenous cultures were, to some extent, protected from the effects of urbanisation. In Limpopo, the people from the Venda region were thus able to preserve many of their mystical beliefs. Sacred lakes inhabited by spirits in the shape of a great water snake lie here, and may not be visited by foreigners.

Another extremely potent tradition here is the extraordinary phenomenon of the great Rain Queen, who goes by the title of Modjadji. This is the name given to the hereditary monarch of the Lovedu people, one of the very few African societies which is always headed by a queen. Nelson Mandela and many other luminaries through history have had an audience with Modjadji. Reputedly the inspiration for the Victorian novel *She* by H. Rider Haggard, the Rain Queen still lives a secretive, secluded life in the Venda district, only occasionally seen or interviewed by outsiders.

South Africa is also home to a group of indigenous religions known as the African Independent Churches. Involving a mix of Christianity and indigenous African spirituality, these are not branches of global religions such as Christianity nor Judaism, though one particularly large church is called the Church of Zion. It has a discrete

THIS PAGE: *A gathering of one of the African Independent Churches, the Church of Zion, where song, dance and chanting mark the great annual pilgrimage to church headquarters at Moria, Limpopo.*

OPPOSITE (FROM TOP): *African outpost; cycad trees are associated with the Rain Queen Modjadji, and have been under the protection of generations of Rain Queens.*

clergy, a unique liturgy and practice, often involving ceremonies held in circular spaces open to the elements. Many of these sects congregate in Limpopo province every Easter at a pilgrimage involving over a million worshippers.

But perhaps oddest of all, Limpopo is also home to a group of people who claim to be one of the Lost Tribes of Israel. The Lembe are an indigenous African people who observe the dietary laws of the Jewish faith, wear head coverings in the same manner, observe the Sabbath and in an intriguing number of ways certainly seem to be right out of the Torah or the Old Testament. Even more remarkably, analysis of their DNA has shown clear affinities with certain Jewish cultures.

birds + rhinos

Although the most renowned game and nature areas of Limpopo tend to be associated with the Kruger Park and its environs, there is a host of other wonderful but poorly-known wild areas within the province. One of the most remarkable is the Nylsvlei district, which lies roughly halfway up the Limpopo segment of the Great North Road.

THIS PAGE: The characteristic rocky ramparts of the Waterberg wilderness region.

OPPOSITE (FROM TOP): South Africa's remarkable raptor population includes species ranging from awe-inspiring eagles to small kites, hawks and kestrels; the rhinoceros, another one of the must-sees when on safari, is fiercely protected in southern Africa against the scourge of poaching, which almost wiped the entire species out.

Nylsvlei has over 250 species of birds, and it is not uncommon for visitors to spot more than 200 of these in a single day. It is another one of the wildlife or nature-related superlatives with which South Africa abounds.

Nylsvlei lies in one of those lesser known but most rewarding of game areas, the Waterberg region. The name Waterberg refers to a very distinctive and beautiful system of elevated plains cut through periodically by sheer cliffs and narrow valleys, with fountains springing from the base of the cliffs. Because the Waterberg's flat segments of land were not big enough for cultivation, it was ignored by the Voortrekkers in search of arable land. Hence it has remained largely forgotten and undeveloped. It therefore remains a superb mountain fastness for all the birds and animals of the bush, and is becoming a highly-regarded safari and game destination. Not only does it offer excellent game, it is also relatively close to the urban centres of Gauteng, making it accessible for people visiting Johannesburg or Pretoria on business. A number of very fine lodges now offer top-rate hospitality in this spectacular region.

The world-famous Lapalala Wilderness Centre, established in 1985 by respected conservationist and artist Clive Walker, is also situated in the Waterberg. Thousands of children, often from disadvantaged backgrounds, have been put through Lapalala's wilderness training courses that teach the importance of conserving nature. The Rhino and Waterberg Museum, wholly dedicated to the rhinoceros, was also opened here in 1998. South Africa, along with several other southern African states such as Botswana and Zimbabwe, has spearheaded protective anti-poaching and wildlife breeding measures to shield the great African mammals, including the rhino, from extinction.

art + the spirit

South African art in general, like music, has become an important cultural export with 19th-century traditional beadwork, exquisite wooden headrests, anti-apartheid art and cutting-edge conceptual work jostling for space in the South African art scene. The northern reaches of Limpopo province are home to a long-held artistic tradition which

has been termed Venda art after the apartheid-era homeland of the same name, and the language spoken in many adjacent areas. The lives and work of more recent artists associated with this tradition offer a privileged glimpse into the inspiration behind the area's ancient carving tradition, which is informed and inspired by a deep spirituality and used for initiation rites, exorcisms and didactic purposes.

One of the most famous names associated with this mystical tradition is that of Jackson Hlungwani, whose remarkable wood carvings combine apocalyptic Biblical images or ideas with traditional African imagery to communicate a powerful contemporary message, expressed through an ancient African spirituality.

history rebalanced: the story of mapungubwe

One of the most insidious aspects of apartheid was its deliberate suppression of the pre-European history of South Africa, despite archaeological findings to the contrary, in order to buttress claims of European racial superiority. Since 1994, however, scholars have been free to study these areas in earnest. The conclusions of the specialists are thus now continually fed into an expanding story of a past much more complex, sophisticated and dynamic than was commonly believed or understood before.

One of the most important archaeological finds in this respect is the site of an 11th-century city-state known as Mapungubwe. Located in the far north of the province near the town of present-day Messina, it was inhabited by one of the earliest African communities to base its economy on trade and mining, and was part of a broader cultural and trade network which spread across southern, central and East Africa.

Another major excavation at Makapansgat Cave in the far north reveals that the cave has had a continuous succession of hominid occupation right up to the emergence of anatomically-modern man. This is the only known cave of its kind in the world, offering such an unbroken record of use. In the near future, this site will undoubtedly join the fossils of Sterkfontein and archaeological sites in Langebaan, KwaZulu-Natal and Eastern Cape as newly-important historical attractions in South Africa.

THIS PAGE (FROM TOP): Beautiful pots outside a simple Venda home; the traditional layout of an African homestead, called a kraal, is evident at this successful community-run cultural village on the edge of Kruger National Park.

OPPOSITE: Dramatic Mapungubwe Hill, site of a major early African trading city-state and now the focus of ongoing archaeological research.

...an expanding story of a past much more complex, sophisticated and dynamic than was commonly believed...

The Outpost

There are few corners of this earth which are left untouched. One of them is occupied by The Outpost in the great Kruger National Park. Located in the northernmost reaches of the Park, high on a hill overlooking the floodplains of the Luvuvhu and Mutale Rivers, The Outpost is as far from the hustle and bustle of modern living as one can get.

Nothing about this property, though, is primitive. Designed by Johannesburg-based architect Enrico Daffonchio, The Outpost integrates futuristic sophistication with the rugged African bush. A kilometre-long (half-mile) raised walkway forms the backbone of the property, around which public spaces and 12 suites congregate, also on stilts. The dining room and pool deck are wall-free, providing views as far as the eye can see.

Safari accommodation is redefined in this property's suites. Abstractly termed 'spaces', each space is carved out of the rock and earth that the property sits on. Walls are canvas screens that can be pulled back for 180-degree vistas, and the only barriers that stand between you and the great outdoors are slim fixtures and gossamer mosquito nets. This open concept is key to Daffonchio's architectural approach.

THIS PAGE (CLOCKWISE FROM TOP):
Taking a bath in The Outpost's open-plan bathrooms is a unique experience; the soft, yellow glow of a suite lit up in the evening; the lodge's lap pool is nestled amidst dense foilage.

OPPOSITE (FROM LEFT): The lounge area is decked out in bright colours which constrast against the muted tones of the bush; airy, open rooms allow one to make the most of excellent views.

...The Outpost integrates futuristic sophistication with the rugged African bush.

In his words, it allows guests to feel close to their environment, but not be threatened by it.

The Outpost is in Makuleke country. For centuries, these ancient people cultivated this region of South Africa before they were forcibly removed in 1969. In the 1990s, they regained possession of their homeland. The Outpost has been awarded a 30-year concession by the Makuleke tribe, after which it comes into full Makuleke ownership.

Not far from The Outpost is Thulamela archaeological site, which holds 14th-century artefacts. Another historical site within reach is the 19th-century trading station Crook's Corner, which was set up along the banks of the Luvuvhu River, where ivory traders used to ship tusks to Mozambique.

Bird-watchers and game enthusiasts will find plenty to see. Rare birds such as Pel's fishing owl, the thick-billed cuckoo and the racquet-tailed roller are frequently spotted here, as are large herds of buffaloes and elephants, the lesser-known Tessebe and Nyala antelopes, and the Samango monkey. Even the most experienced game-viewer will be challenged and thrilled.

The Outpost is for intrepid travellers who feel at home in hiking boots as much as they do in designer shoes. Combining the best of both worlds, this is African safari at its most stylish.

FACTS		
	ROOMS	12 suites
	FOOD	self-service kitchen: fresh and innovative
	DRINK	wine cellar
	FEATURES	property on stilts • wall-free design • plunge pool • pool deck
	BUSINESS	Internet facilities
	NEARBY	rare wildlife • Luvuvhu River flood plains • Thulamela archaeological site • Crook's Corner • Lanner Gorge • Makuleke village (approx. 100 km [240 miles] away)
	CONTACT	10 Bompas Road, Dunkeld West, Johannesburg • telephone: +27.11 341 0282 • facsimile: +27.11 341 0281 • email: theoutpost@global.co.za • website: www.theoutpost.co.za

PHOTOGRAPHS COURTESY OF THE OUTPOST.

Royal Malewane

Wrap yourself warmly in luxury at Royal Malewane. This world-class safari retreat lies on the western fringes of Kruger National Park, and has played host to celebrities, Arab sheiks, Indian princes and American tycoons. Royal Malewane treats everyone like a king, and will roll out the red carpet for you too.

Eight separate luxurious suites dot the property. Nestled among native acacia-thorn trees and other bush vegetation, the suites are connected by elevated walkways to allow guests to get as close to the bush as possible, while preserving it almost entirely. Infinity-edged pools and thatched gazebos with loungers provide ample opportunity for outdoor relaxation, while opulent colonial-style interiors take you back to a bygone era. Sleep in a canopied king-size four-poster bed lined with crisp Ralph Lauren linen, and step into a freestanding Victorian cast-iron bathtub in your own bathroom.

The two top suites are the Royal and Malewane Suites. Regularly requested for by the property's VIP guests, these two-bedroom suites accommodate up to four guests each. There is also a private lounge with dining facilities, and you get to enjoy the dedicated services of a private butler, chef, masseuse,

THIS PAGE (CLOCKWISE FROM TOP):
Separate sinks and freestanding bathtubs are a feature of Royal Malewane's luxuriously-appointed suites; a spectacular sunset enjoyed in solitude; canopied four-poster beds adorn each suite.

OPPOSITE: The sprawling deck of the Royal Suite is lined with plush carpets, cosy couches and armchairs, and boasts a private plunge pool.

game-drive vehicle, ranger and tracker. An outdoor jacuzzi and pool allow you to commune with nature in total privacy. Should any guests require an anonymous arrival, there are landing facilities for private helicopters and executive jets.

Royal Malewane is situated in the unspoilt Thornybush Private Game Reserve. South Africa's Big Five are well-known residents here, and the resort's Master Tracker has an uncanny ability to spot them. He is after all the only Master Tracker in the entire country, and specialises in tracking dangerous game.

Fine dining is the order of the day here. Executive Chef John Jackson delights in full-flavoured, colourful cuisine made with only the freshest of local ingredients. Vegetables and herbs come from his own garden, and everything else is delivered from nearby towns. Breakfast is a stunning buffet spread, including many of John's exotic homemade jams. Lunch is light, followed by an English high tea. Dinner is a formal seven-course affair served on china, crystal and silver, or a sumptuous cookout in the boma.

With so many illustrious people counting themselves among the property's patrons, you know that this is nothing less than the best of what South Africa has to offer.

FACTS		
ROOMS	6 luxury suites • Royal Suite • Malewane Suite	
FOOD	international fare by a private chef	
DRINK	wine cellar	
FEATURES	spa • library • private gazebos and pools • game drive vehicles • highly-qualified rangers and trackers including a Master Tracker	
NEARBY	Big Five and other game-viewing spots • Nelspruit • White River	
CONTACT	PO Box 1542, Hoedspruit 1380 • telephone: +27.15 793 0150 • facsimile: +27.15 793 2879 • email: info@royalmalewane.com • website: www.royalmalewane.com	

PHOTOGRAPHS COURTESY OF ROYAL MALEWANE.

Ant's Hill

THIS PAGE (CLOCKWISE FROM TOP): *Open-plan bathrooms in Ant's Hill's lodge and cottages overlook a dramatic gorge; natural stone and timber are used throughout the property; the infinity-edged pool flows right over the rim of the gorge.*

OPPOSITE (FROM TOP): *The large, airy verandah is lined with plush sofas and comfortable chairs for lounging in; the cosy living room affords an impressive view over the gorge and waterfall.*

A sister lodging to Ant's Nest, Ant's Hill is the second property which husband-and-wife owners Ant and Tessa Baber have added to their growing Ant Collection. Ant's Hill is situated in a private game reserve adjoining Ant's Nest, and the two properties share the same ethos and spirit cultivated by the Babers, as well as many activities. While Ant and Tessa are based at Ant's Nest and leave Ant's Hill in the hands of highly-competent staff, the couple remain closely involved with Ant's Hill.

Ant's Hill is an architectural gem perched on one of the highest hills in the Waterberg. Lovingly designed by Ant himself, the lodge sits on a ridge next to a waterfall, and overlooks a gorge. The view is dramatic to say the least. Plains and hills stretch away into the horizon, and spontaneous game sightings are everyday occurrences. Only natural stone and the best local timber, such as wild olive and acacia wood, were used in the construction of this lodge. Vibrant textiles and creatively-designed furniture from Kenya add a touch of style and sophistication to this rural property.

Like its sister property, Ant's Hill caters to small parties. It can accommodate a maximum of only ten guests, thus promising total exclusivity and flexibility. In the main

short hop away is a romantic honeymoon cottage. Folding doors line two sides of the house, providing panoramic views. Even the bath is positioned for a prime view, and there are both indoor and outdoor showers.

Whether you stay at Ant's Nest or Ant's Hill, you will be lavished with the Babers' genuine hospitality. They possess a passion for the local wildlife and flora which will rub off on you. Horseback rides, game drives and bushveld walks are just some of the activities they organise. A stay with Ant and Tessa is bound to be a truly wonderful experience.

lodge is a spacious double bedroom with a gigantic 2-by-2-m (approximately 3-by-3-ft) four-poster bed, offering views of the valley from the comfort of your sheets.

Large folding doors open up in the summer, and during the cool winter months can be kept shut to retain the warmth emanating from the living room's open fireplace. Curl up and enjoy gorgeous views of the waterfall and gorge from the living and dining rooms. To get closer to the gorge, you can take a dip in the lodge's spectacular pool. Carved out of boulders on a cliff's edge, the refreshing water cascades right over the lip of the gorge. The lodge's verandah also overhangs the gorge, and has large comfy loungers to relax in.

Adjacent to the main lodge is a family cottage comprising two en suite bedrooms, a living and dining room and a sundeck. A

FACTS

ROOMS	main lodge: 1 double bedroom • family cottage: 2 bedrooms • 2 honeymoon cottages: 1 bedroom each
FOOD	bush and boma dining: home cooking
FEATURES	horseback-riding • game drives • family safaris • guided walks • airstrip • infinity-edged pool • massage facilities
NEARBY	Big Five viewing spots • Iron Age villages • bushman paintings • Rhino and Cultural Museum • crocodile farm • hippo colony • cattle farm • local town
CONTACT	PO Box 441, Vaalwater 0530 • telephone: +27.14 755 4296 • facsimile: +27.14 755 4941 • email: antsnest@telkomsa.net • website: www.waterberg.net/antsnest/antshill.html

Ant's Nest

Running along the northern border of South Africa, straddling Botswana and Zimbabwe, is the great Limpopo River. A couple of hours south of the river is the Waterberg Plateau. Once a hideout for outlaws and poachers, the Waterberg became a haven for enterprising gold miners before finally becoming a naturalist's haven. Today, the Waterberg has shaken off any connotations of its dubious past, and enjoys huge success as a wilderness area.

Ant's Nest is a private bush retreat in the heart of the Waterberg, owned and managed by husband and wife duo Ant and Tessa Baber. Overcrowding is not a problem you will have to deal with here; the couple make it their policy to take only one family or party at a time. The Babers personally run Ant's Nest, and lavish guests with their good old-fashioned family-style hospitality.

The original homestead sits in a natural amphitheatre, and has a classic African atmosphere. Right in front of the property is a watering hole frequented by a wide variety of game, which mingle with the Babers' horses and dogs. In the garden is a

THIS PAGE (FROM TOP): Dining under the stars is a regular affair at Ant's Nest's charming reed boma; a heart-warmingly cosy en suite room decorated in timber, stone and local textiles.

OPPOSITE: A watering hole right in front of the house draws game which mingle with Ant and Tessa Baber's own menagerie of horses and dogs.

plunge pool, set amidst sprawling lawns and flourishing native plants. The idyllic scene is best enjoyed from the comfort of the spacious verandahs which surround the house.

Three double bedrooms with four-poster beds and one twin room sleep a maximum of eight guests. Two of the bedrooms are housed in a separate thatched rondavel (a round house). Both have their own verandahs, with the upstairs room boasting fabulous views of the Waterberg hills. The main house hosts the other two bedrooms.

This intimate colonial home was decorated by Tessa, who grew up in Kenya. Cosy furniture fashioned out of timber, stone and textiles fill the comfortable sitting room with its open fireplace, small library and the dining room. Meals are an experience unto themselves. Breakfast is served out in the bush, while the midday meal may be taken at home. Dinner is a sumptuous three- to four-course feast under the starry sky around a campfire in the property's reed boma.

Ant and Tessa have a stable of 30 horses ranging from thoroughbreds to Arab-South African Boerperd cross-breeds and children's ponies. Professional riders and absolute beginners are catered to, and rides are led by two competent guides. Game sightings on horseback rides are often heart-stopping affairs. Ramblers might prefer Ant and Tessa's guided bushveld walks. With the couple's rich knowledge of local flora and fauna, these walks are always informative and exciting. Game drives are also available, as are family safaris with fun and educational activities for children. Any visitor to this homestead will leave with a little bit of the Babers' charm in their hearts.

FACTS		
ROOMS	3 double rooms • 1 twin room	
FOOD	boma: home-style cooking	
FEATURES	horseback-riding • game drives • family safaris • guided walks • airstrip • plunge pool • watering hole • garden	
NEARBY	Big Five game reserve • Iron Age villages • bushman paintings • Rhino and Cultural Museum • crocodile farm • Palala River hippo colony • Charles Baber's cattle farm • local town and church	
CONTACT	PO Box 441, Vaalwater 0530 • telephone: +27.14 755 4296 • facsimile: +27.14 755 4941 • email: antsnest@telkomsa.net • website: www.waterberg.net/antsnest	

PHOTOGRAPHS COURTESY OF ANT'S NEST.

Clearwater Lodges

From the moment guests step into the game-drive vehicles that will escort them right into the heart of Welgevonden Private Game Reserve, it becomes clear why this 33,000-hectare (81,500-acre) expanse is a popular safari destination. Located at the rust-red foothills of the Waterberg, Welgevonden has a particularly attractive terrain of pleats and folds, layered with lush bush willow. Translated, the name Waterberg means 'water mountain', a reference to the rivulets of water that gush down the sides of its hills when it rains. More elevated than most other regions in South Africa, the Waterberg

boasts a cooler climate, which makes safari excursions all the more enjoyable. In the midst of all this is Clearwater Lodges, nestled deep within the reserve.

Clearwater Lodges offers guests two completely different safari experiences. These options are spread out between Clearwater's two properties—Kudu Lodge, set on the open savannah, and Tshetshepi Lodge, huddled in the midst of indigenous forest and hidden against the mountainside.

Kudu Lodge could have leapt out of the pages of *National Geographic*. It is located in the thick of safari action, and promises spectacular views of wildlife in action, where you can observe animals feeding, hunting and at rest. Tshetshepi Lodge, on the other hand, provides a more intimate getaway. At close proximity to a mountain, a stay at Tshetshepi rewards guests with the soothing sounds of water trickling down the

THIS PAGE (FROM TOP): The cuisine at Clearwater Lodges is one of its finest attractions; the main building of Kudu Lodge, set in the open plains of the savannah.
OPPOSITE: A chalet at Tshetshepi Lodge, an intimate mountainside getaway.

Waterberg, which are especially audible after a bout of rain, when streams turn into raging rivers at some spots.

Though the Big Five are often spotted here, guests lap up sightings of smaller species like the chacma baboon, honey badger and scrub hare with as much enthusiasm. Indigenous flora and ancient archaeological sights are other attractions, but there is no denying the draw of the majestic black-maned Kalahari lion, whose charismatic presence in itself often merits a visit to Welgevonden Reserve.

Clearwater Lodges calls its accommodation 'chalets', but that does not mean that guests will be put up at less than luxurious lodgings. To the contrary, chalets in both lodges are decked out in sumptuous European style, complete with five-star trappings. For any luxury safari lodge, outdoor showers are a must-have. As such, Clearwater Lodges has installed one in each chalet for their guests to frolic in al fresco.

South African business veteran Anne Cointreau-Huchon, who made the Western Cape's Morgenhof wine estate world-famous, owns Clearwater Lodges, and the lodge's wine selection benefits from her expert taste in wines. Given her French ancestry, the food here is naturally one of the lodge's best features. Guests are served what is best described as 'wholesome ethnic-gourmet food'. Expect fresh crisp salads, hearty main courses, delicate desserts and, sometimes, exotic meats like ostrich served in filo pastry. Guests can also tuck into lavish high tea spreads or water down at the bar—drinks are complimentary, save for imported bottles.

While not the most extravagantly-priced resort in South Africa, Clearwater Lodges is exclusive—each lodge holds a maximum of only 10 guests at any one time. Not surprisingly, Clearwater Lodges is a member of the prestigious Relais & Châteaux, a status it has truly earned.

PHOTOGRAPHS COURTESY OF CLEARWATER LODGES.

FACTS

ROOMS	10 chalets
FOOD	dining room and boma: ethnic fusion
DRINK	wine cellar
FEATURES	indoor and outdoor showers in all chalets • personal outdoor deck • pool • ranger
BUSINESS	meeting facilities
NEARBY	game-viewing spots • bushman paintings • Johannesburg (a 2.5-hr drive)
CONTACT	PO Box 365, Stellenbosch 7599 • telephone/facsimile: +27.21 889 5514 • email: info@clearwaterlodges.co.za • website: www.clearwaterlodges.co.za

Makweti Safari Lodge

All over the Waterberg wilderness lie spiny candelabra trees. With bright orange or red fruit and large crowns of spindly branches that curve upwards, these trees are impossible to miss. So characteristic is the candelabra tree of Waterberg vegetation that it has lent its name to Makweti Safari Lodge. Makweti is Sotho for 'candelabra tree', and this lodge is the gateway to a thrilling, malaria-free safari experience.

This safari lodge perched on the side of the rugged Makweti Gorge is crafted from natural rock. Teak decks overhang the gorge, which in the summer is a graceful waterfall, and in the winter is a sculptured stone wall. Birds and animals abound, and their presence is often heard before it is seen. The gorge is like an echo chamber, projecting baboon barks and melodic bird calls from black-headed orioles, babblers and starlings into the crisp, clean air.

The peace here is never disturbed. Makweti Lodge accommodates just 10 guests in five secluded thatch-and-stone suites. Each suite is decorated with an array of antique treasures, hand-beaded fabrics and rich, dark woods. All suites come with indoor and outdoor showers, Victorian bathtubs, open fireplaces and decks with uninterrupted views of the bushveld. Scattered throughout the Lodge are antique African art, khelim (flat-woven) rugs and comfortable leather couches.

THIS PAGE (FROM TOP): Suites offer secluded privacy, surrounded by natural bushveld; intimate wildlife sightings are to be expected at the Waterberg.

OPPOSITE (FROM LEFT): Each of Makweti Safari Lodge's five exclusive suites is decorated with dark wood, earth-toned textiles and beautiful African antiques; the boma where the lodge's excellent private chef dishes out traditional local cuisine; the lodge's African heritage is evident throughout the property.

Meals are expertly prepared by a private chef. She will delight you with homemade soups, game and other native fare infused with local spices. Dinner may be served either by candlelight in the formal dining room, or out under the stars in the boma.

The Indaba Lounge, which overlooks the Makweti Gorge and undulating landscapes beyond, is an ideal place to sample one of the lodge's exquisite South African estate wines from its own cellar. Let

the safari come to you—watch animals drinking at the lodge's own waterhole from the comfort of the lounge or laze in the sun at Makweti's filtered rock pool.

Makweti Lodge is set in the pristine Welgevonden Private Game Reserve. Proclaimed a Natural Heritage Site, it shares the Waterberg's Biosphere status, meaning that it is recognised as a centre of biodiversity and cultural heritage. An expert guide will take you on game drives or bushveld walks

through this unspoiled landscape, comprising 33,000 hectares (81,550 acres) of Highveld woodland savannah. The largest crash of privately-owned white rhino roam alongside 16 species of antelope, giraffe, zebra, wildebeest, lion, leopard, elephant, buffalo, brown hyena, cheetah and wild dog, complemented by sightings of over 254 bird species. At Makweti Safari Lodge, your experience in the Waterberg can only be described as unforgettable.

PHOTOGRAPHS COURTESY OF MAKWETI SAFARI LODGE.

FACTS	
ROOMS	5 suites
FOOD	local fare by Chaîne de Rôtisseurs-acclaimed private chef
DRINK	Zebra Bar • Indaba Lounge
FEATURES	lodge carved out of natural rock • wine cellar • watering hole
NEARBY	Highveld woodland savannah habitat • Big Five viewing • 16 species of antelope • private crash of white rhinoceroses • adjacent to Marakele National Park • Johannesburg (3 hrs' drive or 45 mins by scheduled charter)
CONTACT	PO Box 310, Vaalwater 0530 • telephone: +27.11 837 6776 • facsimile: +27.11 837 4771 • email: makweti@global.co.za • website: www.makweti.com

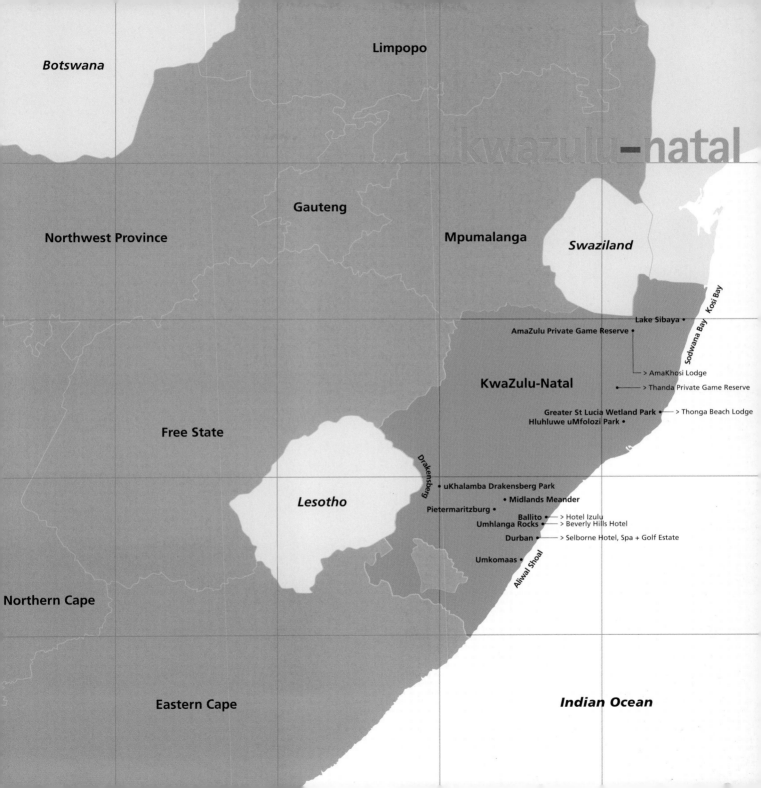

Botswana

Limpopo

kwazulu-natal

Gauteng

Northwest Province

Mpumalanga

Swaziland

Lake Sibaya •

AmaZulu Private Game Reserve •

Kosi Bay

Sodwana Bay

KwaZulu-Natal

> AmaKhosi Lodge

> Thanda Private Game Reserve

Greater St Lucia Wetland Park • — > Thonga Beach Lodge

Hluhluwe uMfolozi Park •

Free State

Drakensberg

• uKhalamba Drakensberg Park

• Midlands Meander

Lesotho

Pietermaritzburg •

Ballito •— > Hotel Izulu

Umhlanga Rocks •— > Beverly Hills Hotel

Durban •— > Selborne Hotel, Spa + Golf Estate

Umkomaas •

Aliwal Shoal

Northern Cape

Eastern Cape

Indian Ocean

the legendary land of shaka

KwaZulu-Natal, one of South Africa's busiest, most densely populated provinces, plays host to some of Africa's most enthralling cultural experiences. Two hundred years ago, the region between the Pongola and Tugela rivers which flow out into the Indian Ocean was the nerve centre and capital of one of history's most extraordinary military geniuses, King Shaka of the Zulu. An illegitimate child made good, Shaka rose to prominence in the early 1800s. At the height of his powers, he controlled an area at least the size of Portugal and many vassal states beyond—a stunning achievement.

The story of this legendary figure is an important theme in KwaZulu-Natal, partly because it is, relatively speaking, fairly well-documented, a situation which allows us a rare window of clarity on Africa's precolonial history. The dearth of records of precolonial societies in Africa often results in highly distorted views of the past being cast as fact. This is at times the result of mere ignorance, prejudice, and in the case of South Africa, the manipulation of history to serve an overweening political or ideological agenda. Recent historical work has finally allowed historical African figures and cultures to be properly understood in their true depth and sophistication, illuminated by the light of academic scholarship.

of heavenly choirs + the dragon mountains

KwaZulu-Natal is thus the setting for a number of impressive tales, offering an embarrassment of riches for both the mind and senses. The province has a huge range of terrain with extreme variations in climate and topography. Its eastern shores are washed by the Indian Ocean, with the focal point being South Africa's busiest port, the laid-back surf-city of Durban; its central sector is sliced along a roughly north-south axis by the mighty Drakensberg mountain range, whose altitude may be gauged from the fact that its highest peak is just metres short of the altitude of the Matterhorn in the Alps. The Alpine-like scenery here is also echoed by names reminiscent of France and Switzerland, such as Mont-aux-Sources.

PAGE 100: The jagged peaks of the Mweni Valley in the mighty Drakensberg testify to the youth, in geological terms, of this dramatic landscape.

THIS PAGE: Man in traditional Zulu regalia on the occasion of a royal wedding.

OPPOSITE: Aerial view of the magical Kosi Bay.

The Drakensberg is also known to the Zulu as The Barrier of Spears, an evocative name which graphically illustrates the sheer cliffs and precipices of this great mountain range. Adding to the appeal of the humid year-round warmth that prevails on the province's coast, the northern segment of the region which borders on tropical Mozambique is peppered with luxury lodges set in lush game areas.

In notable contrast, the KwaZulu-Natal midlands, a place more English than England, has names such as Nottingham Road, Howick and Midmar. Quaint country hotels, marvellous food shops, fly-fishing retreats and a famous craft route called the Midlands Meander nestle in the gently rolling landscape. It is also home to some of the country's best private schools for girls and boys, including Michaelhouse and Hilton, South Africa's equivalent to Eton or Rugby. Another elite school, the Drakensberg Boys' Choir School for talented choristers and musicians, is modelled on the Vienna Boys' Choir and situated here too.

museums + battlegrounds

History is also a thrilling and well-presented attraction. Unlike provinces such as Gauteng and the Northern Cape, history lies a little closer to the surface. The narrative of the second Anglo-Boer War (1899–1902), when Britain went head-to-head with a ragged bunch of frontier farmers called Boers and almost lost, looms large here. But even before this, the indomitable Boer pioneers had fought many extraordinary battles with the Zulu in these parts, most notably the Battle of Blood River, which was also fought in the midlands region.

Whilst some of these campaigns are depicted in museums throughout the battlefields, one must not forget the other intellectual diversions available here. KwaZulu-Natal has a great store of fascinating museums and academic institutes, amongst them the Natal Sharks Board, a scientific institute devoted to studying and managing the predator. Another unique and rewarding visit is the Voortrekker Museum in Pietermaritzburg, which examines the origins, history and culture of Afrikaners. And one of the best places to view South African artefacts and historical documents is Muckleneuk, the former house of sugar magnate Sir Marshall Campbell.

stories of the great mahatma

As if these marvellously diverse features were not enough, KwaZulu-Natal is also home to one of the largest populations of Indian people outside India. This community traces its roots to the system of indentured labour on the region's vast sugar cane plantations in the late 19th century. It is said that you have not really visited KwaZulu-Natal until you have eaten a proper Durban curry. In addition, few people know that this region was also a place of great significance for one of the 20th century's great political figures, pacifist Mohandas Gandhi.

Gandhi, a middle-class lawyer from southern India, was engaged by a Durban trader to cross the ocean from India to oversee a particularly knotty law suit. Gandhi arrived in Natal, as the colonial territory was then called, resolved the case, and went on to become a successful defender of civil and political rights for the large Indian community there. In all, Gandhi spent over 20 years in South Africa, some of them in KwaZulu-Natal and some in the region known today as Gauteng. His name is just one more to be added to the list of luminaries associated with the province.

THIS PAGE: Shark and turtle, denizens of the deep, are both common in the balmy waters of the Indian Ocean off KwaZulu-Natal.

OPPOSITE (FROM TOP): The misty peaks of the Drakensberg; hiking is a popular pastime in 'the Berg'.

a sandy playground

Many people who know South Africa are unaware of this region's great historical travel opportunities, largely because the coastlines both north and south of Durban are so seductive that many never get further than a beachside bar or fashionable restaurant. These coasts, with names like Dolphin Coast, Hibiscus Coast and Strelizia Coast, are extensively developed to take advantage of the warm offshore waters and year-round sunshine, with a long list of exclusive centres to be found from Port Edward in the south right up to the Tugela river mouth in the north.

Many of these resorts are glamorous and fashionable, whilst others are jolly seaside spots. The large city of Durban, however, fast merging with the separate but closely linked provincial capital of Pietermaritzburg, has all that a large, cosmopolitan urban centre should offer. The city is a teeming mish-mash of colliding architectural styles, much of it dating from either the high Victorian or Art Deco period. It has several strong cultural themes, notably the still-dominant Englishness of the place which saw such features as one of the country's first cricket grounds, Lords, being built in Durban. Many people here trace their forebears back to all corners of the British Isles, whilst up to a million others, as mentioned above, came originally from the Indian subcontinent. One thus finds Hindu temples, pungent open-air spice markets or shops selling swathes of shimmering material for saris mixed in with Victorian architecture.

Durban, like a number of the country's cities, has also seen a renaissance since the advent of democracy. Most recently, this has taken the form of a huge new theme park and oceanarium on the beachfront called Ushaka. Here a good mix of family-focused activities co-exists with a brand new aquarium, upmarket shops and restaurants and the rehabilitation of the coastal dunes. Although newly opened, this complex has already proven a major success. A number of additional phases are planned, making these former dock areas some of the hippest places to be seen at.

One of the best things to do in Durban is to visit the Natal Sharks Board, a body devoted to understanding this magnificent creature and negotiating a balance between

THIS PAGE (FROM LEFT): *The Indian community in Durban has left its mark on the city's architecture; spices being traded at the busy Indian market.*

OPPOSITE : *Waves lap gently at the long, sandy beaches of Durban.*

shark and human activities in the area. It is the only institution of its kind in the world, and pioneered the use of shark nets to protect bathing beaches in the early 1960s. Here, you can watch a shark dissection to see its extraordinary internal structure or even go out on ski boats to help with the net maintenance.

an eco-world apart

KwaZulu-Natal also has the unique honour in South Africa of possessing within its domain two UNESCO World Heritage Sites. These are the Greater St Lucia Wetland Park on the northern stretch of the coastline, close to the border with Mozambique, and the uKhalamba Drakensberg Park. The latter is doubly special, because it was awarded World Heritage Site status on the twin counts firstly of historical significance and secondly on the rareness and significance of its biodiversity. Within the borders of this site fall large tracts of the Drakensberg, where botanists and birders talk of rare, exquisite orchids and strongholds of Africa's magnificent raptors.

The Greater St Lucia Wetland Park, occupying a massive 2,750 sq km (1,062 sq miles), is comprised of five distinct eco-systems and, when complete, will be the third-largest conservation area in the country. The five eco-systems here are marine (coral reefs and beaches), shoreline, swamps, the St Lucia Lake itself, which is the largest estuary in Africa, and some wonderful inland areas of sand forest, bushveld and savannahs. At St Lucia, a mind-boggling 100 species of butterfly have been mapped. South Africa in general has a seemingly endless list of such discoveries, a fact which underscores the importance of its precious biodiversity.

Water-dwelling creatures such as hippos and crocodiles abound, and this is also counted among one of the top places in Africa for birding. Since being designated a World Heritage Site, important plans have been made with regard to the preservation

of the unique mix of flora and fauna here, and its presentation to the public. There is a range of accommodation to be had and a host of water-based activities from angling to coral reef-diving at Sodwana Bay. Scientists say that the number of fish species which inhabit these reefs is only four short of those populating the Great Barrier Reef.

of hippos + sardines

North of the St Lucia eco-system lie more wonders, notably two large coastal water features called Lake Sibaya and Kosi Bay, which abuts the Mozambique border. Kosi Bay is particularly enchanting. It consists of a small series of interlinked, semi-saline lakes surrounded by palms, reeds and beautiful bushveld. The lakes are bordered by lush forested dunes, which separate the ocean from the lake system. At night the hippos which frolic in the lakes come onto dry land to graze, and have been known to wander onto the beach. One of the noteworthy creatures to look out for here is the Pel's fishing owl. Horseback safaris here also ensure you get to see the animals close up.

Further south, close to Durban and located on a headland, lies the apparently unremarkable town of Umkomaas. However, this marks the spot from which, in June, dive operators leave the shore and head out to sea to view the world-famous great sardine migration past the Aliwal Shoal. As with Sodwana, Aliwal is placed amongst the top 10 international dive spots, but is perhaps even better known for the annual spectacle of the sardine run which passes here in midwinter. International wildlife photographers have been quoted as saying that no wildlife encounter they have had quite compares with this, for the shoal attracts all the great predators of the deep— rays, sharks and whales—to feast on nature's plenty

Inland, the uKhalamba Drakensberg offers a plethora of wonderful walks, with a new addition being specialised botanical excursions and hikes throughout the mountains. The other reason for the UNESCO award lies in the region's spectacular open-air rock art sites. There are many thousands of such sites throughout the entire country, with this area boasting an especially high number of them.

THIS PAGE (FROM TOP): *Pel's fishing owl, one of the region's many enchanting owl species; road signs, South Africa-style.*

OPPOSITE (FROM TOP): *The Lake St Lucia region, one of South Africa's World Heritage Sites; commercial crocodile farms allow visitors to observe these prehistoric creatures at close range, and protect them from predators, poachers and loss of habitat due to pollution and urbanisation.*

'no end of a lesson'

This was the memorable phrase that Rudyard Kipling used to describe how the British felt at the end of the Anglo-Boer War. The war broke out in 1899, stemming from a struggle over the control of Johannesburg's vast goldfields and Boer desire for political independence. As with the Zulu campaigns some 20 years earlier, historians still find the war to be one of the most striking events in world military history. The tactics of the Boer War are taught at military academies, for many devastating strategies such as the successful use of rural guerrilla warfare by the Boers and the use of civilian internment ('concentration') camps by the British were major early 20th-century innovations. But it was the spectacle of the tiny Boer nation, which fielded only some 80,000 fighting men, keeping the full force of the British empire on the run in KwaZulu-Natal for almost three years, which fascinated the world.

spion kop + isandlwana: names of fear + travail

It was at the Battle of Spion Kop in the KwaZulu-Natal midlands, however, that the full extent of British ineptitude took a terrible toll on the Queen's soldiers. Fought by the cream of Britain's generals, with support from people like Gandhi and observed by a youthful Winston Churchill, the battle was still a rout, and so many British were killed that they were simply piled into trenches where they lay as the dust of battle settled.

Just as riveting as Spion Kop is the story of the two back-to-back battles of Isandlwana and Rorke's Drift that were part of a campaign run by the British against the Zulu in the 1870s. At the battle of Isandlwana, a Zulu force, armed mostly with spears and a few rifles, defeated a large, seasoned, well-equipped British force in spectacular fashion. No man who could not cling to a horse escaped the impi (Zulu warriors), who chased the fugitives to the mission station of Rorke's Drift where the fighting continued. The story, like that of Spion Kop, takes a full day to tell, and should not be cut short. Storytelling is the lifeblood of travel, and the purple hills and valleys of KwaZulu-Natal have many more stories than can be told on a single journey.

There are an estimated 30,000 such sites throughout the entire country...

AmaKhosi Lodge

The Zulu language is spoken from the Cape to Zimbabwe, and is one of the most widely used and understood languages in South Africa today. This did not come about by accident. In the early 19th century, legendary Zulu king Shaka led the Zulu nation to prominence and it reigned over most of what is South Africa today. Shaka's regal legacy lives on in a special safari lodge located on the banks of Zululand's Mkuze River in the 10,000 hectare AmaZulu Private Game Reserve—AmaKhosi Lodge.

AmaKhosi, which means 'the place of the kings' in Zulu, treats every guest like royalty. The banks of the Mkuze River are host to the lodge's six River Suites. Private verandahs and floor-to-ceiling glass walls ensure spectacular views of the flowing river. Each suite comprises a spacious bedroom, separate lounge and a luxurious bathroom with a tub for two. There are also candles and bath salts, making bath time a whole new experience for the senses.

Early morning or late afternoon game drives and bush walks, led by experienced guides, provide ample opportunity to view the abundant flora and fauna nearby. AmaZulu was once a cattle farm, and since 1978 the land has been gradually rehabilitated with its natural wildlife. Today, the Big Five (lion, elephant, leopard, buffalo and rhinoceros) roam freely, as do cheetah, hippo, crocodile, 15 species of antelope and over 400 species of indigenous and migratory birds. Guests who prefer to experience African wildlife from the comfort of the lodge may do so from a game viewing deck.

A resident Zulu chef prepares the meals. Traditional African cuisine with European flair is typical here. The first meal of the day is brunch, an extensive buffet spread with

cold and hot dishes, freshly-squeezed juices and a selection of gourmet cheeses. High tea is taken in the outside lounge and comprises a sumptuous array of quiches, meats, vegetable platters, jams and breads. Dinner is served every alternate night in the lodge's latest addition, a traditional Zulu kraal (paddock) built by the local Zulu community. Enjoy a South African braai by starlight, a novel barbecue experience that encapsulates the essence of this country's glorious outdoor lifestyle.

The Zulu community is very much part of the AmaKhosi Lodge. Zulu school children often delight guests with original Zulu dances, for which the children are paid, and the funds go towards their education. Most staff members are also Zulu. All this is simply part of the lodge's ethos of supporting the local community and showing respect for its culture. At AmaKhosi Lodge, the land, people and wildlife come together in perfect harmony to provide you with an authentic South African Zulu experience.

FACTS		
	ROOMS	6 suites
	FOOD	African fare with European flair by Zulu chef
	DRINK	private bar • mini-bar in suites • sundowners on game drives
	FEATURES	pool • poolside lounges • library • satellite TV • airstrip
	BUSINESS	function room • Internet facilities
	NEARBY	savannah, wetland and mountain habitats • Mkuze River • Big Five game-viewing spots • bird-watching spots
	CONTACT	PO Box 354, Pongola, KwaZulu-Natal 3170 • telephone: +27.34 414 1157 • facsimile: +27.34 414 1172 • email: info@amakhosi.com • website: www.amakhosi.com

PHOTOGRAPHS COURTESY OF AMAKHOSI LODGE.

Thanda Private Game Reserve

Pulsing drums beckon guests into Vula Zulu, a traditional kraal and the setting for the performance of ancient dancing rites. An army of 50 to 100 impi (Zulu warriors), trained by an associate of a Zulu prince, engage in a spirited battle dance that pays tribute to their tribal roots.

The thumps and beats of native rhythms are at the heart of Zulu heritage, and are embraced by Thanda Private Game Reserve. Elements of this age-old tradition are integrated into many aspects of the lodge, and guests are greeted with countless ways to appreciate the rich and still very much alive spirituality of the Zulu people.

THIS PAGE (FROM TOP): Commune with nature in Thanda Private Game Reserve's outdoor showers; the understated entrance lounge to the main lodge.

OPPOSITE: A romantic bedroom with an open fireplace and a four-poster bed draped with gossamer netting.

Subtle references to Zulu culture can be seen everywhere in Thanda, from the décor to the cuisine and activities on offer. A plaque in the form of a Zulu shield proudly presides over the entrance to the lodge. It was unveiled by Zulu king His Majesty King Zwelithini in recognition of the Reserve's commitment to promoting the Zulu nation. When the lodge was being built, over 200 Zulu workers were engaged, many of whom are now fully employed by Thanda. Crafts by local artists decorate the public areas, and are also on sale at the curio shop.

Nine sprawling bush villas are the very embodiment of decadence. In each, a wooden platform reaches out like a hand to

The thumps and beats of native rhythms are...embraced by Thanda Private Game Reserve.

the surrounding vegetation. A thatched sala, complete with a plush lounge seat, perches at the end of the platform and is a superb spot from which to enjoy the tranquillity of nature. A splash pool, viewing deck, lounge, fireplace and a fully kitted-out bathroom with an outdoor shower complete the villa. With four-poster beds draped in soft, rustling fabrics and freestanding bathtubs placed strategically by a bay

window, guests experience luxury resort living in the very midst of the bush. The pièce de résistance is a private boma in each villa where guests can chill out or dine in privacy. Even the food embraces the colourful culture of the Zulu people. Thanda's signature fusion of Western and traditional Zulu cuisine can be relished in the dining room in front of a roaring fire in winter, or under the stars in the boma or the bush. Alternatively, guests can

ask for meals to be served right in the privacy of their own boma.

To get more intimately acquainted with the bushveld, a camp built on the slope of a hill offers four tents as alternative lodgings. With viewing decks and spacious bathrooms with showers, the tents are rustic yet luxurious. They have no electricity, and guests have meals in the dining tent or by the glow of the boma's fire.

Nine sprawling bush villas are the very embodiment of decadence.

THIS PAGE (FROM TOP): *Freestanding baths by panoramic bay windows provide for an excellent view while relaxing in the tub; the main lodge's opulent lounge with its Zulu-inspired décor.*

OPPOSITE: *In each villa, a thatched sala sits at the end of a raised wooden walkway and is furnished with a circular sofa and plush cushions for an all-round view of nature.*

Game drives are a popular way to see the plants, animals and landscape of the reserve. Set just north of Hluhluwe in the province of KwaZulu-Natal, the diverse Thanda landscape encompasses rolling hills, valleys and aloe forests. A drive with one of the lodge's experienced rangers in an open game-viewing vehicle gives guests a clearer understanding of Thanda's wild heritage. For those who prefer to get up close and personal with the flora and fauna, bush walks led by knowledgeable trackers allow for more intimate interaction with nature.

Thanda is 'love' in the Zulu language—a concept that is apparent in this lovingly put together game reserve. The philosophy that drives Thanda is 'for the love of nature, wildlife and dear ones'. Aiming to create a harmonious relationship between man and nature, Thanda Private Game Reserve is equal parts nature reserve and luxury accommodation. To satisfy the former, the land is currently undergoing a process of rehabilitation to return it to its original state.

Looking at it now, it is hard to imagine the degeneration it once went through. Invasive alien plant species, which infested the soil when the land was first bought, have been replaced with flora indigenous to the area. Animals which roamed the grounds in the past—buffalo, cheetah, duiker, impala,

giraffe, hyena, warthog and reedbuck—have been reintroduced. Now birds and wildlife flourish, as a healthy balance has been newly restored to the eco-system. In this natural setting, the Big Five and the Super Seven are thriving like never before.

Guests with varied interests will find a wide array of activities to fill their days after the ubiquitous safari. Nearby, the eastern shores of KwaZulu-Natal are prime spots for whale-watching between the months of June and November. Sodwana Bay, one of South Africa's most exciting diving destinations, has a proliferation of Indo-Atlantic species of coral and marine life. Bottle-nosed dolphins,

turtles and sharks swim in these waters. Non-divers can feast their eyes on various reefs, pinnacles, buttresses, caves and blowholes. Leatherback and loggerback turtles, the stars of Sodwana Bay, lay their eggs here every year as they have for the last 200 million years. Sodwana Bay forms part of the Greater St Lucia Wetlands, South Africa's first World Heritage Site. Home to an abundance of unique plant and animal species, St Lucia Lake has about 1,500 species of fauna, the highest number in all the animal parks this side of Africa.

While in the area, guests should also make a detour to the Elephant Coast, so named for being the habitat of the largest herd of African elephants, living and foraging in the sand forest since time immemorial. Twenty-one eco-systems thrive on the Elephant Coast, including sand forests, lagoons, lakes, wetlands and pristine beaches that are host to animals such as hippopotamuses and birds.

After guests have had their fill of tourist magnets, Thanda offers a variety of activities from freshwater and deep-sea fishing to horseback-riding and bird-watching safaris. Because five superb golf courses pepper the surrounding areas, golf enthusiasts can tee off amidst the serenity of the savannah. The spotless beaches of the Indian Ocean are particularly inviting for beach walks and private barbecues.

Cultural tours to a nearby Zulu tribal village bring guests on a journey into the daily lives of the indigenous community. To see first-hand the close connections between nature and the Zulu people, guests will be led through local historical sites, battlegrounds and the village school. Back in the comfort of the lodge, a library of glossy tomes provides literary insights into fascinating aspects of this ancient people.

If leisurely cruises down tropical estuaries or refreshing dips in private pools are not quite enough to recharge the

batteries, a visit to the wellness centre is sure to soothe body, mind and soul. Lovingly crafted from natural ingredients like plant and marine extracts, the spa's signature treatments have a decidedly exotic appeal. Thanda Spirit starts with a rose petal-filled bath for two, followed by a rose petal salt scrub, an African hot stone massage and a pressure point massage.

A truly sublime experience though, is the Essence of Africa Sala Treatment, administered in the exclusive surrounds of the outdoor sala treatment area. Traditional African maize meal and sour milk are used to exfoliate the body. After an outdoor bushveld shower to wash off the excess scrub, guests are then massaged into a state of utter relaxation with a cocktail of shea butter massage balm and aromatherapy oil—blended the African way, of course.

Thanda Private Game Reserve is the perfect place to restore weather-beaten, overworked souls. The top-rate service and

atmosphere of luxury which are its hallmarks are unparalleled, and prevail alongside a mindfulness for the culture and history of the surrounding environment. The passionate spirituality of the Zulu people echoes strongly throughout Thanda Private Game Reserve. Many guests have spoken of a sense of inner rejuvenation they feel during their stay, which they just cannot quite put a finger on. Perhaps it is the rhythm of the impi, or simply the magic of this wild, untamed land.

FACTS		
ROOMS	9 bush villas • 4 tents
FOOD	dining room, dining deck and boma: Western and traditional Zulu
DRINK	wine cellar
FEATURES	private splash pools • indoor and outdoor showers • private bomas • library • viewing decks • Big Five • wellness centre • Vula Zulu Cultural Experience
BUSINESS	conference facilities • facsimile • Internet facilities
NEARBY	Zulu villages • Hluhluwe • Greater St Lucia Wetlands • Elephant Coast • Sodwana Bay • Cape Vidal
CONTACT	PO Box 652585, Benmore 2010 • telephone: +27.11 704 3115 • facsimile: +27.11 462 5607 • email: reservations@thanda.co.za • website: www.thanda.com

PHOTOGRAPHS COURTESY OF THANDA PRIVATE GAME RESERVE.

Thonga Beach Lodge

There is a somewhat magical air to Mabibi on the Maputaland coast of KwaZulu-Natal, with its mix of coastal forests, lush grasslands, iridescent lakes and sandy beaches. Adjacent to Africa's southernmost coral reefs, Mabibi is the prime tropical dive site in South Africa. Its crystal waters, filled with more than 1,200 species of fish on the reefs, make it one of the best dive destinations in the world. Largely unnoticed, though, this treasure has remained secluded in all its glory, all the better for divers to explore its exciting underwater seascapes.

There is nowhere to stay for 20 km (48 miles) up and down Mabibi beach aside from Thonga, but guests know that this luxury beach lodge is probably the most inspired place to call home for a far longer stretch. Robinson Crusoe chic is at its best here. Rondavel-shaped suites with thatched roofs are nestled between milkwood trees and raised on wooden stilts to protect sensitive dune soils. Bleached wood, other natural materials and glass give an open feel to the suites, as does the private balcony, where guests dine with the wilderness for company.

THIS PAGE (CLOCKWISE FROM TOP):
Soak up the sea breeze at Thonga Beach Lodge's oceanside bar; thatched rondavel suites offer excellent accommodation; Robinson Crusoe-style luxury.

OPPOSITE: At Thonga, nothing stands between you and panoramic views of the Indian Ocean.

Robinson Crusoe chic is at its best here.

Chefs at the lodge take pride in their unconventional cuisine, best described as eclectic. Clean, fresh flavours are presented drenched in colour—menu items include mint-dusted sweet potatoes with coconut salsa, fried green bananas, a Kosi Bay speciality, and Mabibi fish freshly pickled with lime and honey. Meals are served by the pool or in the dining room, where guests can choose to sit inside or out under the shade of milkwood trees. Diehard romantics may opt for a table set on the shores of the Indian Ocean, illuminated only by candles.

Thonga's physical geography gives opportunities for an array of marine activities. Shallow reefs teeming with brilliantly-hued sub-tropical fish like Moorish idols, parrot fish and blue surgeonfish are perfect for snorkelling. The nearby Lake Sibaya, South Africa's largest freshwater lake, is a World Heritage Site and home to a wide variety of aquatic life forms. Guided canoe trips and sunset cruises are the best ways to tackle its vast expanse without breaking a sweat.

After a busy day exploring the beach, the lounge, with its plush couches, crackling fireplace and dramatic views of the beach and forest is an especially inviting spot for a sundowner. Cocktails are served at the ocean bar counter, where guests can relax while enjoying the intoxicating sea breeze. To fully embrace the seductive ocean, marine-based spa treatments at Thonga's sea spa hit just the right spot. A beachside massage with Algologie products, blended from brown and red seaweed and marine sediment from the coast of the Pen Lan Peninsula in Brittany, France, is enough to render anyone weak to the charms of Thonga.

FACTS		
	ROOMS	12 bedrooms
	FOOD	dining room • poolside • private bedroom verandah • beach table
	DRINK	ocean bar
	FEATURES	lounge • pool • dive centre • curio shop • sea spa • library
	NEARBY	Maputaland • Lake Sibaya • Sodwana Bay • Kosi Bay • Mazengwenya
	CONTACT	PO Box 1593, Eshowe 3815 • telephone: +27.35 474 1473 • facsimile: +27.35 474 1490 • email: res@isibindiafrica.co.za • website: www.isibindiafrica.co.za

Hotel Izulu

Thirty minutes north of Durban in the heart of the Dolphin Coast lies Ballito, KwaZulu-Natal's premier coastal holiday resort belt. Flanked by golden beaches and the warm waters of the Indian Ocean, the village of Ballito is affectionately termed 'the pearl of the Dolphin Coast'.

The very first five-star establishment in this heart-warming neighbourhood is Hotel Izulu. Boasting 19 suites, the hotel is an ingenious blend of Tuscan architecture, African features and Balinese influences. The different styles form a convivial mix, and are most often described as 'an African heart with an Eastern spirit'. Five freestanding villas are spread out on manicured grounds. Each villa houses two executive suites, two deluxe suites, a private courtyard and an eight-seater jacuzzi. Luxurious living manifests itself in the Royal Suite. Sprawled across the entire top floor of Villa Ingelosi, it encompasses a bar, dining area, personal deck and a jacuzzi which, incidentally, overlooks the hills and ocean.

Suites are decked out with pure cotton bed linen, silk curtains and grand double baths. The icing on the cake, though, comes in the form of piped music, heated towel

THIS PAGE (CLOCKWISE FROM TOP):
Elegant bathrooms at Hotel Izulu; sprawling luxury villas are set on verdant grounds; a spacious bedroom with a four-poster bed.

OPPOSITE: The sumptuous banqueting hall is an ideal wedding venue.

rails, embroidered bathrobes and Charlotte Rhys toiletries—almost too good to be true.

The royal treatment at Hotel Izulu, however, does not end there. Guests looking for therapeutic relaxation are kneaded, pummelled, exfoliated and rubbed into a blissful state of tranquillity at the Impilo Beauty Spa. The myriad of wellness treatments includes facials, massages, hydrotherapy, manicures and pedicures. For the ultimate pampering session, the African Queen spa package comprises an entire day of rituals that range from a back massage to a jet shower, a steam bath, a Clarins facial and several body treatments. A paraffin manicure and pedicure are thrown in for good measure, while a spa lunch in between keeps rumbling tummies happy during a day of utter decadence.

Hotel Izulu's executive chef Jurgen Snyman is a celebrity in his own right. He is known to push culinary boundaries—curious concoctions such as emulsions, jellies and

foams have graced dinner plates. The 'Big Five' of gastronomy—taste, aroma, texture, succulence and colour—are all carefully interwoven in Jurgen's cuisine at GiGi's, Izulu's à la carte restaurant. Guests looking for less formal dining can grab light lunches at Palm Courtyard or on the terrace under the South African sky. The cherry-hued breakfast room does a full English breakfast or early-morning treats off the menu. Other facilities include a thatch-and-stone banqueting hall which is ideal for romantic weddings, an intimate chapel and a fully-equipped conference centre. Izulu is the Zulu word for 'heaven', and Hotel Izulu is indeed a piece of heaven on earth.

PHOTOGRAPHS COURTESY OF HOTEL IZULU.

FACTS		
ROOMS	19 suites	
FOOD	GiGi's: international • Palm Courtyard: light lunches	
DRINK	bar • wine cellar	
FEATURES	spa • jacuzzi in each villa • private courtyards • wedding chapel • banquet hall	
BUSINESS	conference facilities • Internet facilities	
NEARBY	Zulu Kingdom • Shakaland • Hluhluwe-uMfolozi Game Reserve • Phinda and St Lucia wetlands • Chakas Rock • Zimbali district • Thompson's Bay • Shakaskraal town • Umhlali town • Tinley Manor • Salt Rock • Sheffield Beach	
CONTACT	Rey's Place, Ballito, KwaZulu-Natal 4420 • telephone: +27.32 946 3444 • facsimile: +27.32 946 3494 • email: info@hotelizulu.com • website: www.hotelizulu.com	

Beverly Hills Hotel

Take a near-perfect sub-tropical climate. Add a warm ocean current and generous stretches of perfect golden beaches. Garnish with lush indigenous vegetation and sprinkle with first-class resorts, then serve to appreciative visitors. With such tantalising ingredients on offer, it is scarcely surprising that South Africa's idyllic KwaZulu-Natal coast continues to tempt pleasure-seekers from all around the world. This idyllic playground is a fitting location for the luxurious Beverly Hills Hotel.

Situated in Umhlanga Rocks, the Beverly Hills Hotel combines opulence with genuine warmth in a way achieved by very few hotels. Dramatic ocean views and elegant furnishings are complemented by thoughtful details such as crisp linen, a refreshment centre in every room and quietly attentive staff. With such pampering, it takes only a short time to unwind and truly begin to relax.

Your sense of well-being is further enhanced by the hotel's spectacular dining facilities. The Terrace is an ideal place for an

THIS PAGE (CLOCKWISE FROM TOP):
Suite dreams...stylish fittings and sumptuous comfort are a signature of the Beverly Hills Hotel; a mere step from the soft, sandy beach, the hotel offers spectacular sunset views; the splendid dining room is the epitome of relaxed elegance.

OPPOSITE: *The sweeping staircase in the hotel lobby brings guests to their rooms in style.*

...the Beverly Hills Hotel combines opulence with genuine warmth in a way achieved by very few hotels.

apéritif, while The Sugar Club Restaurant is an excellent venue to adjourn to for dinner. Classic, contemporary cuisine with an eclectic twist is served, featuring fresh seafood from the area. For a relaxed dining experience, elements café bar, situated on the lower terrace, is the perfect venue to meet friends for a casual get-together. Sunday lunch at the Beverly Hills has become something of a legend. Not only is the food served delectable, the view from the restaurant is a splendid one and is guaranteed to make any meal enjoyed at Beverly Hills Hotel unforgettable.

The beach is right at the doorstep of Beverly Hills, and offers guests the perfect opportunity to go for leisurely walks and to soak up the glorious African sun. Hotel staff will even set up loungers on the beach especially for you. More adventurous guests may want to venture further afield and take advantage of the many exciting outdoor and sporting activities offered in the area. These include deep-sea fishing, dolphin watching and microlight flights. For the more energetic, a gym is available on the lower level, and excellent golf courses are nearby. Those in search of nature can head for game reserves teeming with birds and wildlife. The historical and cultural attractions of Durban, such as its Indian quarter, are also within easy reach of the hotel.

The Beverly Hills is also a superb business venue. Two executive meeting rooms offer the best in modern technology and a full range of auxiliary services, such as a florist, photographers, chauffeurs and translators to ensure the success of meetings and seminars, with experienced and professional staff always on hand.

In short, the Beverly Hills Hotel promises the discerning guest a truly sublime combination of spectacular sea views, unabashed luxury, state-of-the-art facilities and friendly service on one of the world's most beautiful coastlines.

FACTS		
ROOMS	73 standard rooms • 7 junior standard rooms • 7 cabanas • 3 cabana suites • 4 suites • 2 Presidential Suites	
FOOD	The Sugar Club Restaurant: classic contemporary • elements café bar: casual	
DRINK	pool terrace • lounge	
FEATURES	beachfront location • swimming pool • gym • curio shop	
BUSINESS	2 meeting rooms • business centre with 24-hour complimentary Internet access	
NEARBY	Gateway Shopping Centre • La Lucia Mall • uShakamarine • dolphin viewing • microlighting • Sharks Board • Umgeni River Bird Park	
CONTACT	Lighthouse Road, Umhlanga Rocks, KwaZulu-Natal 4320/PO Box 71, Umhlanga Rocks 4320 • telephone: +27.31 561 2211 • facsimile: +27.31 561 3711 • email: beverlyhills@southernsun.com • website: www.southernsun.com	

PHOTOGRAPHS COURTESY OF SOUTHERN SUN HOTELS.

Selborne Hotel, Spa + Golf Estate

uests at Selborne Hotel, Spa and Golf Estate, especially golf enthusiasts, will find themselves in paradise. Just outside Durban and a stone's throw from the Indian Ocean, this was the first golf estate in South Africa.

Selborne has a rich history. The Victorian manor house which forms the main section of the hotel was built in 1954 by sugar magnate Vernon Crookes. In the 1970s, the entire property was converted into a cattle farm before becoming a golf course in 1985. The lodge as it is today was created in the late 1980s, when the manor was turned into a guest house, and a further nine suites and a conference centre were added.

The sprawling championship golf course has been hailed as one of the most spectacular in South Africa. A top priority when designing the course was to leave the indigenous coastal forest intact. The course meanders through clumps of indigenous vegetation and rocky outcrops, and is frequently visited by a variety of antelope. Golfers seeking to sharpen their game can enjoy the services of a golf pro in a dedicated indoor golf academy. Equipment, attire and a range of other paraphernalia are available at the in-house pro shop.

A myriad of other activities are also on offer. Swim in the hotel's luxurious pools or

THIS PAGE (FROM TOP): Selborne Hotel, Spa and Golf Estate is housed in a restored Victorian manor house that is now the main lodge, with a golf course which is incorporated into the indigenous coastal vegetation; the rooms in the hotel are elegant and tasteful.

OPPOSITE: The golf course is rated amongst the most stunning in South Africa. Dramatic coastal scenery frames manicured greens, and the calls of countless birds are the only sounds you will hear.

The sprawling championship golf course has been hailed as one of the most spectacular in South Africa.

sunbathe on one of the poolside's many large, comfortable loungers. Beach lovers may want to use the complimentary shuttle to make their way to Selborne's Private Beach Club on the shores of the Indian Ocean, which boasts a wide range of facilities.

Back at the hotel, forest trails take you through the most beautiful sections of the grounds, where you will spot over 150 species of South African birds, such as the purple-crested lourie or the gregarious hadeda. Nature guides from the hotel will be happy to accompany you on a walk.

At the Health and Beauty Centre, you will be pampered from head to toe. Choose between relaxing at the fully-equipped spa or down at the Beach Club, where the sound of waves adds to the tranquillity.

Accommodation comprises 49 exquisite suites and rooms. A number of suites offer breathtaking views of the golf course and grounds, while the Presidential Suite overlooks the signature 18th hole.

Cuisine here will delight any food connoisseur. The hotel's fine dining restaurant serves the best of South African produce prepared in a fusion of culinary styles, and the coffee bar is ideal for a casual meal. Known for its discreet and personal service, Selborne is sure to please.

FACTS		
ROOMS	3 double rooms • 36 garden rooms • 9 garden suites • 1 Presidential suite	
FOOD	restaurant: South African and international • coffee bar: casual	
DRINK	hotel pub • lounge	
FEATURES	pool • sundeck • golf course • golf academy • pro shop • floodlit tennis courts • Health and Beauty Centre • Beach Club • walking trails • wedding chapel	
BUSINESS	conference centre	
NEARBY	golf courses • Durban city • Pietermaritzburg and Howick Falls • watersports facilities • Wild Coast Casino • uKhalamba Drakensberg Park • St Lucia Wetlands	
CONTACT	PO Box 2, Pennington, KwaZulu-Natal 4184 • telephone: +27.39 688 1800 • facsimile: +27.39 975 1811 • email: reservations@selborne.com • website: www.selborne.com	

PHOTOGRAPHS COURTESY OF SELBORNE HOTEL, SPA + GOLF ESTATE.

northern**cape**+**north**west**province**

Botswana

Namibia

Madikwe Game Reserve •

> Jaci's Tree Lodge
> Jaci's Safari Lodge
> Makanyane Safari Lodge
> Mateya Safari Lodge
> Etali Safari Lodge

Pilanesberg Nature Park •

• Mafikeng

• Kgalagadi Transfrontier Park

Northwest Province

Gauteng

> Tswalu Kalahari Reserve

Kuruman •

Kalahari

• Augrabies Falls National Park

Free State

Kimberley •

Orange River

Northern Cape

Lesotho

• Namaqua National Park

Eastern Cape

Great Karoo

place of the ancients

The Northern Cape and neighbouring Northwest Province are vast expanses of arid wilderness which form one of southern Africa's most bewitching destinations. These provinces, forming in themselves only a part of the even more extensive system of ancient 'sand seas' of Namibia and the Botswanan Kalahari, make their impact on the senses as a minimalist symphony of browns, creams, beiges and ochres.

This is a place of immense distances and blazing starlit nights, strange hot gusting winds roaring out of the interior, dozens of strangely adapted plants (including one that lives underground), and a seemingly endless array of desert environments, many of which are amongst the earth's most botanically rich.

Some idea of the great size of these regions may be gauged from the fact that the Northern Cape province alone comprises a third, or 361,830 sq km (139,706 sq miles)—of the entire surface of South Africa, yet it houses less than a million of the country's 48 million souls. Further, in a fascinating paradox, not only do these empty wastelands offer some of modern travel's rarest experiences, but a remarkably long list of them. Each of the five lyrically named regions of the Northern Cape—the Kalahari, the Diamond Fields, the Karoo, the Namakwa and the Green Kalahari—holds its own secrets, miracles and wonders, all well worth taking the time to find.

diamonds on the soles of your shoes

The Diamond Fields and Karoo regions of the Northern Cape are as good a place as any to commence a sojourn here, as this was the scene in 1871 of the great diamond rush of thousands to the centre of this dry plain in search of wealth. In the case of the town that was to become Kimberley, a seemingly insignificant little hillock (kopje in Afrikaans) called Colesberg Kopje was the eroded stump of a giant extinct volcano. Underneath its innocent mound lay unimaginable wealth, which, as Kimberly itself developed in a diggers' frenzy, eventually was to become the monopoly of one of the 19th century's most significant mining operators, Cecil John Rhodes.

PAGE 128: The dramatic sand seas of the Kalahari.

THIS PAGE (FROM TOP): The slow turn of a desert windmill marks the hours in the timeless landscape of the Karoo; these desert and semi-desert wildernesses have an endless range of small, hardy residents.

OPPOSITE: Purple storm clouds loom ominously over the vast expanse of the Kalahari.

The lure of Kimberley today lies in its fascinating mining history, which is the focus of the excellent Open Mine Museum or Big Hole, which, in the centre of the town, is impossible to miss. This is officially the world's largest hand-dug hole, and a visit to the museum is essential. Many of the original corrugated iron buildings which were hurriedly thrown up in the diamond-digging frenzy have been reassembled here in an atmospheric reconstruction of the early mining camp.

of firewater and aliens

A major feature of the region is its fabulous hospitality. Food and drink are very important here, with both having traditions rooted in hardy frontier life. Menus in these parts are heavy with venison, the famed Karoo lamb and other exotic meats: kudu, springbok, ostrich and warthog—an absolutely delicious option, both tender and tasty—and wholesome vegetables done in old-fashioned style, such as mashed pumpkin or fresh, simply-cooked garden peas.

However, it is with spirits that Kimberley comes into its own. This has got to be the only town anywhere where it is legal to be served a drink at the wheel of your car. This extraordinary situation dates back to the diamond rush days when Rhodes and hordes of others had to ride between the various 'big holes' surrounding the town from which diamonds were being extracted. The famous Half pub in Kimberley was sited exactly half-way along the route that Rhodes would ride each day. The hostelry, sensibly, applied for a license to serve drinks to people on horseback—a privilege it still holds today in respect to cars in lieu of horses. The Half and at least one other pub in Kimberley still retains this unusual licence.

Another 'spirit'-related feature of this region is its famous fruit schnapps, mampoer, which is made in the most remote corners of the country. Often made from peaches, or prickly pear fruit, this delicious, devilishly high-proof liquor is a must for warming the vitals on a cold desert night or when telling stories round a campfire. Perhaps it is also responsible for the higher than usual frequency of UFO sightings here too.

heroes of the struggle

The Star of the West, complete with wooden swing doors straight from the OK Corral, is another atmospheric Kimberley pub to seek out. It is situated on the edge of Kimberley's African township, Galeshewe, one of the oldest in the country. Galeshewe was named after a famous 19th-century chief who determinedly resisted the subordination of his people's ancestral lands to colonisation, and has several other political associations. One of the most famous is that of a contemporary of Mandela's called Robert Sobukwe, a gifted linguist and academic who founded a rival movement to the ANC in the late 1950s called the Pan-Africanist Congress (PAC). Sobukwe too was convicted of illegal political activity in 1960, and was considered so dangerous that, when sent to Robben Island, he was kept in solitary confinement and not allowed contact with the men from the ANC. He spent 6 years in solitary before being released under house arrest to live in Kimberley, where he began studying to be a lawyer, later setting up a practice to assist poorer people in the township.

Kimberley was also home to one of South Africa's most gifted men, Sol Plaatje, linguist, writer and social activist who today is ranked amongst the country's most accomplished authors. He is best known for his role in striving to reverse the extreme Land Act of 1913, which was to form the basis of geographical apartheid for the entire 20th century. Soon after the Act, which decreed that less than one-tenth of the total surface of South Africa be owned by black people, Plaatje embarked upon an international campaign in England and America to raise awareness of the implications of this law for the future of black people in his country. Plaatje's home, on the edge of Galeshewe, is just one of the absorbing historical destinations to be found here.

desert adventure central

Both the Northern Cape and the Northwest Province have remarkable frontier towns which are often used as a base for exploring the vast desert and semi-desert wildernesses of this arid western quadrant. The beautiful oasis town of Kuruman in the

Northern Cape, watered by a pure spring at its centre called The Eye, is always bustling with 4x4 desert vehicles setting off into the Kalahari. Kuruman is also associated with the Victorian explorer and geographer, David Livingstone, who lived at the exquisite mission station here as a young man before embarking on his epic journeys into and across Africa.

the boy scouts of mafikeng

In like manner, the Northwest Province border town of Mafikeng has remarkable historical links of great interest to visitors from around the world. During the Anglo-Boer War, the British force at Mafikeng was under siege by the Boers. A senior British officer in the town, Baden-Powell, came up with the idea for the Boy Scouts when confronted with the problem of how to occupy school-age boys who had little to do under the siege except get into mischief. Cleverly, Baden-Powell devised a programme of activities that actually assisted the siege effort. Boys were employed as scouts to do light support work for the professional soldiers, and also fulfilled a variety of other roles. From this ingenious idea grew the seeds of the international scout movement.

THIS PAGE: Enjoying a light moment in a township.

OPPOSITE: The sparse, humble interior of a rural dwelling; a Northern-Cape style hairdo.

The Northwest Province is extremely varied, both in its terrain and the kind of attractions it offers. Some of southern Africa's most famous game areas such as Madikwe and the Pilanesberg game reserve near the glitzy, high octane resort of Sun City, are found here. Madikwe in particular is noted for its conservation of the predatory wild dog, one of very few species in the animal kingdom that nurture the ill and the aged of their communities. Their hunting methods, in contrast, are sometimes described as being extremely vicious. Wild dog hunt live prey as a highly organised pack, each tearing off mouthfuls of the fleeing prey on the hoof—a method of hunting which in fact results in a much quicker death than by strangulation (leopard) or disembowelling (cheetah).

The province also has many associations with legendary historical figures such as Mzilikazi, a rebel Zulu leader who fled to this region from Zululand with his followers to eventually move northwards and settle in the southern parts of modern Zimbabwe. There was also a major wagon trail westwards through these parts, a route that later also became well-known to anti-apartheid activists fleeing the country across the international border here with Botswana. There are many tales, too, of eccentric loners and phenomenally gifted, charming highwaymen who lurked in this land.

THIS PAGE (FROM TOP): Signpost, Kgalagadi Transfrontier Park; wild dog, the signature species of a magnificent conservation project in the Northwest Province where efforts have been focused on saving this animal from extinction; male lion slaking his thirst. OPPOSITE: The ancient watercourse of the Orange River empties into a dramatic gorge at Augrabies Falls in the Kalahari.

the world's fifth-largest waterfall

Returning to the Northern Cape, one finds the Green Kalahari, which borders Botswana and Namibia, home to one of the earliest transfrontier parks, the vast (almost 4 million hectares [approximately 10 million acres]) Kgalagadi Transfrontier Park. Here one sees the Big Five in an untouched desert environment. A sighting of the pugnacious black rhino, a creature which can be distinguished by its pointed, prehensile lip which is used to twist off the leaves of trees and bushes, is guaranteed here. The black rhino sanctuary is located at Augrabies Falls, the world's fifth-largest waterfall, in a gorge along the Orange River. Scientists at the Augrabies Falls National Park study and guard the precious gene pool of this acutely endangered species.

...the world's fifth-largest waterfall...

Jaci's Tree Lodge

Fans of the Swiss Family Robinson will be enamoured with Jaci's Tree Lodge. However, if one expects a tree house experience as seen in the 1960 Disney movie, with hay beds and rope pulleys, one could not be further from the truth. On the outside, the eight exclusive tree houses of Jaci's Tree Lodge might appear rustic. Each tree house envelops a giant tamboti or leadwood tree, supported by stilts up to 4 metres (13 ft) high. Exteriors of rosewood, thatch and stacking doors blend in with the surrounding vegetation. But the rusticity ends here.

Lush silk cushions and suede furnishings adorn the interiors. Mega-watt colours and South African handicrafts are showcased throughout. From vibrant mosaics to walls etched with native motifs, African arts and crafts are recreated with a passion.

Each bathroom is open-plan, with the focus being is an enormous stone bathtub with handmade copper taps. An outdoor jungle shower awaits, where guests can refresh themselves amidst the natural forest vegetation. The deck in front of each unit is built for the sole purpose of relaxing with a drink in hand, soaking up the South African sun by day and admiring the star-filled sky by night. As if guests need more reason to loll about, the gorgeous bar and lounge are cosy hideouts, kept separate from the dining room by a four-sided open fireplace.

THIS PAGE (CLOCKWISE FROM TOP): **The breakaway lounge showcases the vibrant colour schemes and South African crafts in the lodge; this regal dining setting can be found in the main building; the open-plan bathroom of a tree house suite.**

OPPOSITE (FROM LEFT): **Luxurious tree houses boast exquisite furnishings and ample space; boma dining, a staple of any safari experience.**

Sleeping in a tree house...is as close as kids and grown-ups can get to their idea of paradise.

Getting around this network of tree houses is surprisingly easy. Raised rosewood walkways suspended in the jungle canopy that lines the Marico River link the tree houses to the main lodge and its facilities, which include a spectacularly unique breakaway lounge. Jaci's Tree Lodge also shares facilities with its sister establishment, Jaci's Safari Lodge, which is nearby. On languid, balmy days, the cool water of the forest pool surrounded by the untamed bushveld is particularly inviting.

Guests can see and smell the aroma of freshly-cooked food that signals mealtime at the lodge, and the kitchen has peek-a-boo arches that afford guests the novel experience of witnessing the chef at work. Jaci's Tree Lodge offers the option of dining in a boma, or a braai for the quintessential South African gastronomic experience.

A special feature of Madikwe Game Reserve, where Jaci's can be found, lies in its location in a transition zone on the edge of the Kalahari, where rare animal species

abound. Aside from a myriad of bird species, the brown hyena, water monitor and leopard tortoise have made their home here. It also hosts a flourishing population of frogs, from the foam-nest to banded rubber species.

Jaci's Tree Lodge welcomes children of all ages and makes them feel at home, with facilities and programmes which cater specially to their needs. Sleeping in a tree house right in the middle of this pristine wildlife haven is as close as kids and grown-ups can get to their idea of paradise.

FACTS		
	ROOMS	8 rooms
	FOOD	fire grill, plated or crystal dinners
	DRINK	bar
	FEATURES	forest pool • outdoor shower and stone bathtub • ranger • game drives • bush walks • gym
	BUSINESS	conference venue • facsimile
	NEARBY	Top Ten viewing spots • Johannesburg (3-hr drive) • Sun City (1-hr 15 min drive)
	CONTACT	Jaci's Reservations—Madikwe Game Reserve, Northwest Province • telephone: +27.83 700 2071 • facsimile: +27.14 778 9901 • email: jaci@madikwe.com • website: www.madikwe.com

PHOTOGRAPHS COURTESY OF JACI'S LODGES.

Jaci's Safari Lodge

Jaci's Safari Lodge was constructed around an ancient termite mound, under a grove of old, knotted tamboti trees. Perched on the edge of the Marico River, the lodge sits on prime land in the malaria-free Madikwe Game Reserve. So open is the architecture of the lodge that every room faces a dry river bed, which doubles as a walkway for animals en route to the nearby watering hole.

Shaggy thatched roofs, canvas walls and large tented windows blend in with the surroundings, as do the bathrooms whose walls are constructed from natural rock and house handmade rock baths. In each room, an outdoor 'safari' shower and private wooden observation deck overlook a stream.

THIS PAGE (CLOCKWISE FROM TOP LEFT):
The exterior of the Nare Suite, where the bedroom directly overlooks a private pool; a leopard tortoise makes a good playmate for the kids; a magnificent sunset over the pool and deck area; the open fireplace makes an arresting centrepiece in the main building.

OPPOSITE (CLOCKWISE FROM TOP LEFT):
The viewing deck of the Nare Suite opens out to the private pool and overlooks a watering hole; lions taking a leisurely stroll through the bush; generous king or twin-bedded suites ensure a good night's rest.

Guests in favour of the ultimate in privacy can indulge themselves in the Nare Suite. Christened in honour of the resident buffalo bull which makes regular stops at the watering hole in front of the suite, the Nare is the definitive luxury safari suite, with a viewing deck that almost touches the watering hole and a rock pool. In addition to the luxuries of regular rooms, a stay in the Nare Suite is one of the best ways to enjoy the savannah. On request, meals can be prepared in the self-contained kitchen of the suite, and guests can also choose to feast in the outdoor dining area.

Meals are whipped up in an ultra-modern kitchen in the main complex of Jaci's Safari Lodge, in full view of guests who dine

...every room faces a dry river bed, which doubles as a walkway for animals...

The Marico River wends its way through the reserve, which is prime Top Ten territory: sightings of wild dogs, cheetah, brown hyena and rhino in addition to a wide variety of plains game are commonplace, and over 340 species of bird life reside in the area. Madikwe was created also to provide the indigenous peoples living in the area with a more sustainable environment. In an undertaking which was touted as the largest movement of animals since Noah's Ark, Madikwe became the new home in 1991 for 8,000 heads of game from 28 species. The rare and endangered wild dog is a special attraction here.

At Jaci's, children are always made to feel welcome. Staff dextrously balance children's demands and guests' need for privacy. Children are treated to game drives, and when they are back in the lodge, child minders take over. Adults and parents can enjoy their holiday with peace of mind, while the kids have a ball.

against an uninterrupted backdrop of the bush. South African dishes cooked over an open fire are served in a boma, or under a blanket of stars at the bush braai.

PHOTOGRAPHS COURTESY OF JACI'S LODGES.

FACTS		
	ROOMS	8 rooms • Nare Suite
	FOOD	starlight, plated or bush braai dinners
	DRINK	upstairs bar
	FEATURES	pool • outdoor showers • rock bathtub • ranger • game drives • bush walks • gym
	BUSINESS	conference venue • facsimile
	NEARBY	Top Ten viewing spots • Johannesburg (3-hr drive) • Sun City (1-hr 15 min drive)
	CONTACT	Jaci's Reservations—Madikwe Game Reserve, Northwest Province • telephone: +27.83 700 2071 • facsimile: +27.14 778 9901 • email: jaci@madikwe.com • website: www.madikwe.com

Makanyane Safari Lodge

A stay at Makanyane Safari Lodge offers total immersion into the great African wilderness. Situated on 1,800 hectares (4,450 acres) of private land in the midst of Madikwe Game Reserve, this lodge is the latest in safari chic. It blends seamlessly into the surrounding bush, yet pampers guests with luxurious facilities and services.

With a capacity of just 16 guests, Makanyane Safari Lodge affords each of its eight one-bedroom thatched suites true seclusion. Rooms are situated along a shady path that winds through the bush, and are well hidden from each other. Thanks to the clear glass walls in each suite, guests have unobstructed views of the Marico River and the surrounding forest. Attached outdoor showers afford you the novel chance to bathe amidst the natural surroundings. Alternatively, you can throw open the folding doors of the bathroom to usher in the many sights and sounds of Madikwe while you soak luxuriously in the freestanding tub.

The main lodge, which houses the lounge, dining room, library and curio shop, is dramatically positioned to overlook a ravine. The interior design borrows from nature. Ancient leadwood trees, rock fireplaces and thatched roofs ensure the building integrates naturally with its surroundings.

THIS PAGE (CLOCKWISE FROM TOP):
Each suite has an open-plan bathroom and freestanding bathtub; one of the lodge's regular visitors—you might not need to get out of bed to view big game; the tantalising infinity-edged pool appears to spill over into the surrounding bush.

OPPOSITE: Floor-to-ceiling glass walls provide uninterrupted views of the luxuriant bush and its inhabitants.

Guests are given the fullest opportunities to observe wildlife at Makanyane. A prime spot for animal watching is the infinity-edged swimming pool that seems to flow over into the surrounding bush, and game are often seen drinking from the stream-fed watering hole below. On the upper level of the main lodge is an elevated den, which offers panoramic views of the wilderness. Massage treatments can be provided al fresco; guests may choose to have their treatments on the private deck of their suite or out in the wilderness at the sleep-out hide.

Dinner is served outdoors amongst the trees in a lantern-lit boma. On the menu is Executive Chef David Stevens' brand of Euro-African fare, prepared with fresh local produce. House wines are included in the room rate, but wine connoisseurs may opt for other South African labels from the cellar. Guests may also feast on the spread available at Makanyane's bush barbecues and breakfasts served out in the bush.

At Makanyane, the wildlife are the stars of the show. The sprawling South African bush can be explored by 4x4 drive or on foot, guided by an experienced ranger. Rustic hideouts and lookouts are scattered across Makanyane's private grounds, where guests can sip cocktails while observing herds of grazing waterbuck, zebra, impala and a host of other animals.

Perhaps the ultimate safari experience, however, is a night under the starry skies. Guests can set up a bed on the upper deck of a bush-concealed hide, and be lulled to sleep by the nocturnal sounds of the African bush.

PHOTOGRAPHS COURTESY OF MAKANYANE SAFARI LODGE.

FACTS		
ROOMS	8 suites	
FOOD	indoor and outdoor dining areas and boma: European and African fusion	
DRINK	wine cellar	
FEATURES	private lounge • sundeck • infinity-edged pool • indoor and outdoor showers and freestanding bathtub in all suites • rangers on staff • hide-outs and lookouts • indoor and outdoor spa treatments • library • curio shop • gym	
NEARBY	game-viewing spots • Johannesburg (50 mins by air, 3.5 hrs by car)	
CONTACT	Krokodildrift 87KP, Madikwe Game Reserve, Northwest Province • telephone: +27.14 778 9600 • facsimile: +27.14 778 9611 • email: enquiries@makanyane.com • website: www.makanyane.com	

Mateya Safari Lodge

THIS PAGE (CLOCKWISE FROM TOP): *The magnificent sculpture in the main lounge sets the tone for the rest of the lodge; suite interiors are luxuriously decorated with handcrafted mahogany furnishings; the library is a treasure trove of rare 19ᵗʰ-century African literature.*
OPPOSITE: *Watch a brilliant sunset while you dine at the Fire Core, the lodge's boma.*

It is hard to imagine something quite so decadent in the middle of 75,000 hectares (185,300 acres) of wild bush land. Mateya Safari Lodge is a lavish property tucked in the historical Madikwe Game Reserve, which encompasses Stone and Iron Age sites dating back thousands of years.

The lodge is nestled in the Gabbro Hills overlooking the Reserve, and is furnished in rich shades of amber, saffron and bronze. Original pieces of traditional African art are scattered in both public and private areas. Kenyan sculptor Robert Glen's *Near Miss*, a bronze sculpture of an agile lioness reaching for a leaping impala, is the centrepiece of the main lounge, while a regal bronze bust of Queen Mateya, the lodge's namesake, presides over the reception area.

The lodge's five suites are arranged in a radial configuration around one of the hills to maximise game-viewing opportunities from the suites' private infinity-edged pool decks and natural window salas. The rustic façades of the suites, designed to blend seamlessly with their natural surroundings, belie the creature comforts within.

Each suite comes with handcrafted mahogany furnishings, Egyptian cotton linen and a four-poster bed. Guests can choose to go au naturel when taking outdoor showers, soak in the raised marble tub or retreat to the relative safety of the indoor shower.

...regal style is combined with the untamed beauty of the wilderness...

Part of the royal treatment here is having rangers at one's beck and call. Bush walks and game drives in the lodge's 4x4 can be arranged according to your preferences. There are never more than four privileged guests per game party to allow for space, personal attention and total flexibility in itinerary and schedule. The seven gems of the African bush—buffalo, cheetah, elephant, leopard, lion, wild dog, black and white rhino—are common sightings, and guests are also often rewarded with the sight and sounds of over 350 bird species. Bush picnic lunches can be a pleasant additional option to a safari outing.

Back at the lodge, African fusion cuisine is served in the glass-walled dining room overlooking the plains. A more intimate option is room service, laid out under the stars, on the private pool deck of your suite. Dinner at the Fire Core, a circular boma, has the chef demonstrating his culinary prowess over a crackling fire. Those who favour privacy can book the wine cellar, with its impressive selection of wines, for a clandestine meal, and enjoy brandy and cigars in a dedicated section of the cellar.

At the end of a day spent tracking wildlife, the library, with its leather armchairs and rare works of 19th-century African literature, is inviting. A gym awaits those with more energy to expend, while a wellness centre offers head massages, hot stone therapies and other relaxing treatments.

At Mateya Safari Lodge, regal style is combined with the untamed beauty of the wilderness, making a stay here unforgettable.

PHOTOGRAPHS COURTESY OF MATEYA SAFARI LODGE.

FACTS		
	ROOMS	5 suites
	FOOD	dining room and Fire Core boma: African fusion • private dining • picnic lunches
	DRINK	wine cellar with brandy and cigar corner: French and South African wines
	FEATURES	library • infinity-edged pools • indoor and outdoor showers and freestanding bathtub in all suites • ranger services • wellness centre • gym • curio shop
	BUSINESS	business centre
	NEARBY	Johannesburg (3.5 to 4 hrs by car)
	CONTACT	PO Box 21, Derdepoort 2876 • telephone: +27.14 778 9200 • facsimile: +27.14 778 9201 • email: info@mateyasafari.com • website: www.mateyasafari.com

Etali Safari Lodge

Discover the natural way to health and beauty at Etali Safari Lodge. Situated in Madikwe Game Reserve in the Northwest Province, this lodge combines the traditional safari with a heavenly spa experience.

The highlight of this exceptional lodge is undoubtedly its Wellness Centre. Here, holistic therapies will rejuvenate your mind, body and spirit. Upon entering the spa, you are greeted with a cup of herbal tea. Soothing background music and aromas instantly create the right mood. A stylish interior decorated with organic elements such as wood, stone and water evoke the tranquillity of nature.

Enjoy Etali's signature spa treatment that begins with a deep massage against the glow of scented candles. After your muscles are completely relaxed, a textured body scrub is applied to exfoliate your skin. While enjoying the scrub, pamper yourself with a facial and scalp massage. This supreme indulgence of the senses is rounded off with an aromatherapy steam sauna and a shower.

Luxuriate in the spa's other tantalising spa packages as well. Roll around in the mud with Etali's Warthog Hour, a fun and revitalising private mud bath. When your body has soaked up the mud's beneficial nutrients, slough off the mud and slide into a bath for two with a glass of fruit tea or, if you prefer, South African bubbly.

Guests who want a spa treatment in the privacy of their suite will find the Essence package just perfect. This package comes in two parts. First, a warm herbal bath is specially prepared for you to soak in. Then,

...this lodge combines the traditional safari with a heavenly spa experience.

a portable plinth is brought to your open-air deck for you to stretch out on while a therapist slowly massages away any tension knots that remain in your body.

For an all-day spa treatment, try Innersence. It begins with an invigorating mud treatment, followed by a sensuous shower for two. Relax as a manicurist trims and polishes your nails, and then take a break for lunch or dinner. After your meal, end the treatment with a languorous massage in the privacy of your suite.

There are only eight suites at Etali, set apart for total exclusivity and decorated with cool, earthy tones. Each suite's bathroom is designed to double as an exquisite spa treatment room so that couples may enjoy

spa packages in complete privacy. A whirlpool on your deck is the perfect spot to laze in between treatments, and an outdoor shower allows you to bathe while gazing at antelopes or a fiery sunset.

The cuisine at Etali is an exotic fusion of African and Asian. Organically-grown vegetables, fruit and herbs are staples, and the chef uses only the best local produce in season. There is no set menu, and every meal is a gastronomic surprise. Weight-

THIS PAGE (FROM TOP): Etali Safari Lodge's sun terrace is perfect for enjoying a tall, cool drink while gazing out at the African bush; giant stone jars line the lodge's entrance like sentinels.

OPPOSITE: Etali's open design allows guests to get up close and personal with the animals. Here, an elephant takes a drink from the private pool of a suite.

conscious guests will find plenty of healthy fare here. Meals are light, fruit and vegetable juices are served all day and tasty low-fat or low-carb options are available.

Should you decide to tear yourself away from the lodge, Madikwe Game Reserve offers plenty to see. Designated a game reserve in 1991, Madikwe covers a pristine 75,000 hectares (185,330 acres) of wilderness and is one of the largest game reserves in South Africa. The reserve consists of different habitats—vast plains of open woodlands and grasslands, rugged mountain ranges and rocky hills. Since the replenishing of Madikwe's native animal stock in 1991, more than 8,000 animals from 28 species have been introduced in the largest game translocation exercise in the world at that time.

The beauty of Madikwe Game Reserve can be savoured through a full range of safari activities at Etali. Game drives with an experienced ranger will take you up close to

THIS PAGE (CLOCKWISE FROM TOP):
Elegant, contemporary fittings in muted tones complement the lodge's more rustic features as well as the bush landscape; the outdoor dining area by the main pool catches the last rays of the evening sun; large comfortable beds lined with crisp linen promise guests a good night's sleep.

There is no set menu, and every meal is a gastronomic surprise.

leopards, rhinoceroses, lions, elephants and giraffes. The world's most endangered canine, the African wild dog, is frequently seen here. Over 300 species of birds have been spotted, and more are believed to exist. If you have time for only one game drive, make it the sunset drive to the watering hole. Hordes of game throng the place at this hour, feeding, bathing and preying.

To explore the bush at a more leisurely pace, opt for one of Etali's bush walks. Led by knowledgeable local guides, these walks reveal a treasure trove of secrets about the land, its flora and smaller creatures. Learn about the medicinal value of bush plants and the magical powers attributed to them. Identify grass and bird species and taste the bittersweet fruit of the maroela tree, which is used to produce juice, jam and beer.

Etali means 'a new beginning' in Lingala. With all that this superb safari lodge has to offer, a new beginning certainly awaits you each and every day.

MARINATED LAMB LOIN ON A BED OF ROASTED MINT VEGETABLES WITH BLUEBERRY SAUCE
Serves 4

800 g (1 lb 12¼ oz) lamb loin, deboned (allow 200 g per person)
Marinade
10 g (¼ oz / ⅛ cup) ginger, grated
4 cloves garlic, chopped
2 sprigs fresh rosemary
150 ml (5 fl oz / ⅝ cup) olive oil
100 ml (3⅜ fl oz / ⅜ cup) balsamic vinegar
50 ml (1¾ fl oz / ¼ cup) soya sauce
Vegetables
200 g (7 oz) carrots
200 g (7 oz) baby marrow
100 g (3½ oz) fine beans
1 red pepper
1 yellow pepper
2 butternut pumpkins
50 ml (1¾ fl oz / ¼ cup) extra virgin olive oil
50 ml (1¾ fl oz / ¼ cup) raspberry vinegar
20 g (¾ oz) chopped fresh mint leaves
10 crushed peppercorns and salt to taste
Sauce
1 L (2 pt 1⅞ fl oz / 4¼ cups) lamb stock
400 g (14 oz) blueberries in brine
40 g (1⅜ oz / ¼ cup) butter
handful of basil leaves

Marinade Mix all the marinade ingredients together in a bowl. Marinate the lamb in the mixture for at least 2 hours or longer if desired.

Heat a griddle pan and sear and seal marinated lamb on all sides. Place on a baking tray. Preheat oven to 180 °C (356 °F). Bake lamb for 8 minutes.
Vegetables To prepare roasted mint vegetables, cut carrots, baby marrow, fine beans, red and yellow peppers and butternut pumpkins into bite-size pieces. Drizzle vegetables with olive oil and raspberry vinegar, and sprinkle with mint. Roast in oven until done but still crisp. Season to taste with peppercorns and salt.
Sauce To prepare blueberry sauce, bring lamb stock to a boil and simmer until reduced by half. Drain the blueberries and discard the brine. Add blueberries to the sauce, reduce further until sauce thickens, and whisk in butter.
To serve Slice lamb into 1-cm (½-inch) thick pieces and arrange on bed of roasted mint vegetables. Drizzle with blueberry sauce. Deep-fry the basil leaves. Garnish with deep-fried basil and serve with a starch of your choice.

FACTS	ROOMS	8 suites
	FOOD	dining room: African and Asian fusion
	DRINK	wine cellar
	FEATURES	Wellness Centre • private whirlpools and decks • pool
	BUSINESS	Internet facilities
	NEARBY	woodland, grassland and mountain habitats • watering hole • Big Five and other game-viewing spots • bird-watching spots • giant termite mounds
	CONTACT	Tshukudi Area in Madikwe Game Reserve, Northwest Province • telephone: +27.12 346 0124 • facsimile: +27.12 346 0163 • email: info@etalisafari.co.za • website: www.etalisafari.co.za

PHOTOGRAPHS COURTESY OF ETALI SAFARI LODGE.

Tswalu Kalahari Reserve

THIS PAGE (CLOCKWISE FROM TOP LEFT):
*The cosy interior of one of six
bedrooms in Tswalu Kalahari
Reserve's Tarkuni lodge, which
sleeps a total of 12 guests;
a suite or legae in the Motse,
the Reserve's cluster of suites;
the expansive verandah of the
family suite at the Motse
which overlooks the Reserve's
main watering hole.*

OPPOSITE: *The dining area at
Tarkuni, with a private
swimming pool and deck.*

The Kalahari's fame has spread far beyond South Africa. Located in the wide open reaches of the Northern Cape, the Kalahari is an expanse of red and white sands that is home to an amazing array of fauna and flora.

Amidst this spectacular landscape sits Tswalu Kalahari Reserve. Founded in 1995 by Englishman Stephen Boler, the reserve was bought over in 1998 by the Oppenheimers, a diamond-mining family, following Boler's death. Covering 100,000 hectares (247,100 acres), it allows guests to view wild animals in their natural habitat.

Tswalu means 'new beginning' in the Tswana language, and Tswalu Kalahari Reserve certainly opens up new possibilities. Providing luxurious accommodation for guests while remaining firmly committed to conservation in this protected area, Tswalu is a model for eco-tourism in today's world.

...Tswalu is a model for eco-tourism in today's world.

Tswalu's accommodation is ideal for small groups and families. The Motse is a cluster of eight legaes or suites, and the entire cluster can accommodate a maximum of 20 people. Six of the legaes are for two guests each, while two legaes were designed with families in mind, each accommodating four people. Walls are made from compacted desert sand, and roofs are thatched to blend in with the surroundings. Each legae overlooks the reserve's main watering hole, which at certain times of the day and night, teems with wild animals and birds.

For total exclusivity, book Tarkuni. Available for a maximum of 12 people, this lodge comprises six beautiful bedrooms, a lounge, dining room, patio and heated swimming pool. Children are also well catered for. Two bunk beds are included, as are nannies' rooms. A chef is on hand to prepare meals according to your taste, which are served at your leisure.

A multitude of outdoor activities awaits. Open-sided safari vehicles take you on game drives, during which you might find yourself staring at a Kalahari lion or desert black rhino. For those who want to venture where a vehicle cannot go, horseback rides and bush walks with local guides are available. Discover the many secrets that the Kalahari holds, such as bush medicines and the hunting methods of the San community. To refresh yourself, sit down to a bush meal or take a break in Lekgaba Outlook. As day fades, join your fellow guests for regular sundowners on Namakwari's lantern-lit dunes.

FACTS		
	ROOMS	Motse: 8 suites • Tarkuni: 6 bedrooms
	FOOD	dining area and boma: African • Lekgaba Outlook: personal chef
	DRINK	wine cellar
	FEATURES	outdoor heated pool • children's room with child minder • library • gift shop • private game vehicle • telescope for stargazing • private plane
	NEARBY	abundant wildlife • watering holes • meerkat colonies • Moffat Mission • Kuruman Eye fountain • caves • archaeological sites • Sishen Golf Club
	CONTACT	PO Box 1081, Kuruman 8460 • telephone: +27.53 781 9234 • facsimile: +27.53 781 9238 • email: res@tswalu.com • website: www.tswalu.com

PHOTOGRAPHS COURTESY OF TSWALU KALAHARI RESERVE.

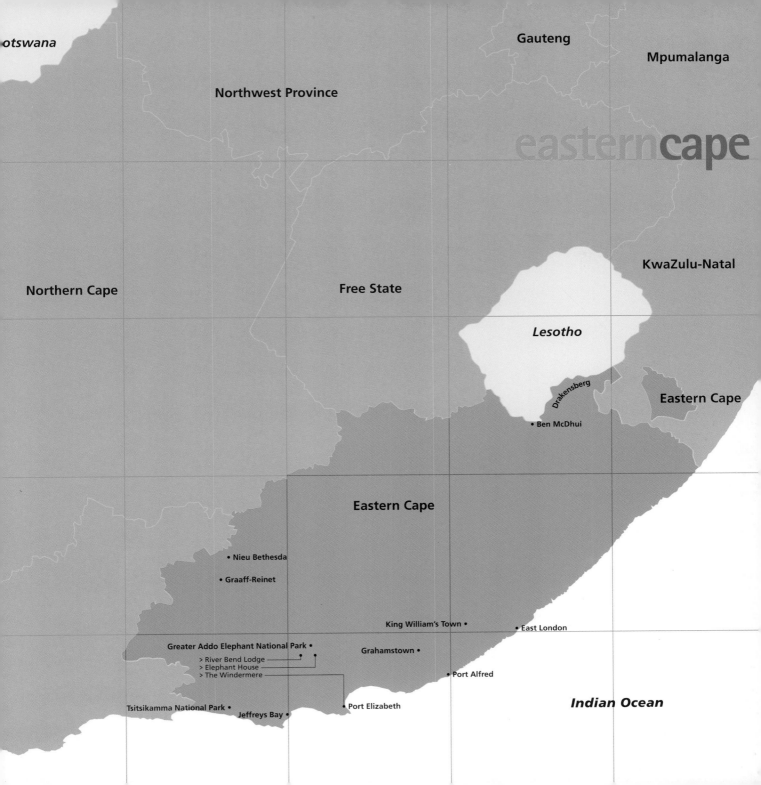

the home of cool

The Eastern Cape region of South Africa is poorly understood, largely because it is often overshadowed by the glamour of its neighbouring province, the Western Cape. Yet not only is the Eastern Cape host to some of the most exquisite sectors of the country's world-famous Garden Route, on which the Storms River mouth and thicketed Tstitsikamma Mountains can be found, but also a truly exceptional—even for South Africa—variety of irresistible lures for everyone from keen fossil hunters to hardcore surfers and the average five year-old intent on a day spent hunting for shells on the beach.

And as if that were not enough, the Eastern Cape is also the birthplace of political giant Nelson Mandela. In fact, not only is this area home to Madiba—a word which denotes his clan—as he is popularly known, but also to an awe-inspiring panoply of other truly eminent leaders and political thinkers.

birthplace of political genius

Many prominent anti-apartheid figures were nurtured in the Eastern Cape. Aside from Nelson Mandela, an even earlier political luminary from this region was Govan Mbeki, father of South Africa's second elected president Thabo Mbeki. Mbeki senior also spent many years on Robben Island, forming part of the 'senior guard' in the famous maximum security jail who were given the responsibility by the ANC leadership in exile for the tutoring and mentoring of younger political prisoners in many areas of knowledge such as history, philosophy, political theory and other topics. This was the famous 'university', which resulted in many prisoners completing distance-learning degrees, and thus being well-equipped to take up leadership roles upon their release.

An impressive range of key political figures followed Mbeki senior, including two of the most important figures, other than Mandela, to have shaped South Africa's late 20th-century history: the scholarly Oliver Tambo and Mandela's political mentor, the retiring Walter Sisulu. Unlike the other great political personalities of the province who attended mission schools in the region, Sisulu had very little formal schooling.

PAGE 152: The Storms River Mouth is one of South Africa's most enchanting waterscapes.

THIS PAGE: Hands across the apartheid divide. Nelson Mandela, who hails from the Eastern Cape, shakes hands with the last president of the apartheid regime, FW de Klerk.

OPPOSITE: A bungee jumper takes a heart-stopping plunge from a crane basket suspended high above the ground.

Sisulu had travelled to Johannesburg to seek work, where he became involved in trade unionism and social activism. Happily married to an equally committed wife, Albertina, who was also from the Eastern Cape, Sisulu developed unique and novel approaches to both political theory and practical hands-on social activism, attitudes which profoundly affected Mandela when he arrived in Soweto. Mandela and Sisulu were to be comrades through the turbulent 1950s and early 1960s, and thereafter in the same cell block on Robben Island for over 27 years.

Whilst Mandela and Sisulu faced life imprisonment after their conviction in 1963 for anti-government, pro-democracy political activism, Oliver Tambo, the third member of this gifted trio of leaders, had been instructed to take his family and flee South Africa to head the ANC in exile.

Still later in the early 1960s came the famous name of Robert Sobukwe, founder of the Pan-Africanist Congress (PAC), a rival party to the ANC, followed by student leader Steve Biko, who hailed from the Eastern Cape village of Queenstown. His tragic death in detention as a result of police brutality in 1977 robbed the country of one of its most singular potential leaders. These stories can now be freely explored, where before simply to possess an image of these figures would have resulted in being placed under police surveillance and a possible jail term.

'the most perfect wave in the world'

One of the most exciting aspects of this province is the number of superlatives, ranging from the sublime to the trivial, that it lays claim to. The Eastern Cape has the highest commercial bungee jump in the world; the world's noteworthiest living prehistoric fish; the world's largest pineapple; the Grahamstown Festival, rivalling its inspiration, the famous Edinburgh Festival, in size and atmosphere; and the world's best supertube, according to former world surf champion Shaun Tomson. Here along this exquisite stretch of the country's eastern coastline lie two iconic names for the world of surfing—J-Bay (Jeffreys Bay) and Cape St Francis.

Endowed with cult status as a result of the classic 1970s movie *Endless Summer*, in which hardcore surfer Bruce Brown roamed the world in search of the perfect wave, these two coastal hamlets are known to surfers the world over. In July, one of the international surf calendar's major competitions, the Billabong Pro, takes place at J-Bay, attracting surfing's top names and invoking an orgy of beach-focused activities such as parties, rock concerts and all-night drinking binges where surf and epic waves are the main topics of conversation, followed by equally epic hangovers. And although J-Bay is world-famous for its supertubes, St Francis is the spot to try out Bruce Brown's own favourites—waves which are known as Bruce's Beauties.

In fact, the entire coastline here offers a magnificent array of surf experiences, with Port Elizabeth and Port Alfred high on the list, followed further north by another place of pilgrimage for the faithful, the legendary Nahoon Reef at East London, one of surf's juiciest, most consistent right-handers. Added to this is ocean-based eco-tourism, including sightings of porpoises also making the most of those legendary tubes, whale-watching, and a large number of idyllic safe-bathing beaches. Unsurprisingly with this kind of lifestyle, where each turn of the winding road throws up another curve of golden sand and an irresistible swell, this coastal route attracts the environmentalist, surfer or anyone else looking for a place to relax.

white knuckle country

There is also a particularly high concentration of extreme sports to be sampled mostly, but not exclusively, along the coast. Your options include, at 216 m (709 ft) the world's highest bungee jump off the vertiginous Bloukrans Bridge; bridge swinging, where you swing between two precipitous bridges on a harness; black-water tubing or river kayaking through the Storms River Gorge; swooping on a harness through the high coastal forest canopy, reputedly one of only very few such experiences in the world; hiking and South Africa's only ski resort, Tiffendell, on the slopes of Ben McDhui, which borders the land-locked mountain kingdom of Lesotho.

THIS PAGE: Sandboarding along this endless coastline is addictive, especially at über-trendy surf mecca Jeffreys Bay.

OPPOSITE (FROM TOP): The days of police and army peace-keeping patrols during elections are now but a distant memory; elder statesman Walter Sisulu, Mandela's staunch colleague through the 1950s and 27 years of prison, with his wife and a young member of the family. Steve Biko, anti-apartheid activist and son of the Eastern Cape, remembered.

The highlight of all these is the magnificent Otter Trail, a 42-km (26-mile) hiking trail that is spoken of in reverent tones by many. The trail lies along the margin of land and ocean, leading one out of the hustle and bustle of city life, with only the inquisitive Cape clawless otter and the rest of nature for company. It is invariably booked up at least a year in advance, and cancellations are rare. However, many other equally pleasant trails are much less busy, and more accessible.

a history as old as time

The earth's surface is in continual flux, constantly being built anew and reformed by volcanic eruptions and erosion. Africa is the oldest continent, the ancient core of Earth's earliest landmasses. Here in the Eastern Cape, the riveting story of our planet is, quite literally, laid bare, a situation which has scientists from all over the world coming to these dry valleys to unearth the clues buried in the dust.

The main regions for fossil hunting stretch southwest from a place called Aliwal North, with one of the most enchanting towns in the country, Graaff-Reinet, forming the heart of fossil country. Graaff-Reinet is, in addition to its interest from a fossil hunter's

THIS PAGE: Rural dwellings huddle on verdant, undulating slopes.
OPPOSITE (FROM TOP): A skeleton sculpture resting on a sandy bed; a traditional healer harvesting roots and bulbs for medicinal purposes.

point of view, a very beautiful example of 18th-century town-planning. Most of the town has a preservation order on it, and entering the town is akin to taking a step back in time. Even if one finds fossils of little interest, a visit to the gem of the Karoo, as it is known, with its charming inns and delectable food, should not be missed.

However, in 1938 an event occurred at the sleepy port of East London, about halfway up the Eastern Cape's coast, that shook the scientific world to its core—the discovery of a living fossil, which is a survivor of a species otherwise considered extinct in the great offshore canyons of the ancient East African shore. On a hot December day, Marjorie Courtenay-Latimer, a researcher at East London's small marine museum, was called to the docks to look at an extremely unusual fish that had been caught in a fisherman's net. While its unusual leg-like fins, heavy armour of bony scales and strange brush-like tail looked familiar, she had no idea what it was, but knew it had to be something extraordinary. It turned out to be a coelacanth, a fish thought to have been extinct since prehistoric times. Fittingly named *Latimeria chalumnae*, it is on display in the East London Museum.

the art of a place

Graaff-Reinet and fossil country are in the heart of the eerie and starkly beautiful Karoo semi-desert, which crosses several provinces including the Western and Northern Capes, as well as the Eastern Cape. Much has been written, including some of South Africa's finest literature, about the strange experiences which people have had in these vast, largely uninhabited wastes. These parts, though harsh, do have some water, and many of these literary works focus on the difficulties of frontier farming life and the intense relationships that people have both with each other and the environment.

Undoubtedly the most famous of these authors is writer Olive Schreiner (1855–1920), a very early feminist whose ideas still sound radical today. She published her novel *The Story of an African Farm* under the pseudonym Ralph Iron. Schreiner and her gifted brother have a much-valued legacy both in the areas of

THIS PAGE (FROM LEFT): *The solitude and magnificent scenery draw visitors back to refresh mind, body and soul.*

OPPOSITE (FROM TOP): *In rural communities, women nurture vegetable gardens to keep their homes supplied with food; since 1994 potable water has been brought to millions in rural areas—an immense boon to the well-being and productivity of these remote communities.*

female emancipation and the thorny topic of African political rights at the turn of the 19th century. There can be no better introduction to these timeless, desolate valleys than to dip into the book as a start for your journey to the mysterious Karoo.

Close to Graaff-Reinet lies a tiny, remote hamlet called Nieu Bethesda. This unlikely place was once home to one of South Africa's oddest creative personalities, the Outsider artist Helen Martins. Known as the Owl House, Helen Martins' statue-filled home transports one into a magical world of mermaids, fantastical creatures and remarkable human figures. Martins ended her own life in her home during a bout of illness, surrounded by her much loved creations.

Yet another attraction for the art lover is the Eastern Cape's mesmerising heritage of open-air rock art created by the San. The San were largely overwhelmed by both the migrations of other indigenous peoples to their hunter-gatherer grounds, but more tragically by European settlement. It is only in the post-apartheid period that scholars are beginning to unlock the meaning of these long-neglected images of exceptional power, and to appreciate their incandescent beauty. It is occasionally possible when visiting country hotels or guesthouses in the province to view rock art sites on the properties. However, the government has taken steps in preventing general access to many sites in order to protect the art from vandals. An application to the tourism authorities of the province, however, can connect the visitor to organised tours conducted at sites which have been developed specifically for tourism.

heading back to the land

The Eastern Cape is not best known for Big Five game experiences. However, over the past eight years parts of the province have been successfully conserved, with the long-term view of reintroducing the Big Five once again.

This has now happened, resulting in there being a number of very fine luxury lodges offering excellent game opportunities here. In addition to this, the Greater Addo Elephant National Park offers unrivalled sighting opportunities for the elephant lover.

settling the frontier

In the early 1800s, Britain took over the colony of the Cape from the Dutch as part of an alliance with Holland to prevent Napoleon from gaining control of the strategic port. Thus a drive was launched in England to attract settlers for a scheme to create a string of European-owned farms along the Cape's northern frontier. The campaign sought to attract English people from all strata of society who would represent a wide range of professions. The new settlement was to be a microcosm of English society.

In 1820, several boatloads of people who later became known as the 1820 Settlers began to arrive in this dry, remote region, and the settlement grew to become one of South Africa's prettiest towns, Grahamstown.

With its quintessentially English character, Grahamstown is home to one of the country's top tertiary educational bodies, Rhodes University. Rhodes is well-known for its very high standards and its speciality faculties, including journalism and pharmacology. It was also known as one of the most politically liberal universities, with many of its alumni involved in the anti-apartheid struggle.

party, party, party!

Each freezing July in winter, a mammoth party takes place in sleepy Grahamstown. For seven to ten days, 100,000 people descend on the little town, intent upon being part of an arts festival like no other. The annual National Arts Festival, more often called the Grahamstown Festival, is modelled on the Edinburgh Festival and has become one of the world's top arts events. As with Edinburgh there is an official programme, consisting of important theatrical productions, major art expos, top-rate dance performances and debut performances of major new works by all manner of local and international artists. Many of South Africa's favourite performing artists have been nurtured here at Grahamstown, and the very popular fringe festival, again modelled on Edinburgh's, takes all applicants wanting to perform, resulting in the streets being filled with the wild, wacky and weird.

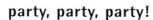

...this coastal route attracts the surfer, environmentalist or anyone else looking for a place to relax.

River Bend Lodge

With so many safari lodges in South Africa today, it is hard to find those that stand out. In the 17,000-hectare (42,000-acre) Greater Addo Elephant National Park, flanked by the majestic Zuurberg Mountains of the Eastern Cape, one manages to do just that.

This is no small claim and is one well earned by River Bend Lodge. The exclusive property offers a complete luxury lodge and African wildlife experience well beyond the traditional African safari. All within the property are a five-star lodge, a health studio, a private nature conservancy, a wildlife rehabilitation centre and a working citrus farm, promising guests a unique experience of the rehabilitated African bush coupled with refined country living.

The lodge itself comprises eight luxurious double suites, each with its own private verandah from where you can lap up views of the bushveld and the open skies. The River Bend Vitality Studio offers soothing massages, rejuvenating facials and beauty treatments administered by an in-house therapist either in a treatment room or the comfort of your suite. Meals too can be taken in your suite or in the dining room. Lunches are often served on the main verandah, which overlooks the property's popular watering hole, or on picnics in the bushveld. Let the chef delight you with his innovative and sensational creations, which taste as good as they look.

At River Bend, great emphasis is placed on conservation and rehabilitation. The

THIS PAGE (FROM TOP): River Bend Lodge is in Greater Addo Elephant National Park, which has the highest concentration of elephants in the world; the Zuurberg Mountain range cradles the park and is home to early Stone Age caves and San paintings.

OPPOSITE: Understated country elegance welcomes guests at River Bend, and is a delightful constrast to the ruggedness of the park.

lodge participates in several breeding programmes and community projects which you have the privilege of viewing, and alternative wildlife activities are on offer. Experienced rangers will take you on wildlife tracking expeditions, game walks and bird-watching trips, in addition to traditional game drives. Game may be viewed in either the Greater Addo Elephant National Park, to which River Bend Lodge has exclusive access, or the property's Private Conservancy and Wildlife Rehabilitation Centre. There is no other corner on earth in which you will find a denser population of elephants. Besides these giants, other frequently-spotted game in the park include lions, leopards, hyenas, rhinos, zebra, buffalo and various types of antelope.

Guests who prefer a more leisurely holiday may choose to visit River Bend's citrus farm or indulge in star-gazing. The Cape region is famous for having some of the clearest skies on the planet, and a telescope is readily available from the lodge. Budding astronomers will delight in identifying constellations of the southern hemisphere. River Bend is also well located for drives to historical Grahamstown and the breathtakingly beautiful Garden Route.

River Bend Lodge redefines what it means to go on an African safari, where elegant country estate accommodation and innovative wildlife activities are combined to create a genuinely unique and unprecedented African bushveld experience.

FACTS		
	ROOMS	8 suites
	FOOD	private chef: New World fusion and Mediterranean
	DRINK	lounge • bar
	FEATURES	pool • watering hole • Vitality Studio • game-drive vehicles
	NEARBY	River Bend Private Conservancy and Wildlife Rehabilitation Centre • River Bend Citrus Farm • Grahamstown • Garden Route
	CONTACT	Greater Addo Elephant National Park, Eastern Cape • telephone: +27.42.233 0161 • facsimile: +27.42 233 0162 • email: reservations@riverbend.za.com • website: www.riverbend.za.com

PHOTOGRAPHS COURTESY OF RIVER BEND LODGE.

Elephant House

Elephants have relished the tranquillity of the Sundays River Valley for thousands of years, and you can share in this pachyderm paradise when you stay at Elephant House. This exclusive thatched lodge is only minutes away from the Greater Addo Elephant National Park, which has one of the highest concentrations of big game in South Africa and almost guarantees you a close encounter with its numerous elephants.

Elephant House is an original mix of English comfort and African charm, with Moorish accents in its thatch and rough plaster. There are eight spacious bedrooms here, luxuriously appointed with antiques, carpets and deep beds. Each room has its own verandah, and the lodge's drawing room leads out onto a wide verandah with enormous sofas. The garden is a visual delight, with arching thorn trees, courtyards and a waterfall.

THIS PAGE (CLOCKWISE FROM TOP):
This nook is characteristic of the lodge's Moorish architecture; bedrooms are embellished with antique furnishings, many of which are from the owners' private collection; this trellised walkway leads from the lodge to its exquisitely-landscaped garden.

OPPOSITE: A roomy verandah looks out onto the well-kept garden at Elephant House.

Elephant House is an original mix of English comfort and African charm...

Along with the relaxing atmosphere, the excellent cuisine is enough to keep one in a languid state. But there is the small matter of elephants, and an excursion to the Greater Addo Elephant National Park is a must. Proclaimed a national park in 1931, this finely-tuned eco-system is today home to more than 400 elephant, as well as buffalo, black rhinoceros, lion, eland, kudu, red hartebeest, zebra and smaller antelope, as well as more than 165 species of birds. Interestingly, Addo is also the last refuge of the flightless dung beetle.

Proposed plans to expand the park will make it one of the most biologically diverse parks in Africa, conserving six of South Africa's seven biomes, a total of 12 vegetation types and South Africa's second-largest elephant and black rhino populations.

Elephant House offers a number of day excursions to various attractions in the area. You can visit the famous Shamwari Game Reserve, a traditional Xhosa village, the

historic St Luke's Church, built in 1895 with beautiful stained-glass windows, and the Moravian mission of Enon. You can also go horseback-riding, bird-watching, hiking, canoeing and boating on the Sundays River, or take a helicopter trip to a deserted beach.

After a hot day in the bush, return to Elephant House for a refreshing dip in the pool or a sundowner on the cool verandah. Evening meals are sumptuous candlelit affairs, prepared with great flair and served with discreet personal attention. And if you are fortunate to visit in September or October, you can enjoy the fragrance of citrus blossoms wafting through the entire valley from fields of citrus orchards.

FACTS		
ROOMS	4 twin rooms • 4 double rooms	
FOOD	dining room: African • poolside lunches	
DRINK	wine cellar	
FEATURES	Moorish architecture • pool • horseback-riding • private game vehicles • bird-watching	
NEARBY	Greater Addo Elephant National Park • Sundays River Valley • Shamwari Game Reserve • Addo Polo Club	
CONTACT	PO Box 82, Addo 6105 • telephone: +27.42 233 2462 • facsimile: +27.42 233 0393 • email: elephanthouse@intekom.co.za • website: www.elephanthouse.co.za	

PHOTOGRAPHS COURTESY OF ELEPHANT HOUSE.

The Windermere

The Windermere is a fashionable boutique hotel that brings to the city of Port Elizabeth a brand new sense of style and occasion. Located in the prestigious waterfront suburb of Humewood with glorious views over Kings Beach, the hotel combines elements of contemporary chic with classic comfort. Port Elizabeth is also the gateway to the Eastern Cape's safari trails and the Garden Route.

When designing the hotel, the owners' brief to the architect was simply this—to create one of the top boutique hotels in the southern hemisphere. And the architect appears to have more than fulfilled this ambitious request. Clean lines and classic shades characterise the décor here, while slate and shale provide a soothing backdrop to modern furniture and lighting.

THIS PAGE (CLOCKWISE FROM TOP):
Curl up with a good book in The Windermere's cosy covered lounge; elegant furnishings make up the bedroom of Suite 101; simple meals can be enjoyed at the hotel's intimate dining area.

OPPOSITE: The contemporary stone façade of the hotel impresses with its clean lines and muted tones.

...the hotel combines elements of contemporary chic with classic comfort.

The rustic texture of stone contrasts beautifully with the smooth marble, ceramic and wood, and the attention to detail is nothing short of exquisite. Every door, window and item of furniture was custom-made for the hotel, and the furnishings in the dining room were all handcrafted by Haldene Martin, hailed as 'Decorator of the Year' in 2004.

There are eight luxury suites here, each outfitted with amenities standard for five-star establishments, such as air-conditioning, heating, telephones, mini-bars, IT ports, CD and DVD players and televisions. The largest suite has a second connecting bedroom, and is ideal for families with children.

It is a short stroll from your suite to one of Port Elizabeth's most beautiful beaches—Kings Beach—named after King George VI and his royal party who swam here in 1947. Kings Beach was recently awarded Blue Flag status, the equivalent of an environmental Oscar, for its pristine condition. Spend lazy days on the beach, or go for a swim at the multi-million rand MacArthur's Baths Pool Complex along the beach promenade. If you want to venture further afield, head to the Greater Addo Elephant National Park for a big game experience. The Windermere will arrange a day-trip to the park, which includes lunch at Elephant House in Sundays River Valley. Return after a day of satisfying game-spotting and enjoy cool sunset drinks on the hotel's spectacular cocktail deck.

You can either dine in the hotel or try one of the many top-rate restaurants nearby. Take a chance with Lady Luck at the Boardwalk Casino, which is a mere 2km (1.2 miles) away, or save your energy for a full round of golf at Africa's only true Lynx golf course, located at the nearby Humewood Country Club.

With the sights and attractions of Port Elizabeth all within easy reach, The Windermere puts the city at your feet in undisputed world-class style.

FACTS		
ROOMS	8 suites	
FOOD	dining room: classic	
DRINK	cocktail deck	
FEATURES	custom-made furnishings • children's facilities • covered parking	
NEARBY	Kings Beach • MacArthur's Baths Pool Complex • Boardwalk Casino • Humewood Country Club • restaurants • bars • shops	
CONTACT	35 Humewood Road, Humewood, Port Elizabeth 6001 • telephone: +27.41 582 2245 • facsimile: +27.41 582 2246 • email: info@thewindermere.co.za • website: www.thewindermere.co.za	

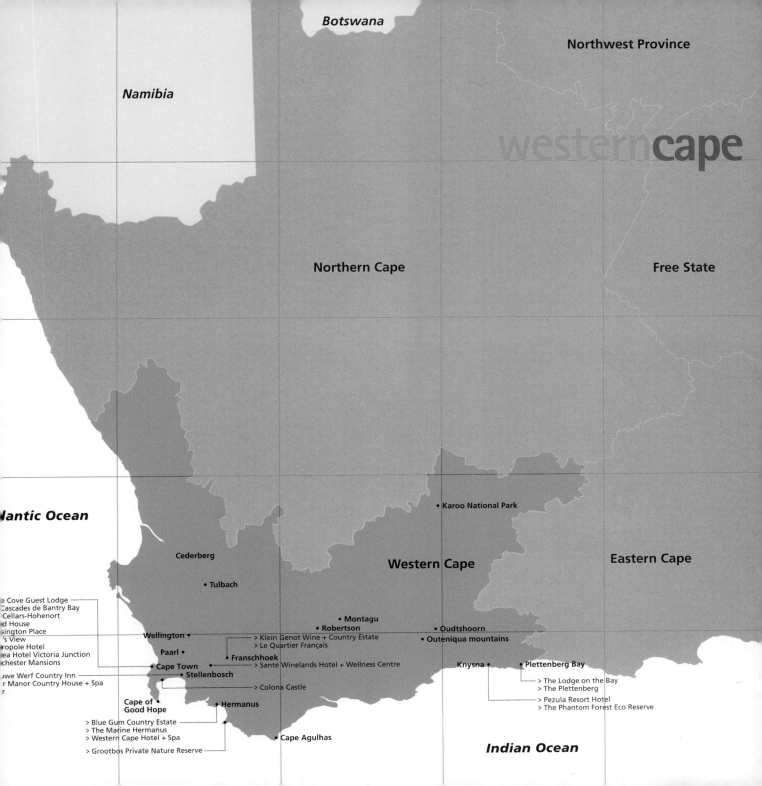

Botswana

Northwest Province

Namibia

western**cape**

Northern Cape

Free State

lantic Ocean

Karoo National Park

Western Cape

Eastern Cape

Cederberg

• **Tulbach**

e Cove Guest Lodge
Cascades de Bantry Bay
Cellars-Hohenort
d House
sington Place
's View
ropole Hotel
ea Hotel Victoria Junction
chester Mansions

uwe Werf Country Inn
r Manor Country House + Spa
r

Wellington •

Paarl •

• **Montagu**
• **Robertson**

> Klein Genot Wine + Country Estate
> Le Quartier Français

• **Oudtshoorn**
• **Outeniqua mountains**

• **Franschhoek**

> Santé Winelands Hotel + Wellness Centre

Knysna •

• **Plettenberg Bay**

• **Cape Town**
• **Stellenbosch**

> Colona Castle

> The Lodge on the Bay
> The Plettenberg
> Pezula Resort Hotel
> The Phantom Forest Eco Reserve

**Cape of
Good Hope**

• **Hermanus**

> Blue Gum Country Estate
> The Marine Hermanus
> Western Cape Hotel + Spa

> Grootbos Private Nature Reserve

• **Cape Agulhas**

Indian Ocean

destination cape town

Forming the southernmost tip of the vast African continent, the Western Cape is at once one of South Africa's most sophisticated and visually breathtaking spots. The legendary 'table top' of Table Mountain can be found here, afire in spring with the majestic king protea, whose blooms are as big as a dinner plate, or shrouded in frigid mists in winter, muting the rustling of the small antelope and countless other wild inhabitants of its steep crags and lush ravines. Aside from its extraordinary backdrop, Cape Town is a feast for the senses. It's a glass of iced chardonnay on a pure white beach, the feeling of sweaty triumph when completing the last few steps of the walk to the top of Table Mountain, or the sudden surge of your horse as it stretches out on the famous riding path along Noordhoek Beach. Cape Town is also the glamour of its annual international fashion week, and the indescribable feeling of freedom when whipping round the bends of Chapman's Peak drive in an open-top car. It is also that unforgettable moment when Nelson Mandela, the world's longest-serving political prisoner, walked out clothed in dignity and freedom from jail on 11 February, 1990.

a place like home

Although the Western Cape has some of southern Africa's most famed sights and attractions, like the rest of the country, the Cape too has altered radically since the advent of democracy in 1994. Cape Town has now become an open secret for travellers, a place whose pleasures are broadcast most effectively by those who have experienced it first-hand and cannot wait to return. Oddly, South Africa, and the Cape in particular, strike a familiar note with a surprisingly wide range of international travellers. English tourists alight in Cape Town to find a wonderful slice of Victoriana, strongly flavoured with the ribald overtones that mark the major port around Table Bay, where they feel right at home. Visitors from mainland Europe are intrigued by the hints they see of over 350 years of contact with Holland, Germany and France in particular. Here as in Europe, food and wine are taken extremely seriously, and everywhere there

PAGE 170: *Blouberg Strand in Cape Town is a glowing symphony of sky and sea.*

THIS PAGE: *This cosy dwelling in a winery near Stellenbosch is a prime example of Cape Dutch architecture.*

OPPOSITE: *Striking aerial view of Cape Town's fashionable Atlantic seaboard.*

are traces of European immigrants who set foot on these shores centuries before. One can see a master jeweller on a street corner whose shop bears a German sign, a road with a French name, or glimpse church belfries and spires which seem to have come straight from the Swiss Alps.

Yet mixed in with these echoes of Europe is another reality—the intoxicating sights and sounds of Asia. Along with the Dutch, who were the first colonial settlers, came many from the islands of Java and Bali as well as other Dutch East India Company (Verenigde Oostindische Compagnie or VOC in Dutch) outposts like Malacca on the west coast of Peninsular Malaysia, and also southern India. They were slaves who were owned by the wealthy officials of the VOC, and with them they brought their culture, religious beliefs, cuisine and exceptional skills in furniture-making and silversmithing. Thus the Cape, as befits its geographical location, looks both east and

west, and all this has given rise in the last 350 years to an utterly unique cultural brew which still holds novelty for both the fiercely loyal inhabitants of the city as well as the increasing numbers of visitors discovering Cape Town for themselves.

the many playgrounds of the cape peninsula

The Cape, however, is much more than glamorous Cape Town. For the visitor, the province can be divided into a variety of distinct regions, each with a selection of its own irresistible pleasures. If it is not the pull of the Atlantic seaboard with its mile upon mile of sun-drenched coastal roads, trendy restaurants and pavements thronging with the well-heeled, it's the lure of the great sheltering arc of False Bay, scudding with flotillas of windsurfers, its coast studded with windswept villages and small harbours, many with waterside restaurants that top gourmets' lists.

As if the Cape did not have enough to offer, it also has a number of highly unusual extreme sports options. One of these is the activity of surfing a giant wave that hits the Cape coast only when certain weather conditions prevail at sea. The other takes place high above the pleasure-seekers on Clifton Beach. Adjacent to Cape Town International Airport is the world's best collection of non-commissioned fighter aircraft. A super-sonic flight in these planes will cost many thousands of US dollars, much of which is to cover the fuel needed.

Then there is the spine of the Table Mountain range which snakes along the peninsula, and on whose leeward side can be found the toniest suburbs with names like Bishopscourt, location of the official home of the Bishop of Cape Town, who in days gone by was Nobel Peace Prize laureate Desmond Tutu, Newlands and Rondebosch. Further along this side of the mountain, one enters huge forested areas, where one glimpses grand homes through the trees beyond imposing gateways and private drives, and where can also be found some of the Cape's oldest vineyards. The ancient name of Constantia is one which was well known

THIS PAGE (FROM TOP): Archbishop Desmond Tutu, peace and anti-apartheid activist, and creator of the eloquent term 'the rainbow nation of god' for the post-apartheid state; the atmospheric streets of the old 17th-century Muslim quarter, the Bo Kaap.

OPPOSITE: The glamorous Clifton Beach is close to one of the Cape's most fashionable districts and fine dining strips; a huge part of Cape Town's appeal lies in the many areas of wild or semi-wild open space that lie between the suburbs and classic urban streetscapes.

in Europe's 18th- and 19th-century salons for its sweet golden wine known as Vin de Constance. Specifically imported for the nobility in many parts of Europe and lauded by such luminaries as writers Jane Austen and Charles Dickens, this heavenly, viscous nectar is now being made again. The wine is in such demand that purchasers are limited to six bottles at a time. The avenues of ancient oaks, manicured hills under vine, exquisite tasting room and stately views at the vineyard make a visit to the cellar well worth the trip, and the wine itself is sufficient reward for the journey.

At the heart of the peninsula is the city centre, nestled against the slopes of Table Mountain and encompassing a kaleidoscope of architectural styles, from spectacular African Art Deco to Victorian whimsy and the pastel painted shop-houses of the 17th-century slave quarter overlooking Table Bay. The town has the layout of a 17th-century European market town, which has prevailed since the Cape was first settled in 1652 by the Dutch. The Dutch established a garden where they grew all manner of plants, fruits and vegetables which were used to supply the ships from all of Europe's maritime powers which plied the trade route to the East. Known as The Company Gardens, this gorgeous park-like space remains, along with a large number of buildings dating from those early times. Cape Town is therefore one of the few South African cities built for walking in rather than driving around. The city centre's tourism office offers a number of delightful walking tours, which enable one to follow the footsteps of famous visitors from centuries past. Close by The Company Gardens, for example, is the

church in which David Livingstone worshipped as a young explorer, and cobbled Greenmarket Square nearby might well have seen a young Charles Darwin wander past during his short stay here on the return trip of the *HMS Beagle* to England after its epic voyage around the globe.

A 10-minute walk northwestwards from the Gardens takes one to the ramparts of the Castle, the oldest European-built structure in the country, which was once home to the governors of the Cape. In the early 1800s, it was the residence of Lady Anne Barnard, wife of one of the early governors during the period of British rule. Lady Barnard was a far-sighted person who understood how important her diplomatic role in this distant colony was. The settlement, taken over by the British as part of an effort to keep the strategic port from Napoleon, was home to many Dutch settlers who disliked the new overlords. Lady Barnard became known as a tireless hostess, convening parties, balls and soirées of note in an effort to beguile the residents of her new domain. She was universally spoken of with respect and delight, and even in death, reputedly, makes a routine appearance at any parties held in her old home. The Castle has undergone a major refurbishment recently, and now houses a large display of superb antique furniture from many periods in Cape history.

The last part of the city proper which needs introduction is the famous Cape Town Waterfront, which has been one of the most successful port redevelopment projects in the world. The earliest harbour buildings date back to 1860, and restoration took

THIS PAGE AND OPPOSITE TOP:
Panoramic view of the Victoria & Alfred Waterfront, a spectacular redevelopment of the 19th-century harbour.
OPPOSITE (BELOW): **The Capetonian spirit at its very best.**

place in 1990. Once a wilderness of rusting hulks salvaged from the Cape's ferocious seas, desolate, abandoned warehouses and seedy sailor's taverns, the huge Victoria & Alfred (the queen's son, not the famous husband) Basin is now a playground for all. There are wine emporiums, hundreds of shops and designer boutiques, craft markets and upmarket hotels with excellent views of Table Mountain. It is also the departure point for those wishing to visit Robben Island, the infamous site of Mandela's incarceration. The Waterfront is one of Cape Town's key places to meet, entertain or 'park off' (hang out), as a South African would put it.

exploring the hinterland

Aside from the Cape Peninsula itself, the Cape provincial interior is also brimming with lively spots. Among the most prominent are the well-known Winelands towns of Stellenbosch, Paarl and Franschhoek, located a short 30-minute drive inland from the city. These are the oldest wine-growing areas, with estates which date back to the late 1600s. Part of the appeal of these places is the exquisite old manor houses that were built here in the idyllic low mountain ranges, with their superb grape soils. Some of these are now exclusive little hotels, which have been furnished in keeping with the historic style of a well-to-do 17th-century country farm and home. The towns' names are evocative, especially Franschoek, which means 'French corner', and commemorates the arrival here of a number of French Protestant families who were fleeing religious persecution in Europe. They brought with them the art of grape cultivation, improving upon the first rough wines made by the Dutch for sale to the many ships using the Cape as a place to replenish supplies.

No visit to the Cape is therefore complete without a trip to the Winelands, which in recent years have expanded beyond what seemed possible 10 years ago. Now the term Winelands includes large new areas much further inland. Areas such as Tulbach, Robertson and Montagu now all have significant areas of land under vine and other Mediterranean crops like olives. The Cape has long been one of the world's top fruit-

producing areas, and added to this more recently have been cheeses and cured meats. It is as important to schedule a day or two of Winelands exploration as it is to do the Chapman's Peak drive. The serried ranks of mountains here have a pinkish tinge which, when combined with the bright blue of the sky, the purple of the heath-like Cape wild flowers and the swirl of white clouds, make this a place where stress simply melts away. The Winelands can be enjoyed from the comfort of intimate hotels tucked away in the hills, many well over a century old, as well as by sampling a new crop of stylish restaurants, some of which are among the top 50 in the world.

the cape whale coast + floral wonderland

As if the endless variety of areas under vine in the interior of the province were not enough, each of the Western Cape's two coasts offers yet more. The east coast is one of the world's top spots for ocean-based eco-tourism. Large pods of Southern right whales come here to calve in the spring. The very fact that there are enough of these magnificent creatures to warrant a whale-watching industry is a conservation success story. Once, this species of whale faced extinction. Today, thanks to vigorous international policing of whaling, their numbers have increased to healthy levels, though it will still take several decades for their population to reach equilibrium. For now, though, mesmerised visitors make their way to the various bays and small towns

THIS PAGE: View of the Hantam region, a tiny section of the great spread of spring wild flowers that stretches for hundreds of miles that is the Cape's west coast in balmy September.
OPPOSITE: All over the Cape, sun-filled restaurants known for their exquisite food and wine look out onto beautiful scenery.

along the coast in the hope of catching a glimpse of the mammoth creatures. On the country's opposite coastline, however, the windswept Atlantic seaboard is washed by one of the world's most dangerous seas. The cold ocean currents off the west coast flow straight from freezing Antarctica. Large sections of the African coastline, which stretch far beyond the northern boundaries of South Africa's neighbours like Angola, are guarded by treacherous reefs, on which countless ships have foundered, sending passengers to watery graves below.

Back on dry land, one of nature's most memorable displays takes place every spring. The dry, arid strech of this West Coast desert and semi-desert region is, confusingly, an area of impressive biodiversity. This is partly due to the age of the region, but the most exciting element for the visitor is what is known as the Namaqualand wild flower display each spring, which extends largely along the coast for hundreds of miles. The wild flower display would literally take days of driving to see in its entirety, but even a short trip from Cape Town at this time of year will bring you to the southernmost fields of orange, purple and white daisies, and varieties of fynbos, a popular name meaning 'fine bush' in Afrikaans, which refers to the Cape Floral Kingdom. If one happens to be in the Cape at any time other than spring, then a visit to 'South Africa's Kew Gardens', the magnificent Kirstenbosch National Botanical Gardens, provides a glimpse of South Africa's breathtaking botanical heritage.

celeb city

It is the combination of unspoilt wilderness and urban cool in the city itself which makes the Cape so appealing to many of the world's celebrities. The list of famous people who either own a home here or rent one when in need of refuge from the limelight is a growing one. The supermodel caravan trails through here at regular intervals—sometimes for work, since Cape Town has become a major destination for fashion shoots from around the globe. Juliette Binoche and Samuel L. Jackson settled in for some months to film *Country of My Skull*, a movie about South Africa's Truth and

THIS PAGE: Cutting-edge design and trendy hangouts pepper Cape Town's byways.

OPPOSITE (FROM TOP): Coffee society and the wonderful aroma of freshly-ground beans may be found on literally every corner; the worldwide passion for retro style is evident on the Camps Bay promenade.

Reconciliation Commission. Nicolas Cage, Patrick Swayze and John Cleese have also been spotted. London-based stage actor Anthony Sher hails from the Cape, as do various branches of the Oppenheimer clan. America's famous political dynasty, the Kennedys, have holidayed here, as does at least one Schumacher, partying and reputedly househunting too. Aside from the obvious attractions, Capetonians themselves are famous for not being fazed by the famous, and this has to be part of the appeal.

Cape Town also regularly plays host to the world's top jazz and music cognoscenti. Around Easter, Cape Town is host to a branch of the well-known Dutch North Sea Jazz Festival. Now an established date on the world's jazz calendar, the Cape Town event, although no longer linked directly with the North Sea management in Holland, attracts a stellar lineup, usually including the incomparable son of the city Abdullah Ibrahim. Once known as Dollar Brand, this matchless composer and pianist grew up during the most savage years of apartheid in a Cape Flats ghetto to become an implacable anti-apartheid activist in exile. A former protégé of Duke Ellington, he returns on invitation to play his haunting compositions to an adoring home audience. But the festival attracts many other superb local international talents, including dewy-eyed budding divas, African jazz masters and grizzled swing lineups who remember the days when a black band playing in a white suburb used to have to pretend to be waiters if the police sprang a raid.

party city

Every December Cape Town lapses into a languid mood, where the biggest decisions are whether to have rock lobster or prawns for lunch. The sun is hot, the sky blindingly blue, the evenings long and light, and meals are always al fresco. Moving out of the city, one can easily find a picnic spot in a forest, on a precipice hanging off Table Mountain, tucked in the lee of a huge rock on a pure white

THIS PAGE (FROM TOP): *Outrageous costumes are a key attraction of the annual Mother City Queer Project party; the Cape Minstrel Parade on New Year's Eve sees thousands of minstrel troupes parading through the city; the North Sea Jazz Festival is a major date on the international music calendar.* OPPOSITE: *Glamorous Camps Bay on the city's Atlantic seaboard is set against the dramatic backdrop of the Twelve Apostles.*

beach or nestled in a vineyard. The trendy shopping and restaurant spot of Cape Quarter and Camps Bay Terrace are also popular areas for eating and carousing.

If one ventures out, one can find a number of now-famous regular party dates which also need to be put firmly on the schedule. Two of the biggest take place in December—the Mother City Queer Project (MCQP) annual costume party and the Cape Minstrel Parade, which happens every New Year's Eve and which, despite being an all-male affair, is reminiscent of Carnival in Rio.

The MCQP was part of a city initiative to provide services and information to Cape Town's substantial gay community. The party, like the Easter Jazz Festival, is now a hotly anticipated event that attracts international tourists in droves. Usually scheduled for mid-December, it is as if the festive season is officially declared open by the fantastic spectacle of this huge party, which always follows an outrageous dress-up theme.

The Cape Minstrel Parade, a great annual street event, is a mix of the music hall tradition crossed with an urge to fill the streets with music. Somewhere along the line, the various groups began to compete with the flamboyance of their outfits, and today, each troupe, which can have up to many hundreds of members, wears a bright, clownsuit-like uniform with a hat, which is judged as part of a huge costume competition. In the months before New Year, seamstresses everywhere work feverishly to make hundreds of uniforms in time for the parade, which launches on New Year's Eve in the streets of the old Slave Quarter with a torrent of brightly-coloured troupes pouring through the tiny cobbled thoroughfares in their thousands. The parade is an excuse for a party of many days that involves a complex process of judging troupes and their costumes. Sometimes, small posses of minstrels can still be seen parading through the streets a full week into January busking or just celebrating the Cape's incomparable midsummer nights. The dazzling array of attractions in Cape Town caters to travellers of every taste and inclination, marked by the exuberance and vibrance of the new South Africa.

Aside from its extraordinary backdrop, Cape Town is a feast for the senses.

The Lodge on the Bay

THIS PAGE: Enjoy a glass of chilled South African white wine on the private balcony in The Lodge on the Bay's New York-style Mercer Suite, which opens out right onto Robberg Beach.

OPPOSITE (FROM TOP): The rooftop deck of the resort comes with a jet spa bath and plenty of space to bask under the clear blue skies of the sun-kissed Western Cape; the dramatic rugged coastline that marks Plettenberg Bay.

Situated on Robberg Beach in Plettenberg Bay, The Lodge on the Bay is right in the heart of South Africa's famous Garden Route. This coastal region between Mussel Bay in the south and Storms River Mouth in the north is a forested belt cut by mountains, cliffs and sandy beaches. From The Lodge on the Bay, guests enjoy uninterrupted views of the Indian Ocean and the deep-blue Tsitsikamma mountains, punctuated only by dune forests and dolphins or migratory whales passing along the coast.

This exclusive retreat was once the holiday home of talented designers Yvette and Siegfried Kopp. When converting the residence into a resort, they opted for a minimalist look rich in texture and detail to complement the stunning natural surroundings. Siegfried and his charming wife Yvette are personally involved in running the resort, and make it a point to get to know their guests.

Each suite is decorated in a different style, and all except one boast breathtaking sea views. In addition, all suites come with private balconies, loungers, an outdoor dining table, a mini-bar, CD and video players, bathtubs big enough for two and luxury bath products.

For pure tranquillity, check into the resort's Zen Suite. Surrounding this suite is a private garden in which grows fynbos, the native coastal vegetation of the Cape. Tucked away in the garden is a patio with its own plunge pool and an outdoor shower. The interior of the Zen Suite is a serene combination of maplewood and limestone.

Guests who do not want to leave urban sophistication behind will love the Mercer Suite. Emulating renowned interior designer Christian Liaigre's signature Mercer Hotel in New York, this suite is decorated with dark wood, red roses, white linen and silk blinds. In the sprawling limestone bathroom are soft grey cotton kimonos and a spacious shower

enclosure with a skylight. Lining the generous bath are broad limestone ledges, bearing a constantly replenished supply of Aveda bath products for guests' grooming pleasure. The Lodge on the Bay was voted amongst South Africa's top ten resorts with the sexiest bathrooms by *Style* in 2003, and the Mercer Suite's bathroom undoubtedly helped clinch that accolade.

For total exclusivity, try the resort's Aalto Suite. This glorious penthouse comes with two balconies, a kitchen and a king-size bed. With 180-degree picture windows, you will enjoy an unobstructed view of the ocean from wherever you stand in the suite.

With only six suites accommodating a total of 12 guests, one can be assured of complete privacy and seclusion. A ratio of two staff to each guest ensures that your every need and desire is attended to promptly.

Should you decide to leave the luxurious confines of your suite, the resort welcomes you to its Japanese day spa. Pamper yourself with soothing treatments ranging from facials to full-body massages, reflexology, shiatsu and other body therapies. Ladies may want to treat themselves to a pedicure and manicure or a hydrotherapy petal bath, while gentlemen might prefer a deep sports massage. In between treatments, sip on the endless cups of rooibos tea the spa's staff pour for you. Complete your spa experience with a lounge in the sauna or jacuzzi, or the resort's saltwater swimming pool.

Breakfast comprises a wide range of delicious dishes served on the breakfast deck, and has been declared one of the best breakfast menus in the Cape. Light, healthy lunches are served by the pool, and can be ordered at your leisure. Room service

is available all day, and the menu is African fusion. If you desire a nice bottle of wine to go with your meal, a well-stocked cellar will leave you spoilt for choice.

Plettenberg Bay offers a host of outdoor activities. Hike or bike along one of the many trails that snake across the cliffs of the rugged coastline and the blue mountains of the interior. From July to November, Southern right whales visit the warm waters of the Bay to calve and can be viewed directly from the balcony of your room or the deck of a specially-chartered boat. Beachy Head

Drive on Robberg Beach, a short walk from the resort, is also a popular whale-watching spot. Water sports enthusiasts can take their pick of kayaking, water-skiing, windsurfing, scuba-diving or snorkelling. Deep-sea fishing is also available, as are river and rock fishing. The resort's experienced and knowledgeable staff will offer advice and help with all arrangements. On the rare occasion that it rains, simply snuggle up with a book or movie from the resort's extensive library, which is stocked with over 1,000 books and videos.

THIS PAGE (FROM TOP): *The lounge area of the Scandinavian-inspired penthouse Aalto Suite; elegant minimalist fittings in the sea-facing Ando Suite.*

OPPOSITE: *The sophisticated Mercer Suite is modelled after the historic Mercer Hotel in New York, and repeats the design theme of using dark wood against pale backgrounds.*

Getting to and from The Lodge on the Bay is easy. Daily flights to Plettenberg Bay and George connect the resort to Johannesburg and Cape Town. Transfer time from George airport is a manageable one and a half hours, while Plettenberg Bay airport is a convenient 10 minutes away. Drivers have the pleasure of travelling on what is arguably South Africa's most pristine national route, which provides a link with Port Elizabeth. The two-and-a-half-hour drive takes you down a sharp, winding road with magnificent views of the Bay. To savour the gorgeous scenery extending the length of the Garden Route, it is recommended that you take detours from the motorway and explore the many secluded coves, forest walks and mountain passes along the way.

FACTS

ROOMS	6 suites
FOOD	restaurant: African fusion dinners • private dining • breakfast buffet
DRINK	wine cellar
FEATURES	Japanese day spa • video and book library • saltwater pool • sundeck with jet bath
BUSINESS	Internet facilities • facsimile • printer • photocopier
NEARBY	dolphin- and whale-watching • hiking and mountain-biking trails • watersports facilities • 2 18-hole golf courses • beaches • stables
CONTACT	77 Beachy Head Drive, Plettenberg Bay 6600 • telephone: +27.44 501 2800 • facsimile: +27.44 501 2850 • email: reservations@thelodgeonthebay.com • website: www.thelodgeonthebay.com

PHOTOGRAPHS COURTESY OF THE LODGE ON THE BAY.

The Plettenberg

Heated infinity-edged pools seem to flow into the sea, dolphins frolic in the bay and sandy sun-bleached beaches beckon. The Plettenberg is everything you'd expect from a hotel set in a playground for the rich and famous, and there are three reasons to come here, they say: The view, the view and the view. Built on a rocky headland in Plettenberg Bay, The Plettenberg has breathtaking views of the sea, mountains and miles of golden beaches.

There are 38 superbly furnished rooms and suites with varying sea views, including the luxurious Blue Wing. All are tastefully decorated in fresh nautical blues and soothing creams, and most suites have French doors and step-out balconies. All suites also come complete with under-floor heating and air-conditioning.

If you're after exceptional luxury and total seclusion, book right into Beach House, the new look-out villa with its own swimming pool and three en suite bedrooms, a large sitting room with a fireplace, a dining room and a service kitchen. And since room service is available 24 hours a day, oysters and champagne at midnight are just a mere phone call away.

Beach House is decorated with simplicity and elegance, and has beautiful

THIS PAGE (CLOCKWISE FROM TOP):
Sand at The Plettenberg boasts a cool, stylish design to match its contemporay cuisine; the pool at Beach House overlooks the crashing surf of the ocean beyond; a cosy room adds to the character of Beach House.

OPPOSITE: An intimate meal by the pool makes for a singular dining experience.

...there are three reasons to come here, they say: The view, the view and the view.

bleached wooden floors which add a warm touch of natural rusticity. The main bedroom leads out onto a sundeck and private swimming pool, with spectacular views of the bay and mountains.

The interior is full of artefacts that look as if they had been bathed in brilliant sunshine and caressed by the sea for generations—lime-washed and weathered furniture, sturdy wooden tables, driftwood mirrors and woven baskets by the dozen.

The Carchele Spa at The Plettenberg specialises in marine treatments and features a steam room, wet room and steam shower scented with cinnamon, cedarwood and vanilla. And do check out the Vichy shower,

which comes with six individually controlled pressure jets. Guests here have been heard to comment on the atmosphere of tranquillity and serenity which pervades the spa.

One of the best things about staying at The Plettenberg is the dining experience, which can only be described as truly exceptional. The hotel's signature restaurant is Sand at The Plettenberg, which looks out across Formosa Bay. The restaurant is relaxed in feel and contemporary in style, and serves global cuisine with an emphasis on fresh seafood and local delicacies.

Chef Christiaan Campbell uses only the freshest local produce. There are summer vegetables, herbs and asparagus from

nearby farms, prawns, crayfish, oysters and line fish straight from the sea, and succulent lamb. For those with a sweet tooth, the gratin of passion fruit mousse, trio of sorbets and chocolate tart are irresistible.

For a romantic dinner just for two, slip downstairs to The Plettenberg's state-of-the-art wine cellar, where you and your partner will be surrounded by bottle upon bottle of the best South African wines, featured in the establishment's award-winning wine list.

Nature-lovers will be pleased to know that all year round, dolphins play in the bay, ride the waves and delight onlookers. During whale season from July to October, you can catch sight of these majestic

creatures from the hotel terrace or your own private balcony. You can also arrange to head out to sea on a marine eco-safari to view the marine life, such as grinning seals lying flipper-up in the water and, of course, pods of frolicking dolphins.

Plettenberg Bay and its surrounds are a natural paradise, offering vast expanses of unspoiled Cape flora, delicate eco-systems, wetlands and lagoons. There is a wonderful network of hikes and trails for walkers and ramblers, and you should factor in at least a morning's visit to Robberg Nature Reserve. You may also want to visit Stanley Island, the only privately-owned island off the coast of South Africa, which has an assortment of antelopes and birds.

For avid golfers, choose from two superb courses near The Plettenberg, one of which was designed by the legendary Gary Player. Adrenaline junkies can choose from a range of thrills around here, including open-cockpit gliding, cycling, surfing, and bungee jumping off nearby Bloukrans Bridge, believed to be one of the world's highest jumps at 216 m (236 yds).

From Plettenberg Bay it is a short distance to the charming and laid-back seaside town of Knysna, which is set on an extensive lagoon that opens to the sea through soaring sandstone cliffs known as The Heads, just a few of the spectacular sights that await visitors to The Plettenberg.

MUSSEL AND RED PEPPER CHARLOTTE

Serves 6

40 pieces steamed mussel meat

Crêpes
110 g (3¾ oz / ⅞ cup) cake flour
1 egg
1 egg yolk
300 ml (10⅛ fl oz / 1¼ cups) milk
pinch of salt
pinch of freshly-ground black pepper
3 tsp canola oil

Roasted red peppers
4 large red peppers
40 ml (1⅜ fl oz / ⅛ cup) extra virgin olive oil
salt and freshly-ground black pepper to taste
100 ml (3⅜ fl oz / ⅜ cup) extra virgin olive oil

Herbed butter
1 tbsp fresh mixed herbs, chopped
60 g (2⅛ oz / ¼ cup) unsalted butter, softened
1 clove garlic, crushed
pinch of salt

Crêpes Sift the flour into a mixing bowl. Beat the egg and egg yolk and combine with the milk. Beat the milk mixture into the flour, then add the salt, pepper and finally the oil, beating constantly. Pour the batter by teaspoonfuls into a frying pan, and fry 6 thin, small- to medium-sized pancakes. Set them aside to cool when done.

Roasted red peppers Place the red peppers, 40 ml (1⅜ fl oz / ⅛ cup) extra virgin olive oil and seasoning in a roasting pan and toss together. Roast the red peppers at a high temperature until the skin of the peppers wrinkles. Remove from the oven and allow to cool until you are able to handle them comfortably. Carefully remove the skins and seeds. Set half of one pepper aside for the red pepper oil, then slice the remaining peppers into thin strips.

Red pepper oil Place the reserved half red pepper and 100 ml (3⅜ fl oz / ⅜ cup) extra virgin olive oil in a blender and blend until a smooth purée is obtained. Pass the resulting purée through a fine muslin cloth. Set in a conical strainer and leave to slowly filter through. Add salt and set aside.

Herbed butter Mix the herbs, butter, garlic and salt together, then mould the mixture into the shape of a small cylinder. Place butter cylinder in the refrigerator until set.

Line 6 buttered moulds with the crêpes. Mix the peppers and mussel meat together, reserving a few mussels for the garnish. Fill each crêpe with the pepper-mussel meat mixture. Cut the cylinder of herbed butter into 6 generous slices, and place 1 slice on top of each charlotte. Fold over the overlapping edges of the crêpes and wrap each mould carefully with cling film. Place the mould in a steamer and steam the charlottes for 15 minutes.

To serve Gently turn out the charlottes with a spatula onto serving plates. Heat the reserved mussel meat and place on top of the charlottes. Spoon over a little of the red pepper oil and serve at once.

Wine Waterford Sauvignon Blanc 2001

OPPOSITE: Sunlight bathes the façade of The Plettenberg, which has seen the passing of countless tides sweeping in from the Atlantic Ocean.

FACTS

ROOMS	37 luxury rooms • Beach House: 2 en suite bedrooms
FOOD	Sand at The Plettenberg: seafood
DRINK	Sandbar • wine cellar: award-winning wine list
FEATURES	heated pools • Carchele Spa
NEARBY	Tsitsikamma National Park • Robberg Nature Reserve • Stanley Island • Monkeyland sanctuary • Outeniqua Choo Tjoe steam train ride • scuba-diving • golf courses • Knysna Elephant Park • Knysna town
CONTACT	40 Church St, Plettenberg Bay 6600 • telephone: +27.44 533 2030 • facsimile: +27.44 533 2074 • email: plettenberg@relaischateaux.com • website: www.plettenberg.com

Pezula Resort Hotel

Soaring above the tranquil town of Knysna on South Africa's famed Garden Route is a headland offering breathtaking ocean and lagoon views. This spectacular region, which is home to majestic mountain passes and lush forests, is clad in an aromatic mantle of unique Cape fynbos, with bushes and trees which teem with flowers, birds and insects.

On this clifftop nestles the Pezula Resort Hotel. It would be hard to find another place with such a blend of natural splendour, idyllic seclusion and excellent service.

Pezula upholds exceptional standards of luxury and privacy. Each suite comes with its own balcony and extraordinary views. The gourmet menu, too, reflects the hotel's careful attention to detail. Only the freshest organically-grown produce is used and meals are specially prepared to bring out their full, natural flavour. A wide selection of fine Cape wines as well as international labels are also available.

South Africa's glorious climate delights its visitors, and the beautiful Garden Route is no exception. Summers are warm with plenty of sunshine, and winters are mild and pleasant. This weather allows guests to enjoy Pezula's many outdoor facilities.

THIS PAGE (CLOCKWISE FROM TOP):
A spacious suite with a private balcony that opens onto a neatly kept garden; Pezula's suites are bright, airy and luxuriously decorated; freestanding bathtubs and sinks give bathrooms a sophisticated edge.

OPPOSITE: Pezula's 18-hole championship golf course is set high above the Indian Ocean and Knysna lagoon.

Golfers can tee off at the hotel's acclaimed 18-hole championship golf course, while nature-lovers can observe wildlife in the resort and the neighbouring nature reserve. Birds such as the paradise flycatcher, African marsh harrier and Knysna turaco, as well as mammals from the zebra and bushbuck to the gentle duiker and elusive genet, can often be seen. At certain times of the year, majestic Southern right whales come to the waters of the Cape to calve, and can also be seen from Pezula's cliffs.

For the sporty guest, there are numerous possibilities including cricket and tennis academies as well as an equestrian centre, mountain-biking, hiking, diving, angling for trout, deep-sea fishing, kayaking, yachting and much more that enhances the lifestyle features of the resort. Nearly everyone, of course, will want to visit the magnificent sheltered beach at nearby Noetzie. There, one can soak up the African sun on soft, golden sand or simply go for a relaxed stroll, taking in some of the most stunning coastal scenery in the world.

With its combination of soul-stirring natural beauty, pampered privacy and gentle efficiency, Pezula is destined to become one of the world's legendary retreats, if it isn't one already.

FACTS		
	ROOMS	78 suites
	FOOD	restaurant: gourmet • 24-hr room service
	DRINK	bar
	FEATURES	world-class spa • fitness centre • heated indoor and outdoor pools • sauna • 18-hole championship golf course • chauffeured limousine • private jet • helicopter
	BUSINESS	executive boardroom
	NEARBY	watersports facilities • Tsitsikamma National Park • Outeniqua mountains • Sinclair Nature Reserve • Congo Caves • Robberg Nature Reserve • Knysna forest • Karoo
	CONTACT	Lagoonview Drive, Knysna 6570 • telephone +27.44 302 5332 • facsimile: +27.44 384 1658 • email: info@pezula.com • website: www.pezula.com

PHOTOGRAPHS COURTESY OF PEZULA RESORT HOTEL.

The Phantom Forest Eco Reserve

THIS PAGE (CLOCKWISE FROM TOP):
Be entertained around the fire
by traditional African
drumming every evening at
The Phantom Forest Eco Reserve;
you can pamper yourself at
the Body Boma spa;
boardwalks cut through
the leafy reserve.

OPPOSITE (FROM TOP): The reserve
overlooks the breathtaking
expanse of the Knysna lagoon;
glass ceilings and walls in the
bathrooms of the Tree Suites.

In an area of the Garden Route where verdant indigenous forests spill into gleaming estuaries and rise up beyond vast mountain ranges, there lies a place that whispers a special magic. A place that promises to feed the spirit and delight the senses. Barely visible from afar, the ephemeral Phantom Forest Eco Reserve is tucked away high up upon a forest-clad hillside, overlooking the celebrated Knysna lagoon.

A deep respect for the environment resonates throughout the reserve, and diligent care is taken to minimise any damage to the pristine natural surroundings. Using only sustainable building materials, a harmonious balance between man and nature has been created.

Cocooned amidst the timeless Afro-montane forest and fynbos vegetation are 14 private and exclusive Tree Suites. Each suite is exquisitely adorned and comprises a sitting room, bedroom, private deck and a sensuous bathroom wrapped in a glass roof and walls, affording splendid views of the surrounding forest and night sky. The décor of the lodge can be described as an eclectic mix of African styles, subtly reflecting the various rich and diverse cultures of this mysterious and endlessly captivating continent. Handwoven silks and other glorious fabrics, intricate wooden carvings and rare artefacts gathered from across Africa are all tastefully displayed with a contemporary twist.

The various buildings throughout the reserve are connected by a series of meandering boardwalks, flanked on either side by towering indigenous flora. You may be startled along the path by cheeky vervet monkeys darting mischievously through the canopy above. The birdlife here is abundant, with over 150 species having been recorded thus far. Distinct calls mark their presence, but they are sometimes difficult to spot through the dense foliage. From olive woodpeckers and the renowned Knysna loerie to rummaging porcupines and the rare blue duiker—Africa's smallest antelope—The Phantom Forest Eco Reserve is teeming with wildlife most common to the area.

The dining experience offered here is a guaranteed highlight, and one to be savoured even by the most discerning of palates. Executive Chef Vanie Padayachee and her team are truly passionate about food, and offer sensational dishes which surpass all culinary expectations. The main

dining area is located at the Forest Boma, where an extensive array of mouth-watering New Age dishes is served. The six-course menu is changed on a daily basis, and only the freshest seasonal ingredients are used. Dinner is followed by coffee and liqueur, which can be enjoyed around a burning fire, often accompanied by the rhythmic beating of African drums.

Guests also have the option of feasting at the Chutzpah restaurant, where North African fare is coupled with Moroccan-

inspired décor. All dishes are prepared on a wood-burning outdoor cooking station called the 'rocket'. Richly adorned with brightly-coloured plush scatter cushions and ornate hookah pipes, an exotic ambience pervades the candlelit dining room which is encircled by a sleek, floodlit wrap-around pool that overlooks the picturesque town and estuary of Knysna and the Outeniqua mountains beyond. Before the feast is served, guests can enjoy cocktails along with breathtaking views as the sun casts its last rays across the waters below.

Surrounded by this living, breathing forest with soft dappled light spilling through its leaves, the Body Boma spa is a wellspring of vitality, offering heavenly treatments that promise to pamper both mind and body. The combination of rejuvenating forest air and healing essential oils melts away any hint of stress. The Dead Sea Mud Detox, the Vativer and Black Pepper Shea Butter Back Massage, and the African Sea Escape are just some of the unique treatments that come highly recommended. Lose yourself and slip under a blanket of tranquillity as trained therapists work hand-in-hand with Mother Nature, who brings you treasures from the mineral-rich ancient waters of the Dead Sea to the wild coast of the African Atlantic, and the priceless bounty of the fynbos kingdom.

THIS PAGE (CLOCKWISE FROM TOP): *Staff at Phantom Forest will delight you with their friendly and attentive service; the luxurious lounge area of a Moroccan Tree Suite; Chutzpah restaurant specialises in North African cuisine.*

OPPOSITE (FROM TOP): *The sinuous wrap-around pool glides around the softly-lit dining room; bathrooms in Tree Suites come equipped with twin sinks and double-ended baths.*

The Garden Route is often referred to as 'nature's playground', and there is much to keep the adventurous at heart happy. Why not slip into a canoe with a picnic lunch and drift down the river, home to an astonishingly rich diversity of marine plant and animal life. The reserve also has a nature trail that winds through the heart of the forest. Age-old trees, lush forest ferns, twisted monkey vines and brightly-coloured lichen make it a world of natural wonders. Should all this prove too demanding, then head for a sauna and a relaxing soak in the Bubble Barrel.

The Phantom Forest experience is indeed heightened by its consistent attention to detail and its friendly, efficient service. Staff are always on hand, yet discreet. Your every need is anticipated and met with an ease so natural you might well be forgiven for thinking you were the only guest here. Without doubt, you will definitely feel reluctant to ever leave this little piece of Eden.

PHOTOGRAPHS COURTESY OF THE PHANTOM FOREST ECO RESERVE.

FACTS		
ROOMS	14 suites	
FOOD	Chutzpah: North African • Boma: New Age international	
DRINK	wine cellar • poolside bar	
FEATURES	forest boardwalks • Body Boma spa • Bubble Barrel outdoor jacuzzi • pool	
BUSINESS	Internet facilities	
NEARBY	golf courses • horseback-riding trails • para-gliding facilities • sailing centre • Knysna town	
CONTACT	PO Box 3051, Knysna 6570 • telephone: +27.44 386 0046 • facsimile: +27.44 387 1944 • email: phantomforest@mweb.co.za • website: www.phantomforest.com	

Klein Genot Wine + Country Estate

Only an hour's drive from Cape Town is the historical Franschhoek Valley, the French district of South Africa. The area's first European settlers were the Huguenots, who arrived by ship at the Cape of Good Hope in the late 17th century. They were given land by the colonial Dutch government in a valley called Oliphantshoek, named after the herds of elephants that roamed the area, which was later renamed Franschhoek, meaning 'French corner'.

Today, Franschhoek Valley is a flourishing recreational village in the heart of the Cape's wine country. Located between the majestic Franschhoek Mountains and two rivers, it is home to some of South Africa's best restaurants, art and antique shops and, of course, excellent vineyards and wine cellars. Nestled in this valley is the charming and luxurious guesthouse of Klein Genot Wine and Country Estate.

Set on a working wine farm, Klein Genot is an intimate all-suite guesthouse. Each suite has its own garden, fireplace and king-size bed lined with handquilted French linen. Original artwork graces the walls,

THIS PAGE (CLOCKWISE FROM TOP):
The Franschhoek Mountains form a majestic backdrop for Klein Genot's swimming pool; al fresco dining is possible the whole year round in the Cape's mild, welcoming climate; one of the estate's six tastefully-furnished suites.

OPPOSITE: The estate's tranquil lake is inhabited by indigenous varieties of waterfowl and swans; a rowboat is available for leisurely afternoons on the lake.

...feel free to pick the sun-ripened fruit from right outside your suite.

verdant vineyards produce Klein Genot's predominantly red varieties of wine. The farm also cultivates organic produce, which the estate uses in its cooking. Expect nothing less than fresh garden vegetables and herbs, and for a healthy snack feel free to pick the sun-ripened fruit from right outside your suite.

Indigenous birds roam the grounds at will, while wild waterfowl and swans inhabit the estate's tranquil lake. Afternoon activities are seldom more strenuous than swaying in a hammock or strolling leisurely around the farm. In the evening, the air-conditioned lounge which looks out over the estate is perfect for a pre-dinner apéritif.

More active guests will find a number of activities to engage their interest. Hiking trails criss-cross the mountains and La Motte Forestry Station will organise hikes, cycling trips, horseback rides and fly-fishing in one of the area's two rivers, and trout fishing is also available. All these make Klein Genot the perfect idyllic country getaway.

and bathrooms are suites unto themselves. Generously-sized and decorated with elegant contemporary finishings, they comprise walk-in showers, extra large baths, twin basins and a full range of South African Cape aloe natural products, enhancing the luxurious comfort of the rooms.

Wine lovers will enjoy private wine-tasting sessions at the farm's 5,000-bottle wine cellar. Over 20 hectares (49 acres) of

FACTS

ROOMS	6 suites	
FOOD	dining room: organic home cooking	
DRINK	wine from the estate's cellar • lounge	
FEATURES	private garden • fireplace • lounge	
BUSINESS	Internet facilities	
NEARBY	art and antique shops • vineyards • farms • hiking and biking trails • fishing spots • Pearl Valley Golf Course • tennis courts • boules courts • bowling green • Franschoek Valley • Franschhoek town	
CONTACT	Green Valley Road, Franschhoek • telephone: +27.21 876 2738 • facsimile: +27.21 876 4624 • email: info@kleingenot.com • website: www.kleingenot.com	

PHOTOGRAPHS COURTESY OF KLEIN GENOT WINE + COUNTRY ESTATE.

Le Quartier Français

The Cape Winelands are renowned not only for their wines, but also for their cinematic landscapes. At the heart of the Winelands lies Franschhoek Valley, a French enclave and wine-producing region dating back to the late 17th century, and its namesake town with just one main street and a bustling weekend atmosphere. When the Huguenots settled here three centuries ago, they brought with them their age-old French cuisine and wine culture, a heritage that has come to characterise the region.

There are 101 reasons to visit the historic village of Franschhoek, not least of which is Le Quartier Français. With an endless list of awards and a renowned executive chef in the kitchen, Le Quartier Français, a member of Relais & Chateaux, is a superbly-rated restaurant and hotel.

Guests have pondered long and hard over how exactly to define this property. It has been termed a lodge, a country inn, even an auberge. Whichever way you classify it, it is a stylish establishment that has never had to try too hard to stand out from the rest.

Much has been written about the culinary talents of Executive Chef Margot Janse. Aside from a multitude of accolades she has earned, Le Quartier Français has consistently bagged a place in *Eat Out*'s 'Top 10 Restaurants' every year since 1999. Margot has been given the honour of top chef in South Africa by the country's *Wine Magazine*, and her creative handiwork at Le Quartier Français shows you why. Her cuisine is contemporary and creative, using seasonal local ingredients and changing on a daily basis, depending on who knocks upon her

THIS PAGE (CLOCKWISE FROM TOP):
A deep black pool occupies most of the auberge's central courtyard, which is embraced by breathtaking mountains; the streetside terrace outside the bar provides ample opportunity to linger; private plunge pools are a key feature of the luxury suites.

OPPOSITE: The warm, inviting atmosphere of the restaurant is the perfect setting for an exciting meal.

back door with produce from the local terroir. There are now two restaurants at Le Quartier Français which showcase the hotel's excellent cuisine.

Le Quartier Français revolutionises the concept of traditional à la carte dining by offering three menus with up to eight innovative courses specially created by Chef Margot. Start off with seared yellow fin tuna, caponata and pistachio aïoli, followed by quail en crepinette, rocket and preserved lemon crushed potatoes with five spice jus, and crème fraîche mousse and Breton shortbread with wild berries for dessert, all but a few in the wide palette of flavours which you can savour and enjoy.

iCi serves casual bistro food in a laidback atmosphere, with its streetside terrace, bar and restaurant. Blue bay oysters can be followed by hunter's pot pie with rustic chips, and finished with a vanilla, berry and amaretti splice, all washed down with the best from a wine list which features award-winning wines alongside native Franschhoek creations, giving the menu a firm local flavour. The décor in the restaurants is contemporary and sophisticated, but never stiff or formal. After-dinner entertainment can be had in the screening room, which provides a new viewing experience.

Set against a fragrant rose and lavender border, the Cape Provençal spirit is

echoed in the auberge. The property is unpretentious and cosy, splashed in sun-kissed pastels, fitted with wood-burning fireplaces and wooden headboards painted in cheery hues. The 15 large bedrooms overlook a vintage-style pool, while two exclusive, intimate executive suites are equipped with their very own plunge pools.

Guests in search of a spa won't find one on the grounds of the auberge. Beauty treatments are all dispensed in the comfort of your room. Full-body massages, back, neck and foot massages, reflexology sessions and manicures and pedicures are available, but the best thing that can be ordered from room service is on the bath menu. Handdrawn baths—some with cocktails, candles and incense, others with Champagne and oysters—are the speciality of the house.

Le Quartier Français flows rather like the lifeblood of the village. The Midas touch of owner Susan Huxter extends beyond the eponymous restaurant and hotel, and into two other restaurants in the area. Bread & Wine Vineyard Restaurant serves modern country cooking on the picturesque grounds of a wine farm. Rustic ingredients prepared with a contemporary flair are always tempting, and bread-making classes at the restaurant give guests the opportunity to whip up tall loaves of bread—a satisfying way to spend an afternoon, and a chance for them to take a little piece of the restaurant's atmosphere away with them.

Delicious!, a hip village déli and coffeeshop frequented by both local and out-of-town guests, serves mouth-watering quiches, croissants and main courses. An espresso bar is open daily for coffee and cake, while a full dinner menu is served once a week, and the day's specials are scribbled on a chalkboard menu.

In Franschhoek Valley, wine cellars wait to be explored. Wine-tasting sessions are held almost everyday. In the town, an array of art galleries, antique shops, boutiques and quaint specialist shops offer a truly blissful way to spend the day. Notably, Franschhoek has the largest concentration of acclaimed restaurants in the land, as it is, after all, the food and wine capital of the country.

THIS PAGE: Soft down duvets and homely furnishings in the property's signature lavender colour adorn this suite.

OPPOSITE (FROM LEFT): Each room at Le Quartier Français adopts a summery Cape Provençal style; the tone is set at the reception area, with its bright colours and charming details.

FACTS		
	ROOMS	15 luxury rooms • 2 suites
	FOOD	Le Quartier Français: innovative contemporary • iCi: bistro-style • bar: snacks
	DRINK	bar
	FEATURES	pool • bath menu • in-room beauty treatments • library • screening room boutique • bicycle hire • babysitting services
	BUSINESS	facsimile • Internet facilities
	NEARBY	Franschhoek Valley • Franschhoek town • vineyards • wine cellars • golf courses
	CONTACT	16 Huguenot Road, Franschhoek 7690 • telephone: +27.21 876 2151 • facsimile: +27.21 876 3105 • email: res@lqf.co.za • website: www.lequartier.co.za

Santé Winelands Hotel + Wellness Centre

South Africa's Cape Winelands are renowned for their stunning natural beauty as much as for their fine wines. Against the spectacular backdrop of the Franschhoek Valley is a tranquil and scenic corner where people from all over the world go to be refreshed and revitalised: Santé Winelands Hotel & Wellness Centre.

Situated on a 190-hectare (470-acre) vineyard, Santé Winelands combines leading spa treatments with luxurious accommodation in beautiful surroundings to provide guests with a complete rejuvenation and wellness solution.

To ensure the comfort and contentment of guests, accommodation options include spa suites, four-bedroom vineyard villas and

a manor house. Satellite television and 24-hour room service are standard throughout, while the villas and spa suites offer the quaint charm of real fireplaces.

The cuisine served at Santé Winelands is a celebration of health and good living. Meals are prepared with the freshest of natural ingredients cooked to mouth-watering perfection, with South African dishes and local delicacies taking pride of place on the menu.

A professional approach to wellness treatment is what truly sets the Santé Winelands apart. The heated indoor hydro-pool allows for counter-current resistance swimming, while hydrotherapy baths provide magnetic-field treatment. Other facilities include a Serail, Haman, Vichy Shower, Kneipp therapy footbaths, sauna, leukonium, as well as an excellent gymnasium. The Centre's signature treatment, Vinotherapy, uses grapeseed oil and grape skins rich in

THIS PAGE (FROM TOP): Rooms at Santé Winelands Hotel exude an unmistakeable style and a restful ambience; the magnificent heated hydro-pool is just one of the numerous world-class facilities to be found at the Wellness Centre.

OPPOSITE: Santé Winelands and Wellness Centre are set in the serene and idyllic environment of the Cape Winelands.

antioxidants as an anti-ageing measure. The treatment involves being immersed in a wine casket bath, creating a uniquely soothing sensation. Also offered are body treatments, lifestyle consultations and expert counselling.

In between these sublime treatments, guests may take part in some of the many activities available in the area. These include golf, polo, horseback-riding, mountain-biking, or visits to wine estates with wine tastings. Cape Town, with its beaches and majestic Table Mountain, is only a short drive away.

Santé Winelands also offers an excellent venue for business conferences, where full corporate facilities ensure the success of any meeting. Four meeting rooms and conference venues are supported by digital communication capabilities and on-site audio-visual equipment specialists.

In today's pressurised world, Santé Winelands is a haven of refreshment that offers a holistic treatment experience to revitalise both mind and body.

PHOTOGRAPHS COURTESY OF SANTÉ WINELANDS HOTEL + WELLNESS CENTRE.

FACTS		
ROOMS	10 manor rooms • 39 spa suites • 7 villas
FOOD	Wellness Restaurant: healthy South African • Health Bar: light meals
DRINK	wine cellar
FEATURES	Wellness Centre: 20 treatment rooms • gym • outdoor pools • vineyard
BUSINESS	conference facilities for up to 180 guests • 4 meeting rooms • 1 boardroom • exhibition area
NEARBY	beaches • coral reefs • restaurants • designer shops • bars • cafés
CONTACT	PO Box 381, Klapmuts 7625 • telephone: +27.21 875 8100 • facsimile: +27.21 875 8111 • email: winelandsres@southernsun.com • website: www.santewellness.co.za

Cape Cove Guest Lodge

Cape Cove Guest Lodge encapsulates the best of cosmopolitan Cape Town. Its owners are long-time Cape Town residents, and have created a contemporary African lodge. This truly international lodge is nestled in the foothills of Lion's Head, in the exclusive suburb of Fresnaye, and overlooks the tranquil Bantry Bay and Clifton beaches.

The lodge's owners retained the original design of the property, which was built in the 1960s, but updated it with contemporary elements. Natural materials such as wood, stone, water and glass are used extensively,

and the property blends smoothly into its surrounding environment. Inside, parquet flooring lines the winter and summer lounges, and solid mahogany furnishings in the bedrooms designed by the owners impart a sense of warmth.

The owners' background in art and design coupled with an enthusiasm for the avant-garde has dictated their choice of original art pieces, which hang in well-appointed places throughout the property. Novel combinations of innovative and traditional define the lodge's décor. In keeping with the cosmopolitan spirit of this lodge, artists from all over the world are represented in the hotel. African tribal art is also an integral part of Cape Cove's design.

Cape Cove Guest Lodge encapsulates the best of cosmopolitan Cape Town.

Six spacious suites are offered, each with a balcony overlooking the Atlantic Ocean or the landscaped garden. Floors are covered in parquet or Earthcote resin, on which rest Nguni animal skins. Bedding is pure suede for the day and comfortable linen for the night. Bathrooms are spacious, tiled in granite slate with slick Italian fittings.

You can luxuriate in two pools, one of which is a gorgeous infinity-edged pool with views of the ocean. On one of the sun decks is a bamboo pergola (a patio with a trellised roof) where guests can enjoy massages, and a bar for cocktails by the pool. The main pool leads into an airy summer lounge. In cooler weather, a winter lounge with a fireplace, custom-made leather and suede sofas and a library will keep you warm and cosy.

The owners of this lodge will pamper you with their generosity, and their little touches of hospitality will delight as they impart the charm of Cape Cove to every guest that crosses its threshold.

FACTS

ROOMS	6 suites
FOOD	dinner on Tuesdays and Fridays
DRINK	pool bar
FEATURES	2 pools and sundecks • bamboo pergola • summer lounge • winter lounge • landscaped garden
BUSINESS	Internet facilities
NEARBY	Clifton beaches • Bantry Bay • Victoria & Alfred Waterfront
CONTACT	11 Avenue Deauville, Cape Town 8005 • telephone: +27.21 434 7969 • facsimile: +27.21 434 8191 • email: info@capecove.com • website: www.capecove.com

PHOTOGRAPHS COURTESY OF CAPE COVE GUEST LODGE.

Les Cascades de Bantry Bay

Towering over Cape Town are Table Mountain and the distinctive peak of Lion's Head, which crowns the slopes of Signal Hill. It is on these craggy flanks overlooking the icy blue waters of the Atlantic Ocean that one finds the most exclusive Cape Town neighbourhoods of Bantry Bay and Clifton.

It was here that Belgian couple Luc and Els Deschouwer decided to build their property in the early 1990s, and over the years have extended this residence into what is today a five-star boutique hotel with the most spectacular sea views from every room. Balinese architectural influences are evident throughout the hotel, with a typical example being the pavilion or balé at the poolside. The balé, typically built by a pool or in a secluded part of a tropical garden, is a place for contemplation and relaxation, and boasts large, fluffy cushions on a raised platform overlooking the pool and the ocean beyond, setting the tone for your stay here. Every night, a sea of candles lights up the balé, creating an atmosphere that is at once magical and exotic.

Unlike other large properties in the neighbourhood, there are no platforms held up by crude concrete pillars at Les

THIS PAGE (CLOCKWISE FROM TOP): The shimmering infinity-edged pool; original South African art and sculpture make up the unique décor of the outside lounge; the design of the hotel is distinctly Balinese.

OPPOSITE (FROM LEFT): A stunning view of the ocean at sunset; each of the rooms has a private verandah.

...a five-star boutique hotel with the most spectacular sea views from every room.

Cascades. Instead, Luc and Els have used the natural contours of the hillside to their advantage, and designed a unique place that gently flows down the curves of the rock. On the upper level is the Main Lodge, with six of the property's 10 rooms. The remaining four rooms are in the Villa, adjacent to the Main Lodge but lower down the hillside. Winding steps bring you from the breakfast area and lounge down a series of terraces, past the main sundeck with its magnificent pool and intimate balé, to the Villa with the restaurant and yet another gorgeous infinity-edged pool.

South African artworks grace the walls and hallways of the lodge. Among them are signature textured paintings by Katherine Wood, Shany van den Berg's expressive bronzes and limited edition etchings by Waydeling, which nestle alongside exquisite Indian mahogany chairs, travel chests from Malaysia and kudu leather sofas.

Reed ceilings and the generous use of wood in the Main Lodge and hewn sandstone walls in the Villa transform the property into a cosy retreat. Exclusivity and intimacy are prime features at Les Cascades. The rooms, decorated in soft browns and beiges, all have large private balconies with sea views. Tranquillity, luxury and the ultimate in décor, service, food and South African wines will leave even the most seasoned travellers mesmerised.

FACTS		
	ROOMS	10 double en suite rooms
	FOOD	dining room: international • poolside lunches and afternoon teas • Main Lodge: full English or Continenal breakfast
	DRINK	lounge
	FEATURES	balé • 3 pools and sundecks
	BUSINESS	facsimile • Internet facilities
	NEARBY	Victoria & Alfred Waterfront • Table Mountain • Clifton beaches
	CONTACT	48 de Wet Road, Bantry Bay, Cape Town 8005 • telephone: +27.21 434 5209 • facsimile: +27.21 439 4206 • email: fontain@mweb.co.za • website: www.lescascades.co.za

PHOTOGRAPHS COURTESY OF LES CASCADES DE BANTRY BAY.

The Cellars-Hohenort

Two great traditions have been elegantly combined at The Cellars-Hohenort, a historic hotel nestled in the heart of Constantia Valley, Cape Town. One is the tradition of fine wine, continued in the magnificently restored 18th-century Klaasenbosch cellars. The other is the tradition of fine living, epitomised by the stately Hohenort manor house once owned by the illustrious Spilhaus family, which still continues to welcome visitors into its gracious embrace.

Cellars-Hohenort is situated next door to the famous Kirstenbosch Botanical Gardens, one of the city's top tourist attractions, and the hotel itself looks out across lovely views of landscaped gardens and verdant vineyards. There are 53 luxury rooms and suites here, as well as the Madiba Villa,

THIS PAGE (CLOCKWISE FROM TOP LEFT):
The elegant yet relaxed dining verandah at The Cellars-Hohenort; the historical interior of Hohenort manor house; English country-style gardens adorn the grounds of the hotel.

OPPOSITE (FROM TOP): The hotel prides itself on the voluminous blooms in its gardens; a golf green allows guests to practise their putts.

...the stately Hohenort manor house...still continues to welcome visitors into its gracious embrace.

named in honour of former president Nelson Mandela, whose nickname is Madiba.

Tucked in a quiet corner of Cellars-Hohenort's gardens, the Madiba Villa is a double-storey Cape-style home, offering complete privacy and tranquillity along with 24-hour room service. Madiba Villa has a large sitting and dining room with a fireplace, built-in bar and service kitchen, and two double en suite bedrooms which are exquisitely decorated. The Villa is fully air-conditioned, and has a private courtyard with its own exclusive swimming pool. Guests should also take some time to stroll through the lush gardens at Cellars-Hohenort.

Lovingly tended by Liz McGrath, the gardens were voted to be among one of the top 30 hotel gardens in the world by *Garden Design*. Liz has also applied to the National Monuments Board of South Africa to have the gardens gazetted as a National Monument. The estate dates all the way back to 1693, and among the most impressive features here are the eight magnificent camphor trees that are 200 years old. They were planted at the time of Simon van der Stel, one of the first Europeans to set foot in the Cape, who had tiny camphor slips shipped to South Africa on one of the vessels sailing from the East.

Cellars-Hohenort also has a wonderful indigenous garden, planted in 1997 by members of Kirstenbosch, that features a selection of plants from every region in South Africa. There is also a landscaped Edwardian garden showcasing a variety of traditional English flowers, as well as a gorgeous rose garden sporting a myriad of colours and blooms. The rose garden was planted in 1997, but before the seedlings were put in the ground, a hurricane tore

Cape Malay, which prides itself on serving unique indigenous cuisine. The hotel also houses a charmingly rustic wine cellar, with some excellent vintages, for a romantic tête-à-tête or any other special occasion.

Life at Cellars-Hohenort moves at a languid pace. Therapists at the Carchele Spa are waiting to ease your stress and strains, and there are two swimming pools for lazing about in, as well as a tennis court and Gary Player-designed golf green. There are another 11 golf courses within easy reach of Cellars-Hohenort, as well as a gymnasium for those wanting to work off all that glorious food. For those who prefer to do a little shopping, there is the hotel's gift shop, the Herb Box, a delightful curio shop which is filled with choice local souvenirs. And before a big night out on the town, you can get your hair styled at the perennially popular D & D Hair Salon.

through the property, ripping off their labels, hence the varied, rather random mix that lines the vineyard perimeter.

In Constantia Valley, you will find seven of the finest vineyards in South Africa, so it is no surprise that Cellars-Hohenort has an award-winning wine list. The hotel's small vineyard itself is planted with four different varieties of table grapes. You can sample the fresh products of these gems over a delectable dinner at The Greenhouse or The

THIS PAGE (FROM TOP): **The Cellars-Hohenort prides itself on its vineyard and wines;** *an opulently decorated suite.*

OPPOSITE: **An elegant lounge with historical furnishings reflects the stately character and charm that preside in the manor house.**

Should you feel like venturing a little further afield, you can soak up the African sun on a nearby beach, take a trip to Table Mountain or visit Robben Island, where the apartheid regime kept its political prisoners.

Cellars-Hohenort is also an excellent base from which to explore Hout Bay, Camps Bay and the Victoria & Alfred Waterfront, as well as the Winelands towns of Stellenbosch, Franschhoek and Paarl.

CHOCOLATE PLATE 'LIZ MCGRATH'
Serves 8

Gâteau
250 g (8⅞ oz / 1⅞ cups) dark Callabaut or other good, dark Belgian chocolate
250 g (8⅞ oz / 1⅞ cups) unsalted butter
5 eggs
3 egg yolks
100 g (3½ oz / ½ cup) castor sugar
150 g (5⅝ oz / 1¼ cups) cake flour

Ice cream
250 ml (8½ fl oz / 1 cup) milk
300 ml (10⅛ fl oz / 1¼ cups) double cream
100 ml (3⅜ fl oz / ⅜ cup) glucose
225 g (8 oz / 1 cup) castor sugar
225 g (8 oz / 1 cup) white chocolate
4 egg yolks
melted chocolate for decorating
icing sugar for dusting

Gâteau Melt the chocolate in a bain-marie. In a pan, melt the butter over low heat and stir it into the chocolate. In a bowl, mix the eggs, egg yolks and castor sugar together until well-incorporated. Add the warm, but not hot, chocolate and butter mixture to the egg mixture, then fold in the flour. Spoon the mixture into 8 buttered moulds and refrigerate for a few hours until chilled. Bake in a preheated oven at 200° C (392° F) for 10 minutes just before serving.

Ice cream Bring the milk, cream and glucose to a boil. Add half the sugar, stir well, then remove from the heat and stir in the white chocolate until

melted. Mix the remaining sugar and the egg yolks together and incorporate it into the ice cream mixture. Strain, churn in an ice cream maker according to manufacturer's instructions and freeze.

To serve Decorate a plate with melted chocolate, then turn out the warm gâteau. Add a ball of white chocolate ice cream on the side. Dust with icing sugar.

Wine A sweet red dessert wine

FACTS		
ROOMS	33 double rooms • 4 single rooms • 14 suites • 1 private villa	
FOOD	The Greenhouse: organic, contemporary French and British • The Cape Malay: traditional Cape Malay	
DRINK	The Vine	
FEATURES	Carchele Spa • 2 heated pools • tennis court • golf green	
BUSINESS	conference room	
NEARBY	Cape Town • Winelands • Kirstenbosch Botanical Gardens • Hout Bay • Camps Bay	
CONTACT	93 Brommersvlei Road, Cape Town 7800 • telephone: +27.21 794 2137 • facsimile: +27.21 794 2149 • email: cellars@relaischateaux.com • website: www.cellars-hohenort.com	

PHOTOGRAPHS COURTESY OF THE CELLARS-HOHENORT.

Ezard House

Camps Bay, the Côte d'Azur of South Africa, is a favourite destination for many, with its dramatically staggered landscape leading up to the magnificent peaks of the Twelve Apostles. En route is the luxurious Ezard House, a property which owners Donald and Christina Ezard decided to develop because they were so impressed with the beauty of this coastal region that they wanted to share it with international travellers.

Ten well-appointed rooms offer you unparalleled comfort. The largest of the selection, the Ocean Suite, has an open-plan lounge, a jacuzzi bath, a huge dressing room and a balcony with stunning views. Six luxury rooms each have jacuzzi baths and balconies that either look out over the Atlantic Ocean or the soaring cliffs of the Twelve Apostles. The three standard rooms are anything but standard. Spacious, comfortable and exquisitely furnished, they enjoy as breathtaking a view as either the Ocean Suite or the luxury rooms.

At the bottom of the atrium is an indoor garden filled with leafy plants, which evokes a sense of space. A river that flows off the Twelve Apostles was pooled to create an elegant koi pond and other water features. On the same level is a Yamaha Disklavier, the centrepiece of Ezard House and a telling sign of the owner's background in music.

Up on the roof is an outdoor jacuzzi which looks out over Camps Bay and Lion's Head. One could soak here for hours, enjoying the phenomenal scenery.

All rooms are individually air-conditioned and have under-floor heating, television, DVD players and fridges. Luxury rooms also have heated towel rails. The rooms are uncluttered and the duvets are goose-down, with 300-thread count percale linen.

Ezard House's Kanebo Wellness Centre is where East meets West. Japanese in origin, Kanebo fuses ancient Eastern wisdom with Western technology to pamper the body and nourish the soul.

These facilities are built over the contours of the Twelve Apostles, and on every floor are wide balconies that provide panoramas of the area's stunning landscape. At Ezard House, you experience the Cape at its very best.

FACTS		
	ROOMS	6 luxury rooms • 3 standard rooms • 1 suite
	FOOD	dining room: international
	DRINK	bar
	FEATURES	pool • sundecks • jacuzzi • koi ponds • garden • grand piano • Kanebo Wellness Centre • exercise equipment
	BUSINESS	complimentary broadband Internet access
	NEARBY	Camps Bay • Table Mountain • Victoria & Alfred Waterfront • Winelands • shark-diving • deep-sea fishing • golf courses
	CONTACT	20 Theresa Avenue, Camps Bay, Cape Town 8005 • telephone: +27.21 438 6687 • facsimile: +27.21 438 1378 • email: info@ezardhouse.com • website: www.ezardhouse.com

PHOTOGRAPHS COURTESY OF EZARD HOUSE.

Kensington Place

Cape Town is synonymous with the city's proud sentinel, Table Mountain. and there is no better place from which to explore the sheer rugged beauty of this historic natural monument than Kensington Place. Located in Higgovale, a quiet, exclusive suburb on the foothills of the mountain, this boutique establishment is minutes away from the cable car station that sees hundreds of travellers a year traversing the slopes of Table Mountain.

There are a host of other reasons to stay at Kensington Place. Each of the hotel's eight intimate, individually-decorated suites provide stunning views of the city and harbour—with the exception of Suite Seven—and each have private terraces. Interiors are distinctly contemporary African, with deluxe fabrics and fine finishes throughout. Original art, mostly South African, adorns the walls. International lifestyle and travel magazines have raved breathlessly about the exquisite design and hospitality of Kensington Place, a testament to this hotel's excellent quality.

Room One is decorated in browns and whites, Rooms Two and Five in a palette of aubergines and Rooms Three and Four in shades of green and greys. Fine touches and unstinting attention to detail also characterise the décor and furnishings, which are underlined with cool elegance.

All rooms come with a complimentary array of Molton Brown amenities. Tasselled

THIS PAGE (CLOCKWISE FROM TOP):
A nook in a superior suite; a striking work of art adorns the hotel's only standard suite; the plunge pool and deck are easily accessible.

OPPOSITE: An open-plan bathroom with a sunken bath in a superior suite.

floor-length curtains grace the windows, while Calvin Klein blankets and plush throws line generously-sized beds. Marble-tiled bathrooms add to the air of understated luxury. There is little here to reveal that this property was once a non-descript suburban house, transformed by discerning owner Chris Weir to its current state of glory as a premier Cape Town boutique hotel.

The service here is impeccable. The ratio of guests to staff is one to one, thus ensuring that your needs are anticipated and responded to with amazing efficiency.

Food is served whenever you feel you desire it. An all-morning breakfast spread is laid out daily. Lunches are light, and dinner is offered five nights a week. While most meals here are hearty, healthy Californian-style cuisine can be ordered in advance.

Also a stone's throw away are the sights and sounds of Cape Town, including the fashionable Victoria & Alfred Waterfront. A visit to the prison on Robben Island, where

former president Nelson Mandela was incarcerated, is an opportunity to catch up with recent South African history, and is a poignant experience which could well move you to tears. A little further afield is the famed wine capital of Stellenbosch and the Hottentots Holland Mountains.

Those with a taste for the outdoors can take a trek through the nearby nature reserve, embark on a mountain hike or set off for a relaxing stroll on the beaches. The many travel journalists who have stayed here wrote stellar reviews. Spend some time here yourself, and you'll soon be writing your own.

FACTS		
	ROOMS	8 suites
	FOOD	dining room: South African and international • daily breakfast and lunch
	DRINK	bar • lounge
	FEATURES	plunge pool • garden • fireplace
	BUSINESS	high-speed Internet access
	NEARBY	Table Mountain • Victoria & Alfred Waterfront • Cape Town city centre • Robben Island • Stellenbosch town • Hottentots Holland Mountains
	CONTACT	28 Kensington Crescent, Higgovale, Cape Town 8001 • telephone: +27.21 424 4744 • facsimile: +27.21 424 1810 • email: kplace@mweb.co.za • website: www.kensingtonplace.co.za

PHOTOGRAPHS COURTESY OF KENSINGTON PLACE.

Lion's View

A stone's throw from Cape Town's city centre is the vibrant beachfront community of Camps Bay. Hugged by the slopes of the Twelve Apostles mountain range and the regal peak of Lion's Head, Camps Bay is one of Cape Town's most prestigious and distinctive residential neighbourhoods, where style is the order of the day.

Situated on one of Camps Bay's many serene tree-lined streets is Lion's View, a luxurious designer home for guests. The brainchild of accomplished South African

architect Greg Wright, Lion's View is an innovative two-level residence quite unlike any other. Wright's vision for Lion's View was to create a property that exemplifies today's modern lifestyle. Hence, the property is conceptualised around clean, flowing lines, a palette of soothing colours, minimalist furnishings and open, airy spaces.

Lion's View is divided into two sections—the Main House and the Penthouse Apartment—and guests can opt for either. The Main House is on the ground floor and

THIS PAGE (CLOCKWISE FROM TOP):
The appeal of Lion's View lies in its sleek, minimalist design; the private plunge pool of the Penthouse Apartment; the open-plan kitchen and dining area of the Main House employ subtle lighting and muted tones.
OPPOSITE: The infinity-edged pool of the Main House overlooks Camps Bay and Lion's Head.

comprises five double en suite bedrooms, a spacious lounge, a dining room and an open-plan kitchen. Furniture and fixtures by top designers such as Philippe Starck line the house and its large patios, adding fine touches of elegance. Enveloped by the patios is a seductive infinity-edged swimming pool that overlooks the Atlantic Ocean.

Upstairs is the stylish Penthouse Apartment. Two elegant double en suite bedrooms, a lounge and a fully-equipped kitchen make up this unique residence. On the balcony is a heated plunge pool and dining area set against the towering peaks of the Twelve Apostles.

Guests at Lion's View are ensured total comfort. A housekeeper is always on hand to tend to domestic needs, and should you want greater privacy, a chef can be arranged to provide in-villa meals. The grounds are neatly manicured, and at the entrance to the Main House is a footbridge that traverses a Japanese koi pond.

Although Lion's View is exclusive, it is certainly not remote. A five-minute stroll takes you to Camps Bay, with its signature palm tree-lined waterfront and array of trendy bars, restaurants and shops. There are attractions galore, from cosmopolitan city entertainment to hiking trails up the surrounding mountains. A short drive away are Table Mountain and the cable car that takes you to the top. And just a little further afield are the Victoria & Alfred Waterfront, Hout Bay and the breathtaking Winelands.

FACTS		
ROOMS	Main House: 5 double bedrooms • Penthouse Apartment: 2 double bedrooms	
FOOD	private chef on request	
DRINK	lounge	
FEATURES	infinity-edged pool • plunge pool • indoor and outdoor dining areas • open-plan kitchens • lounges	
BUSINESS	high-speed Internet access	
NEARBY	Camps Bay • Table Mountain • Victoria & Alfred Waterfront • Hout Bay • Winelands	
CONTACT	4 First Crescent, Camps Bay, Cape Town 8005 • telephone: +27.83 459 7707 • facsimile: +27.21 438 0046 • email: info@lionsview.co.za • website: www.lionsview.co.za	

PHOTOGRAPHS COURTESY OF LION'S VIEW.

Metropole Hotel

Once dismissed as nothing more than an old building on Cape Town's Long Street, the 134-year-old Metropole Hotel has been reborn as the hippest boutique hotel on the block. Gone are the heavily-carpeted floors and the ageing floral wallpaper of the old Metropole. Instead, clean lines and cool neutral tones light up the lobby.

Chic colours like lilac and taupe dominate, while sleek textures like suede, ostrich and linen cosset each of the 29 rooms. Super-sized European-style beds are lined with soft French linen. Particularly inviting are the travertine marble bathrooms and the constant supply of fluffy white towels. Most rooms have a Juliet balcony, an ideal spot for watching crowds bustle past on Long Street.

Elements of the Metropole's past still linger. Originally built in 1870 at the height of the Cape Victorian architectural era, it retains the Georgian façade it received from a 1905 facelift. South Africa's oldest working elevator is housed here, and faithfully continues to service guests.

Further renovations were undertaken in the 1960s and 1980s, but the current style

THIS PAGE (CLOCKWISE FROM TOP): In the Metropole Hotel's rooms and suites, contemporary art complements chic urban design; the elegant dining room of Veranda, the hotel's five-star restaurant; one of the hotel's aesthetically minimalist yet functional spaces.

OPPOSITE (FROM TOP): The spacious entrance foyer combines classic and modern design for a stylish new look; the 1905 Georgian façade of the hotel as it has been preserved.

...the 134-year-old Metropole Hotel has been reborn as the hippest boutique hotel on the block.

and feel of the hotel, both inside and outside, are the work of two men, architect Kurt Buss and renowned interior design guru François du Plessis, who are responsible for the metamorphosis of the Metropole into a truly modern urban refuge.

Veranda serves modern South African fare. Described as 'peasant food from around the world' by head chef Roy Thomson, the cuisine is comfort food with a twist. Dishes like duck bobotie and ostrich three ways (tartar, stir-fried and smoked) are favourites, but homesick guests aching for stick-to-the-ribs fare can tuck into the acclaimed special—beer-battered hake and

chips served in traditional English wrapping paper. Window tables offer a gorgeous view of Long Street and Table Mountain, and guests can linger here over a breakfast of ricotta hotcakes or eggs Benedict.

After meals, discerning guests can settle at the Metropole's M-Bar & Lounge for after-dinner cocktails. Furnished with red ostrich leather chairs and a Versace fabric sofa, the scarlet bar provides cool refreshment against upbeat background music. Guests looking to mingle with sophisticated locals need not step out of the Metropole. Word is out that the M-Bar & Lounge and Veranda are two of the hottest hang-outs frequented by Cape Town's glitterati.

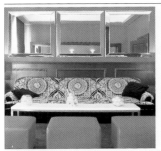

FACTS		
	ROOMS	5 single rooms • 3 standard rooms • 19 superior rooms • 2 suites
	FOOD	Veranda: modern South African
	DRINK	M-Bar & Lounge
	FEATURES	historic building in CBD • satellite television
	BUSINESS	meeting facilities • complimentary Internet and email access
	NEARBY	Cape Town city centre
	CONTACT	38 Long Street, Cape Town 8001 • telephone: +27.21 424 7247 • facsimile: +27.21 424 7248 • email: info@metropolehotel.co.za • website: www.metropolehotel.co.za

PHOTOGRAPHS COURTESY OF METROPOLE HOTEL.

Protea Hotel Victoria Junction

THIS PAGE: *Protea Hotel Victoria Junction's designer lap pool was inspired by New York's Paramount Hotel, which was conceptualised by Ian Schrager, the king of boutique hotels. The pool occupies rooftop space to take full advantage of the Cape's excellent climate.*

OPPOSITE: *Decorated in minimalist style with unstinting attention to detail, the hotel rooms are the epitome of sophistication.*

Cosmopolitan urban dwellers will take great pleasure in Protea Hotel Victoria Junction, a stylish city centre hotel with loft-style accommodation. Billed as the only one of its kind in Africa, it combines high-tech futuristic glamour with good old-fashioned comfort. Next door is the sophisticated Victoria & Alfred Waterfront, Cape Town's most fashionable precinct, into which Victoria Junction blends right in.

Modelled upon the hip and trendy Paramount Hotel in New York, Victoria Junction boasts an ultra-modern façade and interior. Film buffs will be delighted by the bar, restaurant, coffee shop and lounge which are designed to look like film sets. Travellers who need to stay connected will find Internet hotspots scattered throughout the 'film sets', providing instant online access.

At The Set restaurant, which serves a buffet breakfast as well as an à la carte lunch and dinner, guests dine beneath stage lights and movie cameras in stainless steel, brick and marble surroundings. The Out of Africa lounge is set in the plains of the Masai Mara and is a great place to relax at the end of the day, while the exuberant Italian Set is known for brewing some of Cape Town's best cappuccinos. The hotel is also renowned for its imaginative cocktail list. Sample one of the its potent concoctions at Harvey's Diner, a 1950s-style New York diner located behind The Set.

Double-storey loft apartments as well as standard rooms are on offer. Reminiscent of lofts made so popular by New York architects and interior designers, Victoria Junction's lofts are column-free, uninterrupted spaces with raw brick and minimalist steel fittings. Every loft comprises a living room on the first floor, a hi-fi set with a CD player and a Lavazza coffee and espresso machine.

...it combines high-tech futuristic glamour with good old-fashioned comfort.

On the mezzanine upper floor is an en suite bedroom with an oversized bed lined with a crisp white duvet. Business travellers have at their disposal compact executive desks with laptop and facsimile points as well as a high-speed Internet connection. Should you wish to work out in the comfort of your room, exercise bicycles are available.

Other fitness facilities include a stunning lap pool. A strip of turquoise slicing across a brick-coloured sundeck, the pool is perfect for an invigorating swim while comfortable cushioned loungers invite you to spend hours relaxing under Cape Town's endless clear blue skies. For shopping and entertainment, drop in at the myriad shops, galleries, bars and restaurants which grace the Victoria & Alfred Waterfront.

FACTS		
	ROOMS	148 standard rooms • 24 loft apartments • 2 rooms for the disabled
	FOOD	The Set: buffet breakfast, à la carte lunch and dinner
	DRINK	Italian Set café • Out of Africa lounge • Harvey's Diner bar
	FEATURES	lap pool and sundeck • exercise bicycles in rooms
	BUSINESS	2 conference rooms • ISDN lines
	NEARBY	Victoria & Alfred Waterfront • Greenmarket Square • National Art Gallery • Cape of Good Hope Castle • 2 fitness centres • 2 golf courses
	CONTACT	Corner of Somerset and Ebenezer Roads, Cape Town 8001 • telephone: +27.21 418 1234 • facsimile: +27.21 418 5678 • email: reservations@victoriajunction.com • website: www.proteahotels.co.za

PHOTOGRAPHS COURTESY OF PROTEA HOTEL VICTORIA JUNCTION.

Winchester Mansions Hotel

THIS PAGE (FROM TOP): The aquamarine heated swimming pool at Winchester Mansions; the leafy courtyard with gurgling fountains is styled like an Italian piazza.

OPPOSITE (FROM LEFT): Rooms and suites at Winchester Mansions come in a variety of period styles—this is a modern loft; the elegant Mediterranean façade of the hotel.

Once you arrive at the Winchester Mansions Hotel, you most probably will not want to leave. The views are glorious, the style gracious, and the pace of life nice and slow. The hotel looks out across the Atlantic Ocean, and frankly, who would want to go anywhere else when you can have a glass of fine Cape wine in your hand and a fiery red sunset right in front of you?

Winchester Mansions was constructed in the mid-1920s in the style of renowned architect Sir Herbert Baker. Its original Cape Dutch buildings are elegant and genteel. Take your pick from a variety of suites set across three levels, each one featuring specially chosen furniture reflecting a different historical period. You can stay in a contemporary loft-style apartment or a more traditional colonial-style suite. The Robben Island Suite has a double bedroom with a guest room and generous lounge area that looks out across the infamous gaol, where the South African apartheid regime locked away its political prisoners.

Enjoy long lunches in the cool, leafy courtyard surrounded by the trickling sound of water fountains and the happy chatter of guests. Encircled by palm trees, this colonnaded space is piazza-like, a tranquil oasis in the heart of one of the world's most beautiful cities. Come dusk, cocktails and a variety of snacks await on the terrace or in

The views are glorious, the style gracious, and the pace of life nice and slow.

Harvey's Bar, which offers awesome views of the sun setting over the Atlantic Ocean.

Head for a romantic dinner at the hotel's restaurant, Harvey's at the Mansions. It has become something of a hot spot amongst stylish and trendy Cape Town residents, not only because of its great location but also because of its original cuisine. The concept here is Euro-African—African cuisine with a contemporary European twist—and the menu is a delectable showcase of the region's diverse culinary heritage. If you thought leaving your luxurious room was difficult, try leaving the restaurant—especially after a serving of scrumptious Grappa ice cream.

Hosted at Harvey's, the Grapes, Gourmet and Gallery evenings are wine, dine and art evenings which are almost as popular as Cape Town's premier jazz brunch Jazz@The Mansions, starting at 11 am on Sundays.

The day after a meal at Winchester, you can work off all the decadence with a shopping session, a round of golf or even a workout in a nearby gym if you like. Some of the Cape's best beaches are within walking distance of the hotel, and staff will gladly help arrange day-trips and expeditions. Alternatively, visit Winchester Mansions' own spa, The Ginkgo Health and Wellness Spa, where the firm hands of therapists will knead away any stress you may be experiencing. The spa offers a range of facials, massages and hydro-baths, and you can choose to be pampered in the privacy of your suite.

FACTS		
	ROOMS	51 rooms • 25 suites
	FOOD	Harvey's at the Mansions restaurant: Euro-African • The Courtyard: al fresco dining
	DRINK	Harvey's Bar
	FEATURES	heated pool • The Ginkgo Health and Wellness Spa
	BUSINESS	business centre • 2 adjoining conference rooms • 1 executive boardroom • secretarial services • wireless Internet access throughout hotel
	NEARBY	golf course • gym • horseback-riding facilities • para-gliding facilities • sailing facilities
	CONTACT	221 Beach Road, Sea Point, Cape Town 8005 • telephone: +27.21 434 2351 • facsimile: +27.21 434 0215 • email: john@winchester.co.za • website: www.winchester.co.za

PHOTOGRAPHS COURTESY OF WINCHESTER MANSIONS HOTEL.

Colona Castle

You will feel like royalty as you walk into Colona Castle. The entrance hall is a majestic turret, with French doors leading onto a balcony that reveals panoramic lake, sea and mountain views. A five-star Mediterranean-style retreat, Colona Castle graces the mountainside above a tranquil lake district on the False Bay coastline, offering travellers an enchanting base from which to explore the Cape and Cape Town.

The turreted and crenellated Colona Castle was built in 1929 by a Scottish physician, Dr Munro Grier, who fell for the scenic charms of the Cape. In 1996, Nicole and Michael Brand bought the property. Keeping the original foundations and character, they enlarged the entrance tower and refurbished the interiors.

Colona Castle is Tuscan-inspired and filled with the Brands' collection of antiques and objets d'art—life-sized Buddhas, upholstered recliners, lavish mirrors and ornately carved fireplaces. By day, the interiors are suffused with a soft, buttery glow. By night, the exteriors twinkle with a million lights from Cape Town. In summer, cool breezes waft in from the ocean, while open hearth fires warm the lounges in winter.

The five luxury suites, two superior bedrooms and a family suite are all

THIS PAGE (CLOCKWISE FROM TOP):
The fully-refurbished Tuscan-inspired Colona Castle retains its original foundations and its historical charm and character; the exquisite Oriental-themed Chinese suite; tea on the verandah with Table Mountain and Lion's Head in the distance.

OPPOSITE: The three-storey entrance tower which the property's owners furnished with antiques and objets d'art.

individually decorated. The Moroccan bedroom has an evocative North African appeal, while the European-inspired English suite opens onto a large terrace where you can enjoy breakfasts overlooking False Bay.

Dinners at Colona Castle are a grand affair. With its superb position and bold proportions, the dining hall is a special place to eat, and the resident chef's creatively presented cuisine makes use of the Cape's finest and freshest ingredients.

Because Colona Castle is on the warmer False Bay coastline, it is mild in winter and cool in summer. Whales and varying types of marine life populate the Bay, depending on the season. The attractions of Cape Town and its environs are a short drive away, as are the rolling hills of the Winelands. You can visit a penguin colony at nearby Boulders, or head out to the dramatic Table Mountain National Park on the very edge of the Cape of Good Hope, the Western Southernmost Point of Africa.

PHOTOGRAPHS COURTESY OF COLONA CASTLE.

FACTS		
ROOMS	2 superior bedrooms • 5 suites • 1 family suite
FOOD	dining hall: South African, international and fusion
DRINK	poolside bar
FEATURES	historical residence • antique collection • art collection
NEARBY	Cape Point • Boulders Beach penguin colony • Kalk Bay Harbour • St James Beach • Muizenberg Beach • Boyes Drive • PostHuis and Rhodes Cottage Museums • Silvermine Nature Reserve • Stellenbosch and Constantia Winelands • Victoria & Alfred Waterfront • Table Mountain
CONTACT	Verwood Street, off Old Boyes Drive, Lakeside, Cape Town 7945 • telephone: +27.21 788 8235 • facsimile: +27.21 788 6577 • email: colona@link.co.za • website: www.colonacastle.co.za

d'Ouwe Werf Country Inn

Massive urban renewals of late have breathed a new lease of life into the town of Stellenbosch in the Cape Winelands. Once merely an old university town, Stellenbosch is now the heart of the South African wine industry. Its old buildings still sit along oak-lined streets, but art galleries, boutiques and bistros have sprouted, giving the town a modern panache it never thought it would have.

d'Ouwe Werf Country Inn is the best way to get a feel for Stellenbosch's marriage of old and new. Established in 1802, d'Ouwe Werf is the oldest inn in South Africa. The inn stands on the hallowed grounds of the town's first church, which dates back to 1686, and the remains of the church can still be seen beneath the floorboards of the inn's kitchen. d'Ouwe Werf's own history is not without drama. It was razed to the ground several times by fires in the 18th and 19th centuries, but was rebuilt each time. Today, a charred door and some window frames in the Voorkamer (front room) are the only survivors from the hotel's chequered past.

Though the inn's foundations are ancient, the present building is nothing less than sumptuously appointed. No two rooms

THIS PAGE (CLOCKWISE FROM TOP): d'Ouwe Werf's Voorkamer, or front room, is built over the remains of Stellenbosch's first church; one of the hotel's 31 individually-decorated en suite bedrooms; the hotel's 1802 Restaurant is renowned for its traditional Cape cuisine.

OPPOSITE: The inviting waters of the swimming pool and sundeck are set in the hotel's tranquil landscaped garden.

are alike—d'Ouwe Werf freely furnishes each room in either Georgian, Victorian or traditional Cape style. Thirty-one rooms are spread over five buildings, each looking out onto either the lush, verdant garden and courtyard or Church Street. Divided into Superior, Luxury and Classic rooms, many are decorated with exquisite antiques that hint at the hotel's poignant history.

Traditional South African fare—bobotie, smoorsnoek, Biltong pâté and Cape brandy pudding, to name a few dishes—is served up at the 1802 Restaurant, a Stellenbosch culinary institution in its own right. Hearty eaters will find South African dishes satisfying, while diners who prefer lighter meals can tuck into Continental alternatives. The restaurant flaunts an extensive wine list and is one of the few places guests can enjoy a good Cape vintage.

A fine way to while away the daylight hours is to curl up beside the antique stove fire in the high-vaulted Voorkamer with a good book, or browse local newspapers in de Kromme Elleboog, the informal lounge. For outdoor enjoyment, savour a slice of cheesecake, held to be the best in town, in the vine-covered coffee garden.

Days here are easily filled with wine-tasting, shopping and walking. d'Ouwe Werf awaits at the end of each day, its central location in Stellenbosch easily accessible from anywhere on the Wine Route.

FACTS		
ROOMS	31 rooms	
FOOD	1802 Restaurant: traditional South African, Continental and international • coffee garden: light meals	
DRINK	1802 Restaurant • coffee garden	
FEATURES	pool • garden • Voorkamer • beauty salon • lounge	
BUSINESS	meeting room • facsimile • Internet facilities	
NEARBY	Cape Town • museums • art galleries • golf courses • vineyards and wine cellars	
CONTACT	30 Church Street, Stellenbosch 7600 • telephone: +27.21 887 4608/1608 • facsimile: +27.21 887 4626 • email: ouwewerf@iafrica.com • website: www.ouwewerf.com	

PHOTOGRAPHS COURTESY OF D'OUWE WERF COUNTRY INN.

River Manor Country House + Spa

Dubbed the 'town for all seasons', there is never a bad time to visit the picturesque town of Stellenbosch. Many flock to the wine estates dotting the Stellenbosch wine route for a feast of wine-tasting. There are dozens of wineries along the region that offer an array of native pours. Food plays an essential part in the wine-tasting experience. From the heart of the bustling town to the rolling expanses of the wine estates, eateries are a dime a dozen and diverse in character.

From elegant Cape Dutch manors to Victorian villas, sidewalk cafés to country cottages, all type and manner of dining establishments and cuisine can be found in this town. Traditional Cape fare and conventional European cuisine aside, dishes like waterblommetjie-bredie (waterlily stew), hoender pie (a South African version of the classic chicken pie) and bobotie (sweet curry mince casserole) are highlights of the region.

Sitting pretty on The Avenue, a famous oak-lined street within the historical heart of Stellenbosch, is River Manor Country House & Spa. Accorded national monument status, the country house oozes colonial charm, in tune with the rest of its historic surrounds. Barely two minutes' stroll from the lively village centre, River Manor comprises a pair of fine historic residences—River Manor and Moedersloon—furnished in a blend of colonial and African styles. Its 16 bedrooms, some with original Victorian bathtubs, combine the old-world charm of antiques with the modern conveniences of satellite television, mini-bars, air-conditioning and wall safes. Guests are pampered with trays of complimentary sherry and port in their

THIS PAGE (CLOCKWISE FROM TOP):
The warm interior of the conservatory is the perfect setting for intimate meals; soothing creams make bathtime a truly relaxing experience; generously-sized chairs occupy a spacious verandah.

OPPOSITE (FROM LEFT): Quaint touches of colonial charm characterise the décor in each suite; fruit-laden guava trees overlook one of the hotel's two pools.

breakfasts are served in the sun-filled conservatory or under the shade of a leafy guava tree overlooking one of the pools. After a long day spent exploring the surrounding wine farms, golf estates and beaches, guests may return to the manor to sip cocktails on a sunny terrace, or just cool down and relax at one of the two large swimming pools set in the secluded gardens.

This ethereal mood characterises a stay at River Manor Country House & Spa, which makes it the perfect hideaway from the busy clamour of city life, and a true celebration of gracious living.

rooms before dinner and herbal teas at dawn, which they can sip at their own leisure while lounging about in the hotel's luxuriantly soft towelling bathrobes. Wrap-around verandahs offer the perfect spot for sampling local wines, with the sun setting behind the Simonsberg Mountain.

The intimate in-house spa, Gingko Health & Beauty Spa, is situated in the manicured gardens of the country house,

providing a range of professional health, beauty and vitality treatments. Guests with a mind to relax tired muscles can be kneaded and pummelled with The Gingko Elixir Massage—an innovative treatment which combines a myriad of traditional body touch techniques like Swedish, shiatsu and deep tissue. A number of designer Day Spa packages include delectable, healthy light spa lunches. Full English and health

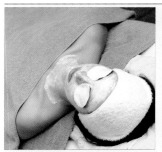

FACTS		
	ROOMS	8 Superior Rooms • 6 Classic Rooms • 2 Petite Rooms
	FOOD	conservatory and poolside: Continental English breakfast • spa menu
	DRINK	2 Honesty bars
	FEATURES	2 pools • health spa • lounges • verandahs • conservatory
	BUSINESS	secretarial services • Internet facilities
	NEARBY	beaches • Cape Town • Franschhoek town • Paarl town • Hermanus town • Tulbach town
	CONTACT	Johan and Leigh Swanepoel, 6, The Avenue, Stellenbosch 7602 • telephone: +27.21 887 9944 • facsimile: +27.21 887 9940 • email: info@rivermanor.co.za • website: www.rivermanor.co.za

PHOTOGRAPHS COURTESY OF RIVER MANOR COUNTRY HOUSE + SPA.

Spier

THIS PAGE (FROM TOP): *One Spier's six luxurious swimming pools, each of which is surrounded by a beautiful private courtyard; De Zalze Golf Club at Spier hosts a challenging 18-hole golf course that cuts across a stunning landscape dotted with vineyards and citrus groves.*

OPPOSITE: *Tee off against a backdrop of majestic mountains and lush vineyards, where a Mediterranean climate practically guarantees year-round games of golf.*

Spier, situated on the banks of the Eerste River, dates back over 300 years. When Cape Town's early settlers left the secure arms of Table Mountain in search of new farmland, the first river they encountered was the Eerste River. Farmers jostled for precious irrigated land along its banks, and when the governor announced that farmers were allowed to keep whatever land they could cultivate in three years, more flocked to the area. In 1685, Spier was born.

Spier prospered until well into the 19th century, after which it gradually fell into disrepair. In 1993, visionary entrepreneur Dick Enthoven bought Spier with the dream of restoring it to its former glory. In 1995, Spier opened for business. Today, Spier can be called a renaissance village, comprising five excellent restaurants and a pub, vineyards and wine cellars, a golf course, a theatre, ecologically designed housing developments, and a range of conservation and educational programmes.

Visitors to Spier have the option of staying at the luxurious and unique four-star The Village at Spier Hotel. In keeping with Spier's village atmosphere, the hotel turned to the traditional, colourful Bo-Kaap architecture seen predominantly in the Muslim quarter of Cape Town for inspiration. Thirty-two buildings housing 155 bedrooms are clustered around six private courtyards, each with its own pool and entertainment

area. Front doors open onto gravel paths and the feel of the entire complex is very down-to-earth. Rooms are decorated in simple country style and are more spacious than those usually found in larger hotels. All rooms have fireplaces for the rare nippy winter evening, and antique furnishings add to the old-world ambience.

Nothing went to waste in the construction of this environmentally-conscious hotel. Wherever possible, natural materials and resources were used for building. Wood was obtained from sustainable forests, and bricks came from a local supplier who did not use the conventional firing pits which are so notorious for emitting pollution.

Construction methods were chosen for their capacity to maximise renewable resources. Alternative energy sources, such as gas fires in rooms, are integral to the hotel's design, and to conserve energy the property is aligned on a north-south axis for ventilation during the hot summer months.

There is no shortage of good food and wine at Spier. From informal pub grub to fine dining, Spier has it all within easy reach. Moyo, the new Pan-African restaurant on the werf at Spier, offers sumptuous buffet spreads and cultural entertainment, while Spier Deli's innovative menu caters to every conceivable dining need, from sit-down meals to lawn picnics. The 150-year-old

There is no shortage of good food and wine at Spier.

course designers, Peter Matkovich, the course meanders through vineyards, citrus groves and dams, wrapped around by stunning mountain views. Every hole offers something special. The green of par three second, the course's signature hole, lies right on the very banks of the spectacular Blaauwklippen River which cuts through most of the course. After a few rounds, revitalise yourself at Camelot Spa, which offers state-of-the-art spa technologies with a wide range of treatments and products.

Equestrians will be spoilt for choice at Spier's Equestrian Centre. Riding tours are available for those who prefer to view the wine country on horseback, while the more sedate have for their pleasure horse and carriage rides around the estate. Beginners may opt for riding lessons, and children can choose to be entertained by pony rides. Young ones will also enjoy the Children's

THIS PAGE (FROM TOP): Moyo is one of several outdoor dining settings to choose from; these elegant rooms are given an Oriental twist through the use of Asian-inspired furnishings.

OPPOSITE (FROM LEFT): Spier's 155 rooms are distributed amongst 32 buildings clustered around six private courtyards.

Jonkershuis Restaurant serves Cape Malay cuisine, while the hotel's Figaro's restaurant is *the* place for fine dining. Nightbirds will find Toto's Bar an excellent rendezvous for drinks and a light snack if they desire.

Golfers will be delighted by De Zalze Golf Club's 18-hole golf course over the Eerste River on the south bank of the estate. Designed by one of South Africa's top golf

Garden, an on-going mini-festival of sorts comprising rock climbing, face painting, arts and crafts, slide shows and other fun activities. Drumming workshops and story-telling sessions are organised regularly.

Two animal sanctuaries offer visitors the opportunity to have a close encounter with wild creatures. Come face to face with a magnificent cheetah at the Cheetah Outreach Programme, or watch how birds of prey are trained to hunt using ancient falconry techniques at Eagle Encounters, a rehabilitation centre for birds that have been injured, poisoned or otherwise illegally removed from their nests.

Tennis is thriving at Spier. Three all-weather tennis courts near the Helderberg mountains are popular among guests. International tennis stars, including Anna Kournikova and South Africa's own Amanda Coetzer, have displayed their prowess right here along with Wayne Ferreira and other high-ranking South African players.

Try travelling to Spier in old-fashioned elegance on the estate's own vintage train. Orginally built in the 1950s in Britain for Rhodesia Railways, this train went on to serve the National Railway of Zimbabwe. The train departs from Monument Station in Cape Town on selected days, and will take you on an hour-long scenic journey through the wine country. It has five beautifully-refurbished lounge coaches and two teak-lined sleeper coaches which can accommodate up to 300 passengers, and is also equipped with a full bar service. The train takes you directly to the heart of the Winelands and the verdant grounds of Spier, where your holiday experience begins.

FACTS		
ROOMS	155 rooms • 3 villas • 4 suites	
FOOD	Moyo: Pan-African • Figaro's: French • Jonkershuis: Cape Malay • Spier Deli: picnics and grill	
DRINK	Toto's Bar	
FEATURES	private pools • entertainment areas	
BUSINESS	boardroom • Internet facilities	
NEARBY	De Zalze Golf Club • Camelot Spa • Craft Market • Equestrian Centre • Vintage Train • Cheetah Outreach Programme • Eagle Encounters • Children's Garden • Manor House arts centre • Spier Wine Centre • Gordon's Bay	
CONTACT	PO Box 1078, Stellenbosch 7599 • telephone: +27.21 809 1100 • facsimile: +27.21 881 3634 • email: info@spier.co.za • website: www.spier.co.za	

PHOTOGRAPHS COURTESY OF SPIER.

Grootbos Private Nature Reserve

Spectacularly sited overlooking the world-renowned whale-watching haven of Walker Bay, the five-star Grootbos Lodge is South Africa's premiere marine and flora destination. The multi-award winning reserve it is set in offers warm hospitality, excellent cuisine and a rich diversity of fauna and flora, making it a nature-lover's paradise. Here, guests can soak in the pristine environs while relishing creature comforts of the most lavish kind. Situated less than two hours from Cape Town, Grootbos provides an ideal destination on the way to the Garden Route.

The 21 luxury suites set amongst indigenous gardens and ancient milkwood trees are characterised by spaciousness, warmth and supreme comfort. All suites have been elegantly decorated and come complete with en suite bathrooms, separate living rooms, fireplaces and mini bars. Large private decks allow one to absorb the tranquillity and sheer magnificence of the views over Walker Bay.

The two thatch-and-stone Grootbos lodges have been stylishly decorated with contemporary African accents. Central also

THIS PAGE (CLOCKWISE FROM TOP):
Walker Bay is home to a host of whales, and at Grootbos you can easily view these majestic creatures at play; stone, thatch and fine timber make up the lodge buildings; spend a lazy summer's day on one of two long sandy white beaches at Walker Bay.

OPPOSITE: Splendid views of the Atlantic Ocean can be enjoyed from the poolside.

to the Grootbos experience is the cuisine. Seafood from the surrounding waters and the freshest vegetables and herbs from the lodge's garden feature strongly on the menu, which is accompanied by fine local wines.

At 1,700 hectares (4,200 acres), Grootbos Private Nature Reserve is home to a magnificent variety of plants and animals, and is close to a pristine 30-km (18.5-mile) coastline with secluded swimming areas, white sandy beaches and archaeological caves. The wild flowers and stunning landscapes of the reserve can be explored by following one of the many self-guided trails, or you can alternatively choose to be accompanied by a specialist Grootbos guide. Guest activities are tailor-made for individual requirements and include flower and nature tours, 4x4 drives and horseback-riding. From July to December, you can view Southern right whales from both land and boat. If guests are yet to have their fill of adventure, an excursion to Dyer Island, the cage-diving mecca for great white sharks, should be sufficient to satisfy even the most ardent thrill seeker. For maritime activities of a tamer kind, a boat takes guests on a marine tour to the same island to view its many protected bird species. Sharks aside, the conservation area of Dyer Island is also home to Cape fur seals, African penguins and a host of different seabirds.

Non-residential guests can similarly enjoy all these on day tours to Grootbos, but to get the most out of this magical destination, a leisurely stay is recommended.

FACTS		
ROOMS	21 suites	
FOOD	restaurant: African • bistro: Mediterranean	
DRINK	bar	
FEATURES	private balcony in suites • pool • library • reading lounge • curio shop • telescopes for stargazing	
BUSINESS	conference facilities • Internet facilities • facsimile	
NEARBY	Walker Bay • Stanford town • Gansbaai town • Flower Valley • De Kelders • Cape Town	
CONTACT	PO Box 148, Gansbaai 7220 • telephone: +27.28 384 0381 • facsimile: +27.28 384 0552 • email: reservations@grootbos.co.za • website: www.grootbos.com	

PHOTOGRAPHS COURTESY OF GROOTBOS PRIVATE NATURE RESERVE.

Blue Gum Country Estate

Situated on 52 sprawling hectares (128.5 acres) on the slopes of the Klein River Mountain is a piece of paradise owned by couple Nic and Nicole Dupper. The Duppers are seasoned directors of holiday properties in the Cape, and have two successful ventures under their belt—Bushmans Kloof Private Reserve in the Cederberg and the renowned Bartholomeus Klip Farmhouse near Wellington. Blue Gum is their third venture, and is fast joining the ranks of the other two. It is close to the flourishing town of Hermanus, in the heart of the dramatic Whale Coast.

One of the secrets to the Duppers' success is their charming hospitality. Expect a cheese and biscuit platter with a glass of sherry in your room at the end of the day. Do not be surprised if you get a phone call in your room from Nic saying that their regular masseuse is free, and asking whether you would like a backrub before dinner. Aslan, the Duppers' friendly white Labrador, is the estate's resident guide who is always willing to take guests on a tour of the estate.

Nic has invested much of his energy in wine-collecting, and Blue Gum has a well-stocked cellar of great South African wines. Nicole personally decorates each room with fresh flowers gleaned both from the fynbos, a natural South African vegetation, and their horticultural delight of a garden.

THIS PAGE (FROM TOP): An European country-style suite at Blue Gum Country Estate; the magnificent Klein River Mountain frames the estate and provides endless opportunities for hiking, biking, riding and nature-spotting.

OPPOSITE: The outdoor dining area overlooks the rolling green fields of the estate.

Everything at Blue Gum harmonises beautifully, like a match made in heaven.

When Nicole is not adding her personal touch to the rooms, she is in the kitchen whipping up a host of gastronomic treats that she has become well-known for. A chef by training, she established her reputation as a fine cook at the award-winning Bartholomeus Klip Farmhouse, and is replicating that remarkable cuisine here. Her roasted butternut and mascarpone cheese ravioli with sage cream sauce has already made headlines, not to mention her fillet of beef on a potato rösti with leeks, mushrooms and a green peppercorn sauce. If you had to pick one reason alone to come to Blue Gum, it would be Nicole's cooking.

Accommodation comprises three luxury rooms and two suites in The Manor House, with five country-style suites in a separate block. All rooms and suites have excellent views, are exquisitely decorated and come with lovely extras such as Crabtree & Evelyn toiletries. Everything at Blue Gum harmonises beautifully, like a match made in heaven.

PHOTOGRAPHS COURTESY OF BLUE GUM COUNTRY ESTATE.

FACTS

ROOMS	3 luxury rooms • 7 suites
FOOD	dining room and outdoor dining area: classic
DRINK	wine cellar
FEATURES	pool • tennis court • library • vineyards • river boat cruises
BUSINESS	boardroom • facsimile • Internet facilities
NEARBY	walking, biking and riding trails • bird-watching spots • fly-fishing dams • beaches • golf courses • scuba-diving and snorkelling sites • shark cage-diving sites • whale-watching sites • watersports clubs • wine estates • coastal villages
CONTACT	PO Box 899, Stanford 7210 • telephone: +27.28 341 0116 • facsimile: +27.28 341 0135 • email: info@bluegum.co.za • website: www.bluegum.co.za

The Marine Hermanus

The Marine Hermanus is arguably the finest spot from which to engage in whale-watching, an activity which can be by turns exciting and calming. Set on the sea front at Hermanus, The Marine overlooks Walker Bay, the preferred haunt of humpbacks and Southern right whales who come here from July to December to mate and calve.

For those who love to watch these gentle giants at play, The Marine is as close as it gets to having whales in your back garden. Take early morning strolls along the cliffs to see them frolic in the waters, or watch them close up from the hotel telescope. At The Marine you can even whale-watch from your bed—the ocean views here stretch all the way to Antarctica.

The five-star Marine has 42 individually-decorated bedrooms and suites, each one as luxurious and sophisticated as the last. Fresh creams and sea blues reflect the hues of the Indian Ocean. There are also beautifully-landscaped gardens—gardening happens to be one of the passions of owner Liz McGrath—a romantic inner courtyard and even more glorious views that look out onto the Overberg mountains, renowned for their unique natural vegetation known as fynbos.

Along with its sister properties The Cellars-Hohenort and The Plettenberg, The Marine is a member of the exclusive Relais & Châteaux group, which means you can expect an array of delightful luxuries like large beds, huge baths, fluffy towels, fresh flowers, a heated pool and of course, excellent service.

Indulge your tastebuds at Seafood at the Marine, the restaurant with a menu that makes the most of the fresh fish and seafood available from the surrouding waters of the

Indian Ocean. There is also the elegant The Pavilion restaurant, which serves contemporary South African cuisine. As you gaze out across the dark ocean over dinner, you'll undoubtedly be grateful that the world's finest land-based whale-watching destination has access to some of the world's finest wines from the sprawling grounds of the nearby Cape Winelands.

In fact, two of South Africa's premier vineyards are right on The Marine's doorstep—Bouchard Finlayson and Hamilton Russell—and you can arrange for a fascinating day-trip to both vineyards.

Along with lively sessions of whale-watching, you should also try a relaxing session at the Carchele Health and Beauty Spa. This world-class marine therapy salon is in keeping with fine French traditions that require their centres to be located within a few metres of the ocean in order to benefit from the minerals in the air and seawater. You can enjoy a variety of therapies using natural seaweed and plant extracts. After a therapy session, one delighted visitor was heard to comment: "My skin felt like a baby dolphin's bottom." There's no end, it seems, to the benefits of a visit to the spa.

You can while away the day with Champagne by the heated swimming pool, or take a romantic walk down memory lane to visit the Old Harbour, which displays a number of World War I cannons. You can also visit nearby Danger Point, and the lighthouse here marks the point where the ill-fated *HMS Birkenhead* went down.

At the southern end of the bay is De Kelders, the site of a cluster of caves once occupied by strandlopers or 'beach walkers', who were the original inhabitants of this coastline. Archaeologists have spent years digging through deep shell middens here to try and learn more about the strandlopers' hunter-gatherer lifestyle.

The region also offers a glimpse of nature at its most impressive. Hermanus offers miles of sandy white beaches and

THIS PAGE: The Marine Hermanus is set against a dazzling background of imposing mountains and the pounding waves of the Indian Ocean.

OPPOSITE: A leisurely breakfast or spot of afternoon tea is enhanced by the expansive vistas which are in full view.

hikes along cliff-hugging paths, while the nearby Fernkloof Nature Reserve has over 40 km (25 miles) of walks through the beautiful Overberg mountains, which form an imposing backdrop to the town.

Every day during whale season, the local whale crier, sporting a jolly giant Bavarian hat, calls in the arrival of each new whale by blowing loudly on a kelp horn. During the whale-watching festival in October, the town is abuzz with holiday-makers, whale-lovers, families and travellers.

The Marine was built in 1902 by Walter McFarlane, who moved here from the nearby agricultural village of Elgin in the 1880s. The hotel started with a modest 21 rooms and underwent many changes over the years, until it fell into the loving hands of David Rawdon in the early 1980s. He renovated and ran The Marine for a total of 13 successful years before selling it to Liz McGrath, who steered the hotel into the new millennium and secured its position as one of the world's finest.

GRILLED CRAYFISH WITH PEPPADEW BUTTER, SAUTÉED BABY POTATOES AND ROASTED ASPARAGUS
Serves 6

6 whole crayfish tails
2 L (4 pt 3⅝ fl oz / 8½ cups) seawater
30 ml (1 fl oz / ⅛ cup) olive oil
salt and freshly-ground black pepper to taste
500 g (1 lb 1⅝ oz) baby potatoes
50 g (1¾ oz / ¼ cup) butter
handful of fresh parsley, chopped
48 spears green asparagus
olive oil for roasting

Peppadew butter
80 g (2⅞ oz / ⅜ cup) peppadews, finely chopped
200 g (7 oz/7/8 cup) butter, softened
salt and freshly-ground black pepper to taste

Crayfish Blanch the crayfish for 5 minutes in the boiling seawater. You can substitute with salted water if seawater is not available. Butterfly the crayfish and clean the heads thoroughly. Rub the flesh with olive oil and place under the grill for 1 to 2 minutes. Season the crayfish thoroughly with the salt and freshly-ground pepper before transferring to an oven preheated at 180° C (356° F), and roast for 5 minutes.

Peppadew butter Mix the peppadews into the butter. Add salt and freshly-ground black pepper. Roll the peppadew butter firmly in cling film. Leave to set in the refrigerator for at least 20 minutes.

Sautéed baby potatoes Cook the baby potatoes in boiling salted water for about 10 minutes. Remove from heat and drain. Sauté the potatoes in 50 g (1¾ oz/ ¼ cup) butter until they are golden-brown and tender. Sprinkle the potatoes generously with the chopped fresh parsley just before serving.

Roasted asparagus Blanch the asparagus spears in boiling salted water for 1 minute, then refresh in ice water. Sprinkle the asparagus with olive oil and roast them in the oven at 180° F (356° F) for 2 minutes.

To serve Arrange the sautéed baby potatoes in the centre of each plate and top with 8 asparagus spears in a fan. Rest the crayfish on top of the potatoes and asparagus. Dot the crayfish and potatoes generously with peppadew butter.

Wine Beaumont Chardonnay 2000

FACTS

ROOMS	8 Premier Suites • 6 suites • 6 Luxury Double rooms • 22 single and double rooms
FOOD	The Pavilion: South African • Seafood at the Marine: fresh seafood
DRINK	'floating wine cellar' at The Pavilion • The Orangery
FEATURES	reading room • marine helipad • Carchele Health and Beauty Spa • heated pool
BUSINESS	conference room
NEARBY	Fernkloof Nature Reserve • air charters • Bouchard Finlayson and Hamilton Russell vineyards • Old Harbour • Danger Point • De Kelders • golf courses
CONTACT	Marine Drive, PO Box 9, Hermanus 7200 • telephone: +27.28 313 1000 • facsimile: +27.28 313 0160 • email: hermanus@relaischateaux.com • website: www.marine-hermanus.com

PHOTOGRAPHS COURTESY OF THE MARINE HERMANUS.

The Western Cape Hotel + Spa

BELOW: *The Western Cape Hotel & Spa glows like a beacon on the Arabella Country Estate.*

OPPOSITE (FROM TOP): *Rooms are equipped to pander to guests' every need, and no single detail is neglected; the shuttered lounge at AltiraSPA and Wellness Centre lets guests relax fully after a reinvigorating session.*

Almost a self-contained complex, the five-star Western Cape Hotel & Spa sits on the rambling Arabella Country Estate, next to Bot River Lagoon, South Africa's largest and arguably most scenic natural lagoon. There's more than enough in this ultra-modern hotel to keep guests busy for days on end.

For starters, the hotel overlooks the award-winning 18-hole championship golf course designed by renowned architect Peter Matkovich, whose course is set along the banks of the Bot River Lagoon and surrounded by indigenous plants. Little wonder then that many come with the sole objective of recharging body and spirit at the AltiraSPA. Ranked among the top 100 spas in the world, the AltiraSPA encompasses a state-of-the-art fitness centre, lap pool, hydro-pool complex and 18 treatment rooms. Spa-goers game to try out the exotic and intriguing should have a go at the brine pool, a healing salt water flotation tank where complete, utter relaxation is imparted by a star-lit skylight, dolphin calls and the unearthly sensation of total weightlessness. The Rassoul Chamber in the Hammam Centre is a Middle Eastern ceremonial bath chamber featuring treatments combining mud, steam, water and scented air.

The hotel, carefully designed to blend in with its vibrant natural surroundings, offers spectacular vistas of the lagoon's cascading banks and the estate's verdant peninsula. The rooms, lusciously decked out with a subtle South African influence, have every modern amenity needed. A novel feature is the air-conditioner which is activated by the opening and shutting of the terrace door. The crème de la crème of society stay in one of the two Presidential Suites. A four-poster bed, gas fireplace, walk-in dressing room and sprawling bathroom are built to pamper, as are the jacuzzi and personal sauna.

Come mealtime, guests can choose between casual or formal dining. The open-concept Jamani Restaurant, a casual eatery which serves breakfast, lunch and dinner as well as buffets, begs the question of whether the kitchen is in the restaurant or the restaurant in the kitchen. Those with a taste for fine dining can adjourn to the award-winning Première Restaurant, which offers French cuisine with distinct South African accents made from the freshest ingredients, while providing the discerning diner with elegant seating in a formal setting coupled with exquisite views over the lagoon. The Arabella Country Estate is nestled within the Kogelberg Biosphere and the Rooisand Nature Reserves, surrounded by the Cape Floral Kingdom. 15 minutes' drive away is Hermanus, celebrated as the world's best land-based site for whale-watching. But with that many attractions contained within the hotel, the temptation to spend the entire trip lolling about the Western Cape Hotel & Spa may prove too strong for some.

FACTS

ROOMS	115 deluxe rooms • 26 deluxe suites • 2 Presidential Suites • 2 accessible paraplegic rooms
FOOD	Première Restaurant: French with South African accents • Jamani Restaurant: earthy, warm showkitchen contemporary
DRINK	The Laguna Lounge • Barnabas' Bar • Laughing Waters Pool and Bar
FEATURES	library • Cristobal's Cigar Bar • health spa • helipad • curio shop
BUSINESS	conference facilities • Internet facilities
NEARBY	Cape Town • Hermanus • Kleinmond
CONTACT	On The Arabella Country Estate, PO Box 593, Kleinmond 7195 • telephone: +27.28 284 0000 • facsimile: +27.28 284 0003 • email: reservations@w-capehotel.co.za • website: www.luxurycollection.com/westerncape

South African Airways

Getting to South Africa has never been easier. South African Airways has a network of flights that connects the main cities of South Africa with the rest of the world. The airline offers 14 direct flights to and from London Heathrow to Johannesburg, and nine to Cape Town each week. In addition, there are 20 flights to and from other European cities. From Johannesburg and Cape Town the rest of South Africa is conveniently accessible by domestic routes.

With air travel becoming increasingly routine, travelling Business or even First Class is no longer the domain of a privileged few. Innovative pricing and packaging of flights in the airline industry has put First and Business Class travel within reach for more people. Also, as travellers become more discerning and sophisticated, a high premium is placed on comfort and style. At South African Airways, First and Business Class passengers are promised an air travel experience beyond compare.

Pampering begins even before you board the plane. Cycad Premium Lounges are open to First Class passengers and offer round the clock dining options, a full bar service, showers, soundproof snooze rooms and a fully equipped business centre. The Baobab Lounge for First and Business Class passengers has state-of-the-art workstations with everything you need to catch up with work.

THIS PAGE (FROM TOP): South African Airways boasts a modern international fleet of passenger aircraft to connect South Africa to the rest of the world; lie-flat beds in First and Business Class ensure you arrive at your destination well-rested.

OPPOSITE: The Baobab Lounge is well-equipped with facilities for both work and leisure.

...passengers are promised an air travel experience beyond compare.

On board, First Class passengers enjoy a 180-degree lie-flat bed, as do many Business Class passengers. For meals, First Class passengers choose items from an à la carte menu, and Business Class passengers enjoy a selection from a five-star menu. An exquisite range of Champagnes and wines is served throughout flights. The excellent service continues even after you have alighted. Arrival lounges for First and Business Class passengers provide refreshing showers, business facilities and breakfast.

South African Airways ensures that you are well-looked after right from the minute you begin your journey to when you finally leave the airport terminal. With this world-class airline, your visit to South Africa is guaranteed to get off to a fabulous start.

FACTS

FLIGHTS	43 flights a week to 31 European destinations
IN FLIGHT	movies • video games • music • reading material • duty-free shopping • wine • First Class : 180-degree lie-flat bed, à la carte menu, Champagne • Business Class: 180-degree lie-flat beds on all flights (early 2005 onwards), five-star menu, Champagne
GROUND	First and Business Class: departure and arrival lounges, complimentary chauffeur service to airports in the UK for tickets purchased in the UK • First Class: Cycad Premium Lounge
CONTACT	UK reservations: 0870 747 1111 • South Africa: +27.11 978 1111 • email: ukhelp@flysaa.com • book online: www.flysaa.com

Cape Town + Winelands Itinerary

The varied attractions of the Cape mean that many visitors never get beyond South Africa's most beautiful region. At its heart is the beautiful city of Cape Town, ringed by white-sand beaches and put into perspective by the towering bulk of Table Mountain. The Victoria & Alfred Waterfront, with its restaurants, shops and craft markets, is the most popular tourist attraction in the country, with the diverse plantlife of Kirstenbosch Botanical Gardens coming a close, but rather more rewarding, second. Head out a few miles and you're in the Winelands—Constantia to the south, Stellenbosch and Franschhoek to the east—where some of the country's finest wines are grown and tasted in restored settler dwellings set amidst a spectacular landscape of mountains and vineyards.

Highlights of the region

Cape Town • Winelands • Homestead hospitality

Suggested itinerary by Abercrombie & Kent Travel

- Fly to Cape Town with either British Airways or South African Airways
- Transfer from the airport for a three-night stay at Kensington Place (see page 216), the Metropole Hotel (see page 220) or The Cellars-Hohenort (see page 210)
- Enjoying the independence of your own car, head east along the spectacular coastline to Hermanus, and spend two nights at the Western Cape Hotel & Spa (see page 244) or The Marine Hermanus (see page 240)
- From Hermanus, a short drive brings you to Walker Bay and the unique setting of Grootbos Private Nature Reserve for two nights (see page 236)

- Finally, you can head north into the Winelands for a two-night stay at either the rustic country homesteads of River Manor Country House & Spa (see page 230) or Klein Genot Wine & Country Estate (see page 198)
- Return to Cape Town and catch your overnight flight to London

Eastern Cape + Garden Route Itinerary

Providing the perfect addition to any itinerary in the Cape Town region, the Cape's southern coast is perhaps one of the most beautiful areas in the world. Sheer cliffs and sheltered bays are clothed in indigenous vegetation, whilst small towns and settlements are home to some of the country's best and most refined hotels and restaurants. It's also perfect self-drive country: many of the greatest sights are off the main road, and inland some of the country's most dramatic passes are carved into the mountains.

Suggested itinerary by Abercrombie & Kent Travel

- Enjoy the dramatic setting of Plettenberg Bay with a three-night stay at The Plettenberg (see page 188)
- Continue on for two nights in Port Elizabeth at The Windermere (see page 168)

Abercrombie & Kent Travel specialises in creating tailor-made holidays to South Africa. With offices in both Johannesburg and Cape Town, they are able to offer their clients the benefit of their in-depth local knowledge and 24-hr support. This itinerary is fully flexible and merely offers an example as to the type of programme offered in the Cape. To discuss your holiday in this region, please call Abercrombie & Kent on +44.845 0700 611 or visit www.abercrombiekent.co.uk

Mpumalanga Itinerary

The Kruger National Park and its unfenced borders with Africa's finest game reserves is undoubtedly Mpumalanga's greatest highlight. This is the best place in Africa to spot the Big Five, and the wildlife experience is perfected by sophisticated lodges offering the ultimate luxury bush hideaways. Don't overlook Mpumalanga's other great sights however—the picture-postcard photos of South Africa's magnificent landscapes often come from this area, taken at the spectacular Blyde River Canyon, God's Window, or Bourke's Luck Potholes. For a longer stay, some of the country's finest luxury boutique hotels are found in Mpumalanga's sub-tropical plantation estates, which blend the finer aspects of settler living with an appreciation of rural life.

Highlights of the region
Exploring dramatic countryside • Stay on exclusive ranch

Suggested itinerary by Abercrombie & Kent Travel
• Fly from Cape Town or overnight from London to Johannesburg with British Airways or South African Airways and connect with your onward flight

- On arrival, transfer to Royal Malewane (see page 90), Singita Lebombo (see page 60), or Lion Sands Private Game Reserve (see page 66) for four nights
- Take delivery of your hire car and proceed to the White River area for three nights at Jatinga Country Lodge (see page 72)
- Return to Johannesburg and your onward flight to Cape Town or London

Abercrombie & Kent Travel specialises in creating tailor-made holidays to South Africa. With offices in both Johannesburg and Cape Town, they are able to offer their clients the benefit of their in-depth local knowledge and 24-hr support. This itinerary is fully flexible and merely offers an example as to the type of programme offered in Mpumalanga. To discuss your holiday in this region, please call Abercrombie & Kent on +44.845 0700 611 or visit www.abercrombiekent.co.uk

Limpopo + Northwest Province Itinerary

Experience the spectacular and silent dunes of the Kalahari wilderness. This is an area where a dedicated conservation effort attempts to restore the natural environment to its original condition within a 100,000 hectare- (247,110 acre-) reserve and sustained breeding programmes ensure rewarding game-viewing and astounding birdlife. In the malaria-free Madikwe Game Reserve on the border with Botswana, a dedicated haven for black and white rhino and spectacular wild flowers, you will find the Big Five. Finally, the Magaliesberg Mountains provide a haven of tranquillity and beauty, offering the visitor a fascinating insight into rural South Africa.

Highlights of the region

Desert exploration • Malaria-free game-viewing

Suggested itinerary by Abercrombie & Kent Travel

- Fly from Cape Town or overnight from London to Johannesburg with British Airways or South African Airways
- Transfer via a private air charter to the Kalahari Desert for a three-night stay at Tswalu Kalahari Reserve (see page 150)
- Return to Johannesburg by private air transfer before continuing to the Madikwe Game Reserve for a three-night stay at Jaci's Tree Lodge (see page 138), Jaci's Safari Lodge (see page 140) or Etali Safari Lodge (see page 146)
- Finally, transfer to the Magaliesberg Mountains for three nights at Mount Grace Country House & Spa (see page 36)

Abercrombie & Kent Travel specialises in creating tailor-made holidays to South Africa. With offices in both Johannesburg and Cape Town, they are able to offer their clients the benefit of their in-depth local knowledge and 24-hr support. This itinerary is fully flexible and merely offers an example as to the type of programme offered in Limpopo and the Northwest Province. To discuss your holiday in this region, please call Abercrombie & Kent on +44.845 0700 611 or visit www.abercrombiekent.co.uk

THIS PAGE (FROM TOP) : *Baths at Jaci's Safari Lodge are handcrafted from natural rock; relax in a spa bed at Etali Safari Lodge; Tswalu Kalahari Reserve is ensconced in thornveld.*

OPPOSITE (FROM LEFT): *The spa complex at Mount Grace Country House & Spa features rock and thatched roofs; the open-plan kitchen at Jaci's Tree Lodge.*

index

The publisher would like to thank the following for permission to reproduce their photographs:

Alain Proust/iAfrika Photos 8–9, 52, 82, 130, 132 (right), 137, 174 (top), 176–177 (top), 179
Andrea Pistolesi/TIPS Images 106
Blue Gum Country Estate 178 (top and below)
Cape Tourism 182 (centre)
Carlo Mari/TIPS Images 55, 78
Chad Henning/iAfrika Photos 83, 84
Chris Dei/TIPS Images 54
Chris Sattlberger/TIPS Images 172, 173
Dag Sundberg/TIPS Images 2
Drew Findlay/iAfrika Photos 18
Eric Miller/iAfrika Photos 21, 22 (below), 156 (centre)
Etali Safari Lodge 253 (right below)
François Savigny/iAfrika Photos front cover (elephant), 80
GR Communications 162 (top and centre)
Garth Stead/GR Communications 162 (below)
Geoff Spiby/iAfrika Photos 102, 105
Gerard Vandystadt/TIPS Images 163
Gert Lamprecht/iAfrika Photos 20
Graeme Robinson/iAfrika Photos 158
Guido Alberto Rossi/TIPS Images 59, 107 (left and right)
Guy Stubbs 13 (below), 15 (top and below), 16, 22 (top), 25 (below),

26 (top and below), 27 (below), 28 (top and below), 29, 30 (top), 31, 81, 82 (top), 85 (top), 86 (below), 103, 104 (top), 110, 111, 132 (below), 134 (top), 155, 159 (top and below), 160 (right and left), 161 (top and below), 174 (below), 176 (below)
iAfrika Photos 100, 156 (below), 175 (top)
Jaci's Lodges 252 (right), 253 (right top)
James Gradwell/iAfrika Photos 57 (below)
Jatinga Country Lodge 250 (right top)
Jeffrey Barbee/iAfrika Photos 108 (top)
Jennifer Stern/iAfrika Photos 58 (below)
Jeremy Jowell/iAfrika Photos 14, 183
Keith Young/iAfrika Photos 25 (top)
Ken Woods/iAfrika Photos 85 (below)
Klein Genot Wine & Country Estate 248 (right below)
Leopard Hills Private Game Reserve 5
Lion Sands Private Game Reserve 250 (left top)
Lou Ann Young/iAfrika Photos 57 (top)
Makanyane Safari Lodge front cover (zebra), 33 (centre and below), 136 (centre and below)
Mapungubwe Museum 87
The Marine Hermanus 248 (left below)
Mother City Queer Project 182 (top)
Mount Grace Country House & Spa 252 (left)
MuseuMAfricA 24

Nessa Leibhammer 86 (top)
The Outpost 109 (top)
Paolo Curto/TIPS Images 170
Per-Anders Pettersson/iAfrika Photos 17, 135
The Plettenberg 249 (left and right top)
Rob House 128, 131 (below), 175 (below), 180, 181 (top and below)
Rodger Bosch/iAfrika Photos 12, 156 (top)
Roland Metcalfe/iAfrika Photos 56 (below)
Royal Malewane front cover (tree), 250 (left below)
Sasa Kralj/iAfrika Photos front cover (house), 56 (top)
Shadley Lombard/Esp Afrika 182 (below)
Shaun Harris/iAfrika Photos 18
Singita lodges front cover (chairs), front and back (top and centre) flaps, 4, 58 (top), 251 (top and below)
South African Tourism 23, 28 (centre), 30 (below), 104 (below), 108 (below), 109 (below), 131 (top), 133 (top), 134 (below), 136 (top), 152, 157
Tswalu Kalahari Reserve 253 (left)
Wesley Hitt/TIPS Images 154
Western Cape Hotel & Spa 248 (left top)
The Windermere 249 (right below)
Yazeed Kamaldien/iAfrika Photos 27 (top)
Zaeem Adams/iAfrika Photos 13 (top)

directory

Abercrombie + Kent Travel
telephone : +44.845 0700 611
www.abercrombiekent.co.uk

AmaKhosi Lodge
PO Box 354, Pongola, KwaZulu-Natal 3170
telephone : +27.34 414 1157
facsimile : +27.34 414 1172
info@amakhosi.com
www.amakhosi.com

Ant's Hill
PO Box 441, Vaalwater 0530
telephone : +27.14 755 4296
facsimile : +27.14 755 4941
antsnest@telkomsa.net
www.waterberg.net/antsnest/antshill.html

Ant's Nest
PO Box 441, Vaalwater 0530
telephone : +27.14 755 4296
facsimile : +27.14 755 4941
antsnest@telkomsa.net
www.waterberg.net/antsnest

Beverly Hills Hotel
Lighthouse Road, Umhlanga Rocks,
KwaZulu-Natal 4320/PO Box 71,
Umhlanga Rocks, KwaZulu-Natal 4320
telephone : +27.31 561 2211
facsimile : +27.31 561 3711
beverlyhills@southernsun.com
www.southernsun.com

Cape Cove Guest Lodge
11 Avenue Deauville, Cape Town 8005
telephone : +27.21 434 7969
facsimile : +27.21 434 8191
info@capecove.com
www.capecove.com

Castello di Monte
402 Aries Street, Waterkloof Ridge,
Pretoria 0181
telephone : +27.12 346 6984
facsimile : +27.12 460 6739
info@castello.co.za
www.castello.co.za

The Cellars-Hohenort
93 Brommersvlei Road, Cape Town 7800
telephone : +27.21 794 2137
facsimile : +27.21 794 2149
cellars@relaischateaux.com
www.cellars-hohenort.com

Chitwa Chitwa Private Game Lodges
Sabi Sand Game Reserve, Mpumalanga
telephone : +27.11 883 1354
facsimile : +27.11 783 1858
info@chitwa.co.za
www.chitwa.co.za

Clearwater Lodges
PO Box 365, Stellenbosch 7599
telephone/facsimile : +27.21 889 5514
info@clearwaterlodges.co.za
www.clearwaterlodges.co.za

Colona Castle
Verwood Street, off Old Boyes Drive,
Lakeside, Cape Town 7945
telephone : +27.21 788 8235

facsimile : +27 21 788 6577
colona@link.co.za
www.colonacastle.co.za

d'Ouwe Werf Country Inn
30 Church Street, Stellenbosch 7600
telephone : +27.21 887 4608/1608
facsimile : +27.21 887 4626
ouwewerf@iafrica.com
www.ouwewerf.com

Elephant House
PO Box 82, Addo 6105
telephone : +27.42 233 2462
facsimile : +27.42 233 0393
elephanthouse@intekom.co.za
www.elephanthouse.co.za

Etali Safari Lodge
Tshukudu Area in Madikwe Game Reserve,
Northwest Province
telephone : +27.12 346 0124
facsimile : +27.12 346 0163
info@etalisafari.co.za
www.etalisafari.co.za

The Grace
54 Bath Avenue, Rosebank,
Johannesburg 2196
telephone : +27.11 280 7200
facsimile : +27.11 280 7474
graceres@thegrace.co.za
www.thegrace.co.za

Graskop Hotel
3 Main Street, Graskop 1270
telephone/facsimile : +27.13 767 1244
graskophotel@mweb.co.za
www.graskophotel.co.za

Grootbos Private Nature Reserve
PO Box 148, Gansbaai 7220
telephone : +27.28 384 0381
facsimile : +27.28 384 0552
reservations@grootbos.co.za
www.grootbos.co.za

Hotel Izulu
Rey's Place, Ballito, KwaZulu-Natal 4420
telephone : +27.32 946 3444
facsimile : +27.32 946 3494
info@hotelizulu.com
www.hotelizulu.com

directory

InterContinental Sandton Towers
Corner of Fifth and Alice Streets, Sandton,
Johannesburg 2146
telephone : +27.11 780 5000
facsimile : +27.11 780 5022
icsandtonsunandtowers@southernsun.com
www.southernsun.com

Jaci's Safari Lodge
Jaci's Reservations—Madikwe Game Reserve,
Northwest Province
telephone : +27.83 700 2071
facsimile : +27.14 778 9901
jaci@madikwe.com
www.madikwe.com

Jaci's Tree Lodge
Jaci's Reservations—Madikwe Game Reserve,
Northwest Province
telephone : +27.83 700 2071
facsimile : +27.14 778 9901
jaci@madikwe.com
www.madikwe.com

Jatinga Country Lodge
Jatinga Road, Plaston, White River,
Mpumalanga
telephone : +27.13 751 5059
facsimile : +27.13 751 5119
info@jatinga.co.za
www.jatinga.co.za

Kensington Place
28 Kensington Crescent, Higgovale,
Cape Town 8001
telephone : +27.21 424 4744
facsimile : +27.21 424 1810
kplace@mweb.co.za
www.kensingtonplace.co.za

Klein Genot Wine + Country Estate
Green Valley Road, Franschhoek
telephone : +27.21 876 2738
facsimile : +27.21 876 4624
info@kleingenot.com
www.kleingenot.com

Le Quartier Français
16 Huguenot Road, Franschhoek 7690
telephone : +27.21 876 2151
facsimile : +27.21 876 3105
res@lqf.co.za
www.lequartier.co.za

Lion Sands Private Game Reserve
PO Box 30, White River 1240
telephone/facsimile : +27.11 484 9911
res@lionsands.com
www.lionsands.com

Lion's View
4 First Crescent, Camps Bay,
Cape Town 8005
telephone : +27.83 459 7707
facsimile : +27.21 438 0046
info@lionsview.co.za
www.lionsview.co.za

The Lodge on the Bay
77 Beachy Head Drive, Plettenberg Bay 6600
telephone : +27.44 501 2800
facsimile : +27.44 501 2850
reservations@thelodgeonthebay.com
www.thelodgeonthebay.com

Lukimbi Safari Lodge
PO Box 2617, Northcliff, Johannesburg 2115
telephone : +27.11 888 3713
facsimile : +27.11 888 2181
info@lukimbi.com
www.lukimbi.com

Makanyane Safari Lodge
Madikwe Game Reserve
Northwest Province
telephone : +27 14 778 9600
facsimile : +27 14 778 9611
enquiries@makanyane.com
www.makanyane.com

Makweti Safari Lodge
PO Box 310, Vaalwater 0530
telephone : +27.11 837 6776
facsimile : +27.11 837 4771
makweti@global.co.za
www.makweti.com

The Marine Hermanus
Marine Drive, PO Box 9, Hermanus 7200
telephone : +27.28 313 1000
facsimile : +27.28 313 0160
hermanus@relaischateaux.com
www.marine-hermanus.com

Mateya Safari Lodge
PO Box 21, Derdepoort 2876
telephone : +27.14 778 9200
facsimile : +27.14 778 9201
info@mateyasafari.com
www.mateyasafari.com

Melrose Arch Hotel
1 Melrose Square, Melrose Arch,
Johannesburg 2196
telephone : +27.11 214 6666
facsimile : +27.11 214 6600
info@melrosearchhotel.com
www.africanpridehotels.com

Metropole Hotel
38 Long Street, Cape Town 8001
telephone : +27.21 424 7247
facsimile : +27.21 424 7248
info@metropolehotel.co.za
www.metropolehotel.co.za

Modjadji House
23 Oosthuizen Drive, Floracliffe,
Roodepoort, Johannesburg
telephone : +27.11 674 1421
facsimile : +27.11 672 4570
info@modjadjihouse.co.za
www.modjadjihouse.co.za

Mount Grace Country House + Spa
Private Bag 5004, Magaliesburg 1791
telephone : +27.14 577 1350
facsimile : +27.14 577 1202
mountgrace@grace.co.za
www.grace.co.za

The Outpost
10 Bompas Road, Dunkeld West,
Johannesburg/Kruger National Park, Limpopo
telephone : +27.11 341 0282
facsimile : +27.11 341 0281
theoutpost@global.co.za
www.theoutpost.co.za

Pezula Resort Hotel
Lagoonview Drive, Knysna 6570
telephone : +27.44 302 5332
facsimile : +27.44 384 1658
info@pezula.co.za
www.pezula.co.za

The Phantom Forest Eco Reserve
PO Box 3051, Knysna 6570
telephone : +27.44 386 0046
facsimile : +27.44 387 1944
phantomforest@mweb.co.za
www.phantomforest.com

The Plettenberg
40 Church St, Plettenberg Bay 6600
telephone : +27.44 533 2030
facsimile : +27.44 533 2074
plettenberg@relaischateaux.com
www.plettenberg.com

The Western Cape Hotel + Spa
On The Arabella Country Estate, PO Box 593,
Kleinmond 7195
telephone : +27.28 284 0000
facsimile : +27.28 284 0003
reservations@w-capehotel.co.za
www.luxurycollection.com/westerncape

Protea Hotel Victoria Junction
Corner of Somerset and Ebenezer Roads,
Cape Town 8001
telephone : +27.21 418 1234
facsimile : +27.21 418 5678
reservations@victoriajunction.com
www.proteahotels.co.za

River Bend Lodge
Greater Addo Elephant National Park,
Eastern Cape
telephone : +27.42 233 0161
facsimile : +27.42 233 0162
reservations@riverbend.za.com
www.riverbend.za.com

River Manor Country House + Spa
Johan and Leigh Swanepoel
6 The Avenue, Stellenbosch 7602
telephone : +27.21 887 9944
facsimile : +27.21 997 9940
info@rivermanor.co.za
www.rivermanor.co.za

Royal Malewane
PO Box 1542, Hoedspruit 1380
telephone : +27.15 793 0150
facsimile : +27.15 793 2879
info@royalmalewane.com
www.royalmalewane.com

Sabi Sabi Private Game Reserve
PO Box 52665, Saxonwold 2132
telephone : +27.11 483 3939
facsimile : +27.11 483 3799
res@sabisabi.com
www.sabisabi.com

Santé Winelands Hotel + Wellness Centre
PO Box 381, Klapmuts 7625
telephone : +27.21 875 8100
facsimile : +27.21 875 8111
winelandsres@southernsun.com
www.santewellness.co.za

Selborne Hotel, Spa + Golf Estate
PO Box 2, Pennington, KwaZulu-Natal 4184
telephone : +27.39 688 1800
facsimile : +27.39 975 1811
reservations@selborne.com
www.selborne.com

Singita Lebombo
The Oval, Oakdale House, 1 Oakdale Road,
Newlands, Cape Town 7700
telephone : +27.21 683 3424
facsimile : +27.21 683 3502
singita@singita.co.za
www.singita.co.za

South African Airways
UK reservations   0870 747 1111
South Africa reservations : +27.11 978 1111
ukhelp@flysaa.com
www.flysaa.com

Spier
PO Box 1078, Stellenbosch 7599
telephone : +27.21 809 1100
facsimile : +27.21 881 3634
info@spier.co.za
www.spier.co.za

Ten Bompas
10 Bompas Road, Dunkeld West,
Johannesburg
telephone : +27.11 325 2442
facsimile : +27.11 341 0281
tenbompas@mix.co.za
www.tenbompas.com

Thanda Private Game Reserve
PO Box 652585, Benmore 2010
telephone : +27.11 704 3115
facsimile : +27.11 462 5607
reservations@thanda.co.za
www.thanda.com

Thonga Beach Lodge
PO Box 1593, Eshowe 3815
telephone : +27.35 474 1473
facsimile : +27.35 474 1490
res@isibindiafrica.co.za
www.isibindiafrica.co.za

Tinga Private Game Lodge
PO Box 88, Skukuza 1350
telephone : +27.13 735 8400
facsimile : +27.13 735 5722
reservations@tinga.co.za
www.tinga.co.za

Tswalu Kalahari Reserve
PO Box 1081, Kuruman 8460
telephone : +27.53 781 9234
facsimile : +27.53 781 9238
res@tswalu.com
www.tswalu.com

Valley of the Rainbow
PO Box 20366, Noordburg,
Potchefstroom 2522
telephone/facsimile : +27.13 272 7050
rainbowlodge@telehost.co.za
www.rainbowvalley.co.za

Whistletree Lodge
1267 Whistletree Drive, Queenswood,
Pretoria 0186
telephone : +27.12 333 9915
facsimile : +27.12 333 9917
wtree@icon.co.za
www.whistletreelodge.com

Winchester Mansions Hotel
221 Beach Road, Sea Point,
Cape Town 8005
telephone : +27.21 434 2351
facsimile : +27.21 434 0215
john@winchester.co.za
www.winchester.co.za

The Windermere
35 Humewood Road, Humewood,
Port Elizabeth 6001
telephone : +27.41 582 2245
facsimile : +27.41 582 2246
info@thewindermere.co.za
www.thewindermere.co.za